Even the Janitor Is White

Barry Kanpol
General Editor

Vol. 4

The Critical Education and Ethics series
is part of the Peter Lang Education list.
Every volume is peer reviewed and meets
the highest quality standards for content and production.

PETER LANG
New York • Washington, D.C./Baltimore • Bern
Frankfurt • Berlin • Brussels • Vienna • Oxford

Even the Janitor Is White

Educating for Cultural Diversity in Small Colleges and Universities

EDITED BY

M. Gail Hickey & Brian K. Lanahan

PETER LANG

New York • Washington, D.C./Baltimore • Bern
Frankfurt • Berlin • Brussels • Vienna • Oxford

Library of Congress Cataloging-in-Publication Data

Even the janitor is white: educating for cultural diversity in small
colleges and universities / edited by M. Gail Hickey, Brian K. Lanahan.
p. cm. — (Critical education and ethics; v. 4)
Includes bibliographical references and index.
1. Multicultural education—United States. 2. Minorities—
Education (Higher)—United States. 3. College teaching—Social aspects—
United States. 4. Small colleges—United States.
I. Hickey, M. Gail. II. Lanahan, Brian K. III. Title.
LC1099.3.H52 370.1170973—dc23 2012011108
ISBN 978-1-4331-1861-6 (hardcover)
ISBN 978-1-4331-1860-9 (paperback)
ISBN 978-1-4539-0808-2 (e-book)
ISSN 2166-1359

Bibliographic information published by **Die Deutsche Nationalbibliothek**.
Die Deutsche Nationalbibliothek lists this publication in the "Deutsche
Nationalbibliografie"; detailed bibliographic data is available
on the Internet at http://dnb.d-nb.de/.

© 2012 Peter Lang Publishing, Inc., New York
29 Broadway, 18th floor, New York, NY 10006
www.peterlang.com

We are indebted to a number of people who helped shape and produce this book. A lecture by James Banks inspired the original concept. Our friends and colleagues in the Small College and University Faculty Forum of the National Council for the Social Studies contributed their ideas, energy, and expertise. Barry Kanpol, Dean of the College of Education & Public Policy at Indiana University–Purdue University Fort Wayne, provided encouragement and guidance at critical times.

Gail dedicates this book to her husband Robert, and to the memory of her father Earl R. Hickey (1930–2012).

Brian dedicates this book to his father, Dennis Lanahan, for his unwavering and enthusiastic support of the education of his children and grandchildren.

TABLE OF CONTENTS

Part I
Introduction

History of Multicultural Education in the United States

In the 19th century, the U.S government ordained that all children under the age of 16 would be educated at public expense. At that time, most American citizens were White, Anglo-Europeans with Judeo-Christian religious backgrounds. The 19th- and early 20th-century American school populations were also comprised primarily of White Anglo-Europeans. Within this traditionally European Judeo-Christian sociocultural context, Whites assumed a dominant status, whereas people of color were relegated to subordinate status (Goodman, 2001; Howard, 1999; McIntosh, 1989; Spring, 2004).

Furthermore, within the context of a White-dominant American society, teacher training programs tended to reflect majority-based theories about school achievement and race/ethnicity. Many teachers came to believe that the responsibility for academic failure rests with students and their families (who most educators perceived as less able than Whites), rather than with the teacher or the educational environment. Teachers' unchallenged worldviews regarding White privilege[1] were carried into educational settings, thereby perpetuating racial stereotypes, prejudice toward persons from diverse backgrounds, and lack of cultural awareness.

The U.S. population has undergone significant change since mandatory schooling laws were enacted in the 19th century. Some of these changes have contributed to a reduction of the White-majority population statistics. For example, in 1965, the U.S. Congress passed the Immigration and Naturalization Act, raising the restrictive immigration quotas for non-European nations and initiating a "third wave" of immigration to the United States. Unlike its predecessors, this new immigrant group was made up largely of Asians and Latin Americans. Thus, the 1965 Immigration and Naturalization Act initiated a trend that changed the composition of American classrooms.

Today, more than 42% of school-age children in the United States are minorities, and 20% speak a language other than English (National Center for Educational Statistics, 2007). In larger cities, up to 68% of K-12 public school students claim non-White heritage (National Center for Educational Statistics, 2007). However, more than 75% of K-12 teachers in the United States are White (National Center for Educational Statistics 2007), with the majority of them being Protestant, middle class, and female (National Education Association, 1997). White Judeo-Christian teachers face significant challenges to their own worldviews as a result of encounters with immigrant students and parents (National Education Association, 1997; Zimpher & Ashburn, 1992). Teachers may also face unexpected conflicts between the culture of their classroom and the cultural frameworks honored in their students' homes (Hollins, 1996).

Indeed, existent literature consistently indicates that people from dominant groups (e.g., White educators in the United States) resist engaging in opportunities to effect social change because such activities threaten the status quo (Goodman, 2001; Ndura & Lafer, 2004). This resistance stems from both sociopolitical and psychological factors. Sociopolitically, those persons from the dominant, privileged group (White educators, lawmakers, and parents in this case) are encouraged via societal expectations to be "self-focused"—namely, to obtain a sense of self-worth by feeling superior to non-Whites, to "see others as threats, to protect their resources, and to blame people of color for their failures" (Goodman, 2001, p. 78). Psychologically, persons from the dominant, privileged group resist opportunities to examine and reflect on issues of race and ethnicity due to their own identity-development struggle to protect their sense of self (Goodman, 2001, p. 78).

Researchers contend that teachers in today's culturally diverse American classrooms must recognize their own worldviews and related biases because only then can they hope to understand the worldviews of their students (Banks, 1994; Davidman & Davidman, 2001; Gillette & Boyle-Baise, 1995; McAllister & Irvine, 2000; Nieto & Rolon, 1995). To effectively interact with their students—in addition to confronting their own White-privilege biases—American teachers must examine issues of race, class, and gender (Pang, 1994); learn about students' cultures; and use these understandings to perceive the world through the diverse cultural lenses present in teachers' own communities (Bennett, 1995; Pewewardy & Frey, 2002; Sleeter, 1992; Villegas & Lucas, 2002). Finally, the literature emphasizes that teacher education programs must address how White-privilege racial identity has shaped teachers' human experiences as well as their school experiences (West, 1994) as White educators' cultural experiences and perceptions have shaped schools, curricula, and teaching practices used to date (Banks, 2001; Gay, 2001; Howard, 1999; McCarthy, 1994; Ndura, 2004; Ndura& Lafer, 2004; Nieto, 2000; Sleeter, 1994; Spring, 2004). Racial and ethnic background continues to significantly shape the human experience; the experiences and perceptions of a predominantly White society continue to shape schools and schooling in the United States. As such, racism remains a pervasive social issue that negatively impacts many persons of color in schools and society in the country (Howard, 1999; Ladson-Billings, 1994; Navarrette, 1993; Pang, 1990; Shipler, 1997; Tatum, 1997; West, 1994).

The literature offers various definitions of multicultural education (Gay, 2000); most authors agree that it encompasses ideas about race, culture, language, religion, social class, gender, and disability (Hernandez, 2001; Sleeter & Grant, 1999). Teacher education programs in many states in the United States are now required to address issues of multicultural education as a means of moving teachers toward cultural competency. The development of cultural competency begins with the belief that multicultural education is an essential component of schooling in a culturally diverse society such as the United States (Hernandez, 2001). Teachers who move toward cultural competency are able to demonstrate and articulate how they work to incorporate concepts about cultural differences and equality in the classroom (Gollnick & Chinn, 2002).

However, teacher education programs (which have continued to be largely populated by White students and instructors) have been slow to respond to research-based calls for reform (Nieto, 2002). Early attempts to increase teachers' awareness of students' diversity often took one of two forms: an add-on class in multicultural education or sporadic references to multicultural issues in selected courses (Hickey, 2006). Researchers have found that these early attempts at change may have done more harm than good. Cursory efforts at multicultural training can lead to stereotypic views of other cultures and hostility toward non-White students (LeCompte, 1985), further discourage beginning teachers from seeking employment in urban schools with large non-White student populations (Rios & Montecinos, 1999), and even perpetuate educators' preference for working with White students (Lampe, 1994; Montecinos & Rios, 1999).

Multiple, complex, and sometimes interacting factors have contributed to teacher education programs' delay in responding effectively to the social and pedagogical changes brought about by increased population diversity (Nieto, 2002; Tatum, 2003). For example, the largely White teaching population in most K-12 schools and teacher education programs has presented a major challenge to open discussion about the need for change. Most teacher education students are White, female (especially in elementary education programs), and from the middle socioeconomic class; they have limited experiences with cultures different from their own, and they have difficulty instructing non-White students (Ladson-Billings, 1995; Schmidt, 1998; Scott & Pinto, 2001). White teachers are resistant to conversations about race or ethnicity because they feel they "are going to be blamed, made to feel guilty, attacked, or otherwise maligned" (Tatum, 2003, p. 37). In response to White teachers' discomfort with conversations about race, many university faculty avoid such dialogue themselves and tend to shut down relevant discussions in teacher education classes (Tatum, 2003, p. 38). As Fox (2001) states,

For faculty, especially faculty of color, the work [to promote anti-racist education] can be debilitating. For not only are they [as instructors] bringing out students' emotionally charged beliefs and feelings, but the very subject of discussion is the White students' negative reaction to people, real and imagined, who look very much like the professors standing before them. (p. 1)

At the end of their teacher education program, most White teachers continue to demonstrate little knowledge about cultural groups; furthermore, they have not spent time examining or reflecting on their own cultural background (Bell, 2002). White preservice teachers tend to have negative attitudes toward non-White persons and non-White American ethno-cultural groups (Bollin & Finkel, 1995; Cooney & Akintunde, 1999). Even when preservice teachers do exhibit an ability to situate future students' lives in a broad, extracurricular social context they continue to be unable to recognize institutionalized racism in school settings (Hickey, 2006; Xu, 2000). Even fewer teachers seem able to challenge their own assumptions about race and racism (Bell, 2002) or the invisible privileges inherent in the White middle-class experience (Sleeter, 1992).

American colleges and universities—particularly teacher education programs—are charged with preparing students to enter the teaching profession as well as helping inservice teachers maintain appropriate teaching credentials. Educational experts agree that special efforts need to be directed toward consciousness-raising to enable teachers and teacher training students within the dominant White society to increase their "awareness of self and others, challenge stereotypes, overcome prejudice, and develop relationships with people from different racial backgrounds" (Goodman, 2001, p. 4). According to many experts, teacher education students should study subject matter, pedagogy, and instructional methods along with multicultural education content (Artiles, Trent, Hoffman-Kipp, & Lopez-Torres 2000). Therefore, this volume addresses the major challenges faced by teacher educators who are committed to diversity education. The chapters in this volume invite readers to reflect on their own practice as teacher educators as well as consider ways in which that practice might be improved.

Special Issues: Teacher Educators in Small Colleges and Universities in the United States

Small colleges and universities (SCU) face three major issues when preparing teachers to teach diverse students in diverse situations: a lack of student diversity, a lack of faculty diversity, and geographic isolation.

Chief among the challenges facing SCU is a lack of student diversity in their teacher education programs. Although students who are not Euro-

American, middle class, monolingual, and female do not attend SCU and enroll in teacher education programs for a variety of reasons, economics often play a predominant role. For first-generation college students, teaching may not be a financially viable profession due to low salaries coupled with student loan obligations and family expectations. This financial pressure may be more acute on males who are or expect to be the sole breadwinners in their families. In addition, SCU are often private with higher tuition, further increasing the financial disincentive to teach.

In addition, many SCU are located in socioeconomically and/or ethnically geographically isolated locations. These locations may be rural, urban, or suburban and often surround teacher education programs with homogenous schools and student populations. In such situations, it is difficult to engage in a field experience in which teacher education students can observe and work with diverse students. Moreover, these socioeconomically and/or ethnically geographically isolated locations may further discourage diversity among the teacher education students due to the homogenous community surrounding the campus, which could alienate some students (Hasseler, 1998).

Due to their size, SCU have a difficult time attracting and retaining faculty with expertise in diversity issues due to issues related to salary, student mismatch, community mismatch, and/or ideological isolation. Faculty members with expertise in diversity issues are often highly sought after by many employers and are attracted to larger colleges and universities that can offer higher salaries and more grant funding opportunities. In addition, these faculty members tend to be from different socioeconomic and ethnic backgrounds than the students they teach, and they encounter resistance from students when they present ideas that do not agree with the life experiences of these students. Moreover, faculty members with expertise in diversity issues may not feel comfortable living and working in a community that is socioeconomically and/or ethnically homogenous. Finally, these faculty members may find themselves literally in the minority among their colleagues with regard to beliefs about diversity issues (Hasseler, 1998).

Lack of Scholarship

Although many studies have sought to devise ways in which to prepare teachers to effectively work with diverse learners at large colleges and universities, few have been conducted at SCU. In fact, only two studies have directly addressed the issues faced by SCU.

Hasseler (1998) surveyed department chairs at 90 ChristianSCU with regard to multicultural education in their departments, focusing on courses and field experiences relating to multicultural education, ways in which faculty supported understanding of multicultural education, and the development of effective multicultural teacher education. Hasseler found great variability in how respondents defined and addressed multiculturalism. Furthermore, fewer than half of the departments surveyed required courses in multicultural education, and most respondents relied on professional development to learn about multiculturalism. The study identified several factors that inhibit effective multicultural teacher education, including lack of minority faculty, lack of time to gain expertise, lack of funding, and lack of minority students.

Yoder's (1981) study addressed multicultural education issues at the program level with a descriptive study of Goshen College's Study-Service Trimester. Students at the sophomore and junior level traveled overseas to Central America, the Caribbean, Eastern Europe, and/or China. The Study-Service Trimester program included an on-campus orientation; living arrangements with families in the foreign location; assignments to volunteer for fieldwork in schools, hospitals, agriculture, and forestry; and group sessions for feedback. Yoder concluded that the program was an ideal setting for multicultural teacher education in that it encouraged a responsive teacher attitude with respect for cultural identity and developed such teaching skills as linguistic variations, diverse learning styles, values clarification, and conflict resolution.

Given the dearth of relevant studies in the field of education, the chapters in this volume contribute significantly to the ongoing discussion of multicultural education at American SCU. We believe readers will find the chapters informative and hope they use the chapters as springboards for reflection toward improving teacher training at their own institutions.

Note

1. For a discussion of the concept of White privilege, see Akintunde (1999), Cooney and Akintunde (1999), Goodman (2001), and McCarthy (1994).

References

Akintunde, O. (1999). White racism, White supremacy, White privilege, social construction of race. *Multicultural Education, 7*(2), 2–8.

Artiles, A. J., Trent, S. C., Hoffman-Kipp, P., & Lopez-Torres, L. (2000). From individual acquisition to cultural-historical practices in multicultural teacher education. *Remedial and Special Education, 21*(2), 79–91.

Banks, J. A. (1994). *Multiethnic education: Theory and practice.* Needham Heights, MA: Allyn & Bacon.

Banks, J. A. (2001). Multicultural education: Characteristics and goals. In J. A. Banks & C. A.

McGee Banks (Eds.), *Multicultural education: Issues and perspectives* (4th ed., pp. 3–30). New York: Wiley.

Bell, L. A. (2002). Sincere fictions: The pedagogical challenges of preparing white teachers for multicultural classrooms. *Equity and Excellence in Education, 35*(3), 236–244.

Bennett, C. I. (1995). Preparing teachers for cultural diversity and national standards of academic excellence. *Journal of Teacher Education, 46*(4), 259–265.

Bollin, G. G., & Finkel, J. (1995). White racial identity as a barrier to understanding diversity: A study of preservice teachers. *Equity and Excellence in Education, 28*(1), 25–30.

Cooney, M. H., & Akintunde, O. (1999). Confronting White privilege and color blind paradigm in a teacher education program. *Multicultural Education, 7*(2), 9–14.

Davidman, L., & Davidman, P. T. (2001). *Teaching with a multicultural perspective: A practical guide* (3rd ed.). New York: Longman.

Fox, H. (2001). *When race breaks out: Conversations about race and racism in college classrooms.* New York: Peter Lang.

Gay, G. (2000). *Culturally responsive teaching: Theory, research, and practice.* New York: Teachers College Press.

Gay, G. (2001). Educational equality for students of color. In J. A. Banks & C. A. McGee Banks (Eds.), *Multicultural education: Issues and perspectives* (4th ed., pp. 197–224). New York: Wiley.

Gillette, M., & Boyle-Baise, M. (1995, April). *Multicultural education at the graduate level: Assisting teachers in developing multicultural perspectives.* Paper presented at the annual meeting of the American Educational Research Association, San Francisco, CA.

Gollnick, D. M., & Chinn, P. C. (2002). *Multicultural education in a pluralistic society* (6th ed.). Upper Saddle River, NJ: Prentice-Hall.

Goodman, D. L. (2001). *Promoting diversity and social justice: Educating people from privileged groups.* Thousand Oaks, CA: Sage Publications.

Hasseler, S. S. (1998). *Multicultural teacher education: Problems and possibilities in small college settings.* Paper presented at the annual meeting of the American Association of Colleges for Teacher Education, New Orleans, LA.

Hernandez, H. (2001). *Multicultural education: A teacher's guide to linking context, process, and content.* Upper Saddle River, NJ: Merrill Prentice-Hall.

Hickey, M. G. (2006). Becoming a teacher: Preservice teachers learn practical knowledge by exploring personal images of teaching. In G. Keri (Ed.), *Learning efficacy: Celebrations and persuasions* (pp. 1–21). Greenwich, CT: Information Age Publishing.

Hollins, E. R. (1996). *Culture in school learning: Revealing the deep meaning.* Mahwah, NJ: Lawrence Erlbaum Associates.

Howard, G. (1999). *We can't teach what we don't know: White teachers, multiracial schools.* New York: Teachers College Press.

Ladson-Billings, G. (1994). *The dreamkeepers: Successful teachers of African-American children.* San Francisco: Jossey-Bass.

Ladson-Billings, G. (1995). Toward a theory of culturally relevant pedagogy. *American Education Research Journal, 35,* 465–491.

Lampe, J. (1994). *Multiethnic cultural perceptions and attitudes of teacher education students.* Paper presented at the annual meeting of the Southwest Educational Research Association, San Antonio, TX.

LeCompte, M. D. (1985). Defining the differences: Cultural subgroups within the educational mainstream. *Urban Review, 17,* 111–127.

McAllister, G., & Irvine, J. (2000). Cultural competency and multicultural teacher education.

Review of Educational Research, 70, 1, 3-24.

McCarthy, C. (1994). Multicultural discourses and curriculum reform: A critical perspective. *Educational Theory, 44*(1), 81–118.

McIntosh, P. (1989, July–August). White privilege: Unpacking the invisible knapsack. *Peace and Freedom*, pp. 10–12.

Montecinos, C., & Rios, F. (1999) Assessing preservice teachers' zones of concern and comfort with multicultural education. *Teacher Education Quarterly, 26*, 7–24.

National Center for Educational Statistics. (2007). *The National Center for Education Statistics.* Available at www.nces.gov.

National Education Association. (1997). *Status of the American public school teacher, 1995–96.* Washington, DC.

Navarrette, J. R. (1993). *A darker shade of crimson: Odyssey of a Harvard Chicano.* New York: Bantam Books.

Ndura, E. (2004). Teachers' discoveries of their cultural realms: Untangling the web of cultural identity. *Multicultural Perspectives, 6*(3), 10–16.

Ndura, E., & Lafer, S. (2004). Exploring the self and the other: Achieving the empathic goals of teacher preparation through multicultural education. *Electronic Magazine of Multicultural Education,6*(1). Available at http://www.eastern.edu/publications/emme/2004spring/ndura_lafer.html

Nieto, S. (2000). *Affirming diversity: The sociopolitical context of multicultural education* (3rd ed.). New York: Longman.

Nieto, S. (2002). *Language, culture, and teaching: Critical perspectives for a new century.* Mahwah, NJ: Lawrence Erlbaum Associates.

Nieto, S., & Rolon, C. (1995, November). *The preparation and professional development of teachers: A perspective from two Latinas.* Paper presented at the invitational conference for Defining the Knowledge Base for Urban Teacher Education, Emory University, Atlanta, GA.

Pang, V. O. (1990). Asian-American children: A diverse population. *Educational Forum, 55*(1), 49–66.

Pang, V. O. (1994). Why do we need this class? Multicultural education for teachers. *Phi Delta Kappan, 76*(4), 289–292.

Pewewardy, C. D., & Frey, B. (2002). Surveying the landscape: Perceptions of multicultural support services and racial climate at a predominantly white university. *Journal of Negro Education, 71*(1/2), 77–95.

Rios, F., & Montecinos, C. (1999). Advocating social justice and cultural affirmation: Ethnically diverse preservice teachers' perspectives on multicultural education. *Equity and Excellence in Education, 32*(3), 66–76.

Schmidt, P. R. (1998). *Cultural conflict and struggle: Literacy learning in a kindergarten program.* New York: Peter Lang.

Scott, K. A., & Pinto, A. (2001). Revolutionizing multicultural education staff development: Factor structure of a teacher survey. *Equity & Excellence in Education, 32*(1), 32–42.

Shipler, D. (1997). *A country of strangers: Blacks and Whites in America.* New York: Vintage Books.

Sleeter, C. E. (1992). Multicultural education: Five views. *Education Digest*, pp. 53–57.

Sleeter, C. (1994). White racism. *Multicultural Education, 1*(4), 5–8, 39.

Sleeter, C., & Grant, C. (1999). *Turning on learning: Five approaches for multicultural teaching plans for race, class, gender and disability.* New York: Wiley.

Spring, J. (2004). *The intersection of cultures: Multicultural education in the United States and the global economy* (3rd ed.). Boston: McGraw-Hill.

Tatum, B. D. (1997). *"Why are all the Black kids sitting together in the cafeteria?" and other conversations about race.* New York: Basic Books.

Tatum, B. D. (2003). Opening the dialogue about race at school. In M. Sadowski (Ed.), *Adolescents at school* (pp. 36–39). Cambridge, MA: Harvard Educational Press.

Villegas, A., & Lucas, T. (2002). *Educating culturally responsive teachers: A coherent approach.* Albany: SUNY Press.

West, C. (1994). *Race matters.* New York: Vintage Books.

Xu, H. (2000). Preservice teachers integrate understandings of diversity into literacy instruction: An adaptation of the ABC's model. *Journal of Teacher Education, 51*(2), 135–148.

Yoder, S. (1981, April). *Multicultural education: A model for the small college.* Paper presented at the annual conference of the American Education Research Association, Detroit, MI.

Zimpher, N. L., & Ashburn, E. A. (1992). Countering parochialism in teacher candidates. In M. E. Dilworth (Ed.), *Diversity in teacher education: New expectations* (pp. 40–62). San Francisco: Jossey-Bass

Part II
Diversity in Education Courses:
Understanding Ourselves, Understanding Others

Understanding Ourselves, Understanding Others: First-Year Education Majors' Beliefs about Diversity

Melissa J. Marks

This study focused on the personal and professional beliefs of 41 preservice teachers in an introductory education course at a small, largely homogenous university. The design of the study included pre- and post-surveys using a Likert scale, group responses via a cooperative learning project, and individual reflective papers. The question under investigation was whether preservice teachers' beliefs about diversity could be expanded through exposure to societal issues using social constructivism. The results were mixed. Although the response papers and group responses overwhelmingly suggested that the preservice teachers became more open minded and supportive toward multicultural education (including but not limited to race, gender, sexual orientation, and socioeconomic status), some of the comments reported included underlying prejudices and assumptions. The post-survey data showed some cases where students were less supportive than they initially reported on the presurvey.

In the best of all worlds, teachers should be accepting of every child and the world that each child brings to the classroom. Familial backgrounds, including socioeconomic status, ethnicity, and race, and individual characteristics such as gender, sexual orientation, or disabilities should not bias a teacher against students. However, because personal beliefs unconsciously affect behaviors and attitudes, teachers with strong negative personal beliefs regarding issues of diversity may have lower expectations for some students, negatively affecting the students' educational attainment and modeling a lack of inclusion for all students. This chapter describes a research project investigating whether a specific project in a Social Foundations course affected preservice teachers' beliefs about diverse groups.

The great majority of teachers prepared in the United States are White and from middle-class backgrounds (Frankenberg, 2009; Hyland, 2009; Moss, 2008). Furthermore, the level of integration among students of various races and ethnicities has decreased since the 1980s; thus, many preservice teachers enter the university with limited in-depth exposure to people unlike themselves (Dillon, 2005; Frankenberg, 2009). This lack of experience with others' worldviews may result in a deficit in the knowledge needed to teach a diverse student body. Although gaining knowledge about others and appreciating all persons is merely the introductory level of multicultural practices (Grant & Sleeter, 2006), it is a necessary first step. Similarly, understanding one's own beliefs and biases does not provide direct insights into the practices that preservice teachers may implement, although it is the first step in critical self-reflection that allows preservice teachers to move toward internalizing a social reconstructionist philosophy and teaching with a social justice framework.

A lack of time coupled with university and state mandates often results in limited opportunity to teach multicultural education unless university faculty members are strongly dedicated to it. In some universities, multicultural education is a stand-alone three-credit course, most often emphasizing race/ethnicity, "special needs, language, economics (social class), gender, and finally sexual orientation" (Jennings, 2007, p. 1264). However, Jennings (2007) contends that teaching about race/ethnicity without engaging students about the political and systematic nature of oppression is inadequate for developing teachers' multicultural education competencies. Obviously, this argument extends far past just race and ethnicity to all populations disenfranchised in schools and society.

At the university where the current study took place, the philosophy promoting teaching for social justice needs is integrated throughout all of the classes. In the Social Foundations of Education course, which is the introductory education class, this content is used as a foundation upon which other classes are built. The Social Foundations course offers preservice teachers a broad view of the educational system within the context of society and all of its political, social, and economic complexity. Multicultural context and values are introduced in this class as a foundation upon which other classes build. The Social Foundations course, as an undergraduate course, often challenges students' conceptions of schooling as they begin to recognize that their individual experiences are not universal.

This research study investigates whether a specific project in the Social Foundations course affected the students' beliefs about diverse groups, enabling them to recognize the need for teachers to be proactive in the fight for social justice. However, as prior research indicates (e.g., Joram & Gabriele, 1998; Pajares, 1993; Wubbels, 1992), individuals' beliefs are deeply embedded and resistant to change. Therefore, despite the best intentions, the effects of any course or specific class activities may not change students' previously constructed beliefs. Nonetheless, one does not know if one does not try; hence, the origins of this study.

Methodology

This research study spanned three class periods early in the semester in two Social Foundations of Education courses. A pre/post-survey model was used along with group-generated feedback and individual reflections. The analysis of each of these sets of data is described in the following sections.

Population. As at many small universities, the population at the university where this study took place is quite homogenous. More than 85% of the student population self-identifies as White and Christian (Catholic or Protestant). The great majority lives within an hour's drive of the university, which is located in a small town/rural area. Of the 41 preservice teachers in the Social Foundations classes, all of the students except one self-identified as White, non-Hispanic; in addition, they all self-identified as Christian (Catholic and Protestants). Furthermore, the great majority self-reported that they had attended schools whose population was 80% homogenous or greater. A strong majority of the students are female, but the classes were evenly divided between elementary and secondary majors.

Research Design. In designing the survey, the author decided to be inclusive of many groups. As Jennings (2007) commented, "If university teacher educators attend to some groups but ignore others, preservice teachers are likely to follow in kind, considering some forms of diversity worthy of attention while dismissing others" (p. 1259). To this end, the author decided that the survey should focus on five areas of diversity: race/ethnicity, disabilities, sexual orientation, immigration/language, and socioeconomic status. These issues were examined using a 41-statement survey to which participants responded on a 6-point Likert scale. Nearly half of the statements were reverse coded to maintain validity. The initial survey was given to students during the third week of the term.

After completing the initial surveys, students in the class were randomly assigned to read one of five articles that focused on topics of discrimination, including White privilege, male privilege, and straight privilege. These articles were chosen not only for their content, but also for their emotional appeal rather than a "research" feel. Participants were given the articles to read for homework.

In the second class, students were broken into "jigsaw" groups so that each group had five students—one representing each of the articles. After sharing the underlying ideas of each article, groups were asked to respond to several questions.

- Based on these readings, what issues of diversity do individuals/schools deal with?
- Who do schools serve?
- Who is not being served?
- Why do you think that is the case?
- In an ideal or utopian world, what should be changed?
- In reality, what can we do?

Groups were then given large sheets of paper and markers to record their shared findings and beliefs.

For homework that night, students wrote a one- to two-page paper, responding to several questions.

- Did the articles you read in class individually and within your group change how you view diversity as an issue in school?
- Is diversity an important issue or is it something to "deal with" after you have taught for a few years or if you have non-majority students in your classes?
- Is it important for all students or just students of color/minority/non-majority?
- What do you think you will do in your class regarding diversity?

These papers were collected at the beginning of the third class, after which students completed the post-surveys.

Data Analysis

The initial plan was to analyze the survey data from the pre- and post-surveys using two-tail t tests to determine whether any significant changes in opinion had occurred—ostensibly from reading the articles, discussing it with peers, and reflecting on the issues. However, with only 33 students completing both the pre- and post-surveys, the participant numbers were too low to be statistically usable. Thus, instead, the means of each statement was compared and the direction and strength of the responses analyzed. Movement in a "positive" direction indicated that the students' responses supported a more inclusive stance; conversely, movement in a "negative" direction indicated that the response was less inclusive. The strength was determined based on how great the difference was between the means. After dividing the analyzed pre- and post-survey responses into the five areas of diversity (i.e., race/ethnicity, disabilities, sexual orientation, immigration/language, and socioeconomic status), the author examined the patterns of the responses, exploring whether the students' responses within an area all moved in the same direction and whether the strength of the movement remained constant within an area.

The four group response questions were analyzed inductively. Using this qualitative method allowed for patterns within each question to emerge. In the first two questions, patterns surfaced regarding which diverse groups the students recognized. In addition, in the first question, codes included specific problems and possible actions.

Initially, the author planned on coding the individual response papers based on each question posed. However, the preservice teachers only responded to the first two parts, which focused on whether they experienced a change of beliefs and whether diversity was important to them. In analyzing these responses, binary codes were used. As no student wrote that the learning activity did not affect him or her, the data were coded into "affected" or "not affected" for the first question and "important" or "not important" for the latter question. Almost no students addressed whether they would include a focus on diversity regardless of the composition of their class, whether the issue of diversity affects everyone, and what specifically would occur in their class regarding diversity.

A limitation in this investigation was that these papers were collected and graded for completion. Thus, although preservice teachers got credit regardless of their opinion, their names were attached to the opinions, removing any chance of anonymity offered by the pre- and post-surveys and—to a lesser degree—the group responses. In addition, the data provided within the surveys and across the three data sets did not correspond with all responses moving in a similar direction or with similar strength. To gain a clearer picture "from the insider's view" (Patton, 1990, p. 207), a focus group was held after the data were analyzed.

Findings

Each data set (surveys, group responses, individual response papers) was analyzed separately. The survey results are presented first, followed by an analysis of the group responses and the individual response papers. Finally, feedback from the focus group is provided.

Surveys. Because only 33 students completed both pre- and post-surveys, the data on the surveys could not be analyzed statistically with any validity. Instead, the means and direction of the responses were noted. In discussing the direction of students' responses, the terms *positive direction* or *positive movement* denote that the students' responses showed greater acceptance or less prejudice than their initial response, which is considered to be the "desired" outcome. Similarly, the terms *negative movement* or *negative direction* denote that students' responses were less accepting or increasingly prejudiced. "Strongly agree" and "strongly disagree" were the only indicators on the 6-point Likert scale. Terms such as *more strongly agree* or *more strongly disagree* indicate the direction of the pre- to post-survey responses.

Race/Ethnicity. Five statements pertaining to race and/or ethnicity were included on the survey. Of these, two statements about race/ethnicity moved in a positive direction, as desired. One stated that education has historically been monocultural, reflecting a White bias (3.66–4.22); the other stated that many students of color are improperly placed in special education (2.71–3.32). These issues were both discussed briefly within the articles. Participants' responses to these statements showed strong movement in the desired direction. However, despite the positive movement, the ending mean of the latter question was only 3.32 on a 6-point scale, indicating that, overall, students still did not fully accept or agree with this fact. The first statement showed a more desired outcome as students moved from 3.66 to 4.22.

Student responses to three other statements about race moved in a negative direction. One statement focused on people of different racial backgrounds having/raising children together (5.59–5.38). The next statements stated that people should be able to develop meaningful friendships without caring about whether the other person's race or ethnicity differed from theirs (5.84–5.69). The final statement was, "In general, White people place a higher value on education than do people of color" (4.83–4.41). Thus, it appeared that students' personal beliefs became more racist while their recognition of inequities in school increased.

Immigrants/ELL students. All responses in this category moved in the preferred direction after the project except for one. Students' responses indicated that they more strongly disagreed that allowing immigrants and refugees into the country was bad for America (3.46–3.71) and more strongly agreed that accepting many different ways of life strengthens the nation (4.88–4.97). Although both moved in the same direction, the responses to these two statements received different levels of support, as shown in the final mean score for each (3.71 and 4.97, respectively). Participants' responses indicated that they more strongly believed in the importance of maintaining one's own culture and not fully assimilating (4.25–4.75), although the responses indicated a decline in support for speaking one's native language in school (4.71–4.29).

People with Disabilities. In terms of people with disabilities, students were initially supportive of including everyone in society; those responses remained relatively high. Students' responses became slightly more in favor of ensuring that all public facilities were accessible, regardless of the expense (5.47–5.59); they also accepted that people with physical limitations were no less effective as leaders than those without limitations (5.09–5.30). However, regarding schools, the students' responses were less supportive. Their opinions about putting students with physical limitations into regular classrooms remained almost unchanged (4.72–4.78). Most interesting, students' responses moved in a negative direction as they agreed more that teachers should not have to adapt lessons because it is too much work (5.41–5.06).

Sexual Orientation. Because the issue of sexual orientation is sometimes cast in religious terms and is a politically heated debate presently (e.g., same-sex marriage), the responses from the students in this area were surprising. Students increasingly supported same-sex couples raising children (4.09–4.20) and developing meaningful friendships without caring about the other person's sexual orientation (4.99–5.13). They also believed society should become more accepting of gay/lesbian lifestyles (3.06–3.63) and increased their support for schools discussing homosexuality when teaching topics such as families, sexual education, and civil rights (3.41–3.62); however, despite movement in the desired direction, the responses for these last two statements showed lukewarm support, with means of 3.6 on a 6-point scale. The one response that did not show positive movement related to the statement "Gays and lesbians should not be allowed to teach in public schools" (5.61–5.58), but the high final mean of 5.58 out of 6 (reverse coded) showed relative agreement among students for supporting homosexuals teaching in the schools.

Socioeconomic Status. Similar to the issue of race/ethnicity, students' responses about socioeconomic status were mixed. Responses moved in a positive direction for some of the questions while moving in a negative direction for others. For example, students' responses showed increased agreement on statements asserting that teachers often expect less from students in lower socioeconomic status groups (3.29–3.94) and that traditional classrooms often reflect middle-class expectations, norms, and ways of life (4.25–4.75). Likewise, students' responses showed stronger agreement that people of lower socioeconomic status should have the same opportunities to acquire an excellent education and medical care as wealthy individuals (4.99–5.13). However, their belief that people who live in poverty lack the motivation to get themselves out of poverty remained unchanged (3.71), showing a lack of agreement or disagreement. Most surprising was that students' responses showed a stronger agreement to the statement, "Students from lower socioeconomic status backgrounds are typically not as intelligent as their middle-class peers" (5.27–4.79).

Gender. Regarding gender issues, most students' responses showed that they initially recognized the need for equality between genders. Although the responses to the surveys sometimes moved in the undesired direction, the overall support was still high, rating between 5 and 6 on a 6-point scale. Students supported equal opportunities in math and science education (5.60–5.67) and supported equal earnings between men and women (5.55–5.88), but they responded that, because males are frequently the heads of the household, they deserve higher wages (5.68–5.47). Likewise, participants generally disagreed that men make better leaders than women (5.53–5.38, reverse coded), but their responses moved in the undesired direction.

Group Responses. The group responses showed a very different picture than some of the quantitative data did. In the five-member jigsaw groups, students were asked five questions but were told that these questions were merely "jumping-off" points for deeper discussion. Nonetheless, most groups chose to focus on the questions and answer them. Their answers were written on large sheets of newsprint. This section summarizes the responses to these questions.

The first question, "What issues of diversity do individuals/schools deal with?" was asked in order to investigate how the students defined the issue of diversity. Most groups listed the issues of sexism, racism, homophobism, and socioeconomic status or listed examples pointing to these issues, such as "treating rich people better than poor." Some groups listed specific problems, such as, "perception of minorities and lower class, segregation, respect of teachers/students, population of city schools, curriculum," whereas others listed what should be done, such as "equal opportunities for both genders and all sexual orientations and races; awareness of different cultures and their beliefs, values, practices; acceptance of different social classes." Based on these responses, it appeared that the preservice teachers understood the general issue of diversity in schools.

The second question, "Who do schools serve?" was a loaded question as students first needed to determine what being "served" by a school meant. Most groups decided that being served educationally meant being "given opportunities to succeed" and, thus, indicated a favored or privileged status. Students not being served were those students for whom opportunities were either denied or given to as "second-class citizens." In the nine groups, all but one group noted that Whites were favored. Other favored groups were athletes, wealthy students, and straight students. One group indicated that "the majority of that school's geographic location" was favored, although the group also listed White, Christian, athlete, and male as indicators. Only one group believed that "very smart (gifted) and very academically challenged" were the best served in schools. Similarly, those not served included students from lower socioeconomic status and minority groups, homosexuals, and women. One group noted that "invisible systems [were] present that discriminate against them." A couple of groups listed "undermotivated" students as well. Again, the preservice teachers' responses reflected the readings that they had completed, which mirrored the current inequalities occurring in schools today.

When asked why some students were served less than others, some group responses reflected the idea that lowered expectations for poorer students and students in urban areas led to lessened service. One group wrote, "Schools are focused on the White middle-class, and standards have resulted in a middle-class system; teachers are unfamiliar with their students' backgrounds and cultural differences"; other groups blatantly stated, "We (the majority) are still living in the past; in denial about the fact that deep down, we're still racist" and "how you're raised (e.g., if you grew up in a racist/sexist home, that's what you know)." Ironically, one group's response seemed to be based on their collective acceptance of racist underpinnings: "Minorities do not get the same education, so the entire minority group is stereotyped." Again, the preservice teachers appeared to understand, at least superficially, why some groups were receiving a less-than-equal education.

Almost all of the groups combined their answers for the last two questions: "In an ideal or utopian world, what should be changed?" and "In reality, what can we do?" Most of the answers focused on the term *equality*, such as "make everyone have equal opportunities regardless of race, religion, gender, etc." Many groups focused on making the educational opportunities and schools more equal, including the qualifications of the teachers.

The concept that students do not enter kindergarten with equal experiences, equal supports, and differing backgrounds was not part of the preservice teachers' understanding as expressed within the group responses. Instead, their responses indicated that they believe that equal schools will produce equal achievement without systemic changes in school curriculum, instruction, and organization.

Interestingly, no group used the term *we* in answering the question. The amorphous *teacher* should generally treat people equally; no comments referred to changes of curriculum, strategies, or school organization. This lack of self in the discussion, along with the lack of specifics, may indicate the preservice teachers' naïveté, ignorance, and/or lack of self-awareness and school awareness. Although not surprising in an introductory class, this finding reaffirms the fact that, even with exposure and interaction with multicultural readings and activities, preservice teachers' deepest assumptions and beliefs (and therefore their most automatic actions) are difficult to change.

In addition, no specifics regarding what should be done were included. Equal qualifications of teachers and equal opportunities for students were among the most prevalent suggestions. The only suggestion regarding how such equality was to be achieved was a general suggestion of additional training. It appears that the preservice teachers saw the problem as that of other teachers, not of those sitting in their class.

Response Papers. Like the group responses, the students presented supportive, inclusive pictures of how they wanted their classes and schools to be. In each and every paper, the students wrote that the discussion that ensued as part of the cooperative learning project in class had affected their thinking about the issues of diversity. The student responses were divided into two categories: those which indicated that it expanded students' views (e.g., "I never realized what a big issue diversity was. I always thought about it in terms of Blacks and Whites") and those which indicated that it confirmed what students already knew (e.g., "I went to a diverse high school, but this reminds me of how aware I need to be as a teacher"). Every student noted that it was important for diversity to be focused on immediately, not after teaching for a few years.

Despite these promising initial findings, further analysis found that the preservice teachers did not delve into the additional questions posed as part of the assignment—specifically, those regarding whether diversity was important for every student and what they planned to do within the classroom to support their students and create a culturally responsive classroom. This lack of response may be interpreted in a variety of ways, including laziness, lack of knowledge, and/or avoidance due to difficulty or discomfort.

Focus Group. Because the quantitative data gathered conflicted with the qualitative data, the author invited students to participate in a focus group. In this group, the author showed participants the quantitative data, focusing on the disparities within topics (e.g., race/ethnicity, homosexuality) as well as the responses that moved in the non-desired direction. The author asked them why they thought the disagreements occurred and why some of the responses moved in the direction that they did. Seven students participated in the discussion.

The students' comments were insightful. One student shared that, the first time she took the presurvey, she went through quickly, choosing mainly "1s and 6s." When she took the post-survey, she said she understood the issues more thoroughly and knew her own biases better; therefore, her answers were less reactive and more thoughtful. Most of the other students agreed that they had developed a heightened awareness by the time of the post-survey and that their answers reflected what they knew to be true about themselves: specifically, they may not be as open minded and unprejudiced as they would like to believe themselves to be. Therefore, although the project was successful in promoting greater awareness about diversity, the survey was not a reliable tool because it was read through changed vision.

Another student had a completely different take on the problem. She said she agreed that no one liked to be seen as a racist or homophobe or sexist; therefore, in the response papers where they wrote their names and within the groups where they were interacting with their peers, their answers may have been less than completely honest. She explained that the difference in the surveys, which were completely anonymous, may have been because the readings showed how much prejudice still exists. Although most of the students in the focus group appeared to disagree, this could be the reality of the situation, in which case the project uncovered students' prejudices and reinforced the acceptability of these undesired beliefs.

One other theory emerged: Students were angry about what they had read because it did not match their experiences; they felt the authors were exaggerating the problems. For example, one student who went to a high-socioeconomic status private school said that issues of poverty were never seen at school, and the article expressing the prejudice and mistreatment of poor people was "ludicrous." The emotional resentment toward that particular reading may have pushed the student to agree or disagree with statements on the post-survey more strongly than on the presurvey. Other students recognized this point but did not appear to agree with it. Nonetheless, it is obvious that students' experiences led them to react emotionally to many of the articles.

Conclusion

The intent in pursuing this research study was to broaden students' awareness on issues of diversity, develop their multicultural competencies, and expand their recognition that societal biases infect schools. After listening to the students' group discussions and reading their group answers and individual papers, the author fully expected the responses on the surveys to move in the desired direction. Although some of the indicators on their surveys, in their group responses, and in their individual papers show growth and support of currently disenfranchised populations, the results in other areas illustrate that students appeared to become less inclusive rather than more in other areas. Furthermore, responses that showed "middle" scores (3.3–3.7 out of 6) indicated a lack of strong feeling either way on issues that affect students and their families.

The Social Foundations course is the first time that the issues of diversity are openly discussed for some of these students. Changing their beliefs is not going to happen overnight; however, the exposure that occurred in this project will likely set the foundation for future classes that continue to build on students' multicultural competencies. These same students will fill out the survey in future classes as they learn more about diversity and teaching. Thus, as these students continue in the teacher education program, the author will be analyzing these students' units and implementation of lessons to see whether ideas introduced in this class emerge.

References

Dillon, N. (2005). The loss of diversity. *American School Board Journal, 192*(12), 34–38.

Frankenberg, E. (2009). The segregation of American teachers. *Education Policy Analysis Archives, 17*(1). Retrieved from http://epaa.asu.edu/epaa/v17n1/

Grant, C., & Sleeter, C. (2006). *Turning on learning: Five approaches to multicultural teaching plans for race, class, gender, and disability.* Upper Saddle River, NJ: Prentice-Hall.

Hyland, N. E. (2009). One white teacher's struggle or culturally relevant pedagogy: The problem of community. *The New Educator, 5,* 95–112.

Jennings, T. (2007). Addressing diversity in US teacher preparation programs: A survey of elementary and secondary programs' priorities and challenges from across the United States of America. *Teaching and Teacher Education, 23,* 1258–1271.

Joram, E., & Gabriele, A. J. (1998). Preservice teachers' beliefs: Transforming obstacles into opportunities. *Teaching and Teacher Education, 14*(2), 175–191.

Moss, G. (2008). Diversity study circles in teacher education practice: An experiential learning project. *Teacher and Teacher Education, 24,* 216–224.

Pajares, F. (1993). Preservice teachers' beliefs: A focus for teacher education. *Action in Teacher Education, 15*(2), 45–54.

Patton, M. Q. (1990). *Qualitative evaluation and research methods* (2nd ed.). Newbury Park: Sage.

Wubbels, T. (1992). Taking account of student teachers' preconceptions. *Teaching and Teacher Education, 8*(2), 137–149.

CHAPTER TWO

Start with Their Story: Using Autobiography to Develop Meaningful Multicultural Pedagogy

Kristi Stricker

This qualitative inquiry examines the ways in which student-written autobiographies facilitate the development of preservice teachers' understanding of their own multicultural experiences. The findings from this study indicate that autobiography has the potential to help preservice teachers begin to understand the power of their own social locations and develop an awareness of the importance of understanding the experiences and social locations of their future students. In addition, the analysis indicates that the autobiography activity provides methods instructors with the opportunity to model the notion of a caring classroom by demonstrating sensitivity to differing levels of understanding and awareness that the teacher candidates themselves hold.

Numerous scholars have written about the possibilities autobiography holds for developing teachers' understanding of themselves and their students (Asher, 2007; Connelly & Clandinin, 1990, Connelly & Clandinin, 2000; Grumet, 1980). Specifically, Grumet (1980) explains that autobiography enables the student to become the active interpreter of his or her past whereas Connelly and Clandinin (1990) suggest that narratives assist in explaining the ways in which people experience the world. As such, autobiographies have the potential to help preservice teachers understand how their own social locations, such as race, class, and gender, affect their personal life opportunities (Asher, 2007). The importance of encouraging this sort of autobiographical self-reflexivity is evident in the research, which suggests that preservice teachers often hold unexamined values and beliefs that can be attributed to their lived experience (Banks, 1998; Sleeter, 2001). The implications of such personal unexamined beliefs for teachers and the students they teach is apparent in Parker Palmer's (1998) work, in which he writes, "In fact, knowing my students and my subject depends heavily on self-knowledge. When I do not know myself, I cannot know who my students are. I will see them through a glass darkly, in the shadows of my unexamined life—and when I cannot see them clearly, I cannot teach them well" (p. 2). In other words, self-knowledge is a necessary precursor to understanding the lived experiences of others.

This chapter explores how autobiographical essays can elucidate the ways in which preservice teachers experience the world and, consequently, how such experiences affect the teacher candidates' understanding of the experiences of their future students. In addition, the chapter discusses the ways in which student autobiographies can be utilized to model effective pedagogy by fostering the development of positive relationships in the classroom and exposing the prior knowledge and understandings of the teacher candidates.

Context

To set the context for understanding the student narratives analyzed in this study, it is important to recognize that all of the participants attended a mid-sized private university in a Chicago suburb. The university, founded in the mid-1800s, has traditionally served as a teacher's college with the specific mission of preparing teachers for Lutheran schools. Historically, the Lutheran mission and heritage of the university have attracted students who wish to continue their Christian education. Although the percentage of students enrolled in the College of Education who expect to teach in public schools continues to grow each year, a considerable percentage of the students choose to complete the theology requirements necessary to be eligible for placement as church workers and teachers in Lutheran schools. It is also important to note that many of the students enrolled in the College of Education attended small homogenous Lutheran schools and have had little exposure to the diversity they will experience during their clinical studies and student teaching.

The autobiographies examined for this study were drawn from student work samples in required methods courses for secondary teacher candidates. Each student participant was required to write a sociocultural autobiography. The autobiography assignment required each student to reflect on the experiences, people, and factors that have been influential in their personal histories and discuss the ways in which gender, race, age, nationality, language, and cultural context may have impacted their lives. After the preliminary exploratory analysis, the narratives were coded and analyzed according to the criteria for the qualitative narrative analysis described by Creswell (2008). The sections that follow explore the results of the analysis and ways in which autobiography can enhance instruction in secondary methods courses.

Understanding Race and Ethnicity

The analysis of the preservice teachers' autobiographies reveals much about the multicultural understandings they hold. This section considers the teacher candidates' understanding of the construct of race and the ways in which the candidates deconstruct their own racial identities. Based on the analysis of the student-written autobiographies, multiple themes related to race emerge, the first of which is the lack of recognition of race as an influencing factor in the candidates' own lives. In particular, it was not uncommon for the candidates to either ignore the construct of race in their writing or to assert that their race was not an important factor in their lives. This notion is evident in the following student excerpt: "My parents are both White and almost fully German, which means I am also White and just about 100% German. So far in my life, my race and ethnicity have not had an impact on my life." Similarly, a second candidate wrote:

> Another thing that I did not really notice when I was growing up was race and ethnicity. The majority of people in my town were White (like me) and from the same area as me. Of course there were people who were not White, but we never had a problem with that and we never excluded them.

The lack of racial awareness among preservice teachers with majority status is not uncommon. As Levine-Rasky (1998) writes, "This silence is reflected in the way in which teacher candidates regard their own biographies. It is rare for them to conceive themselves as classed and raced social actors moving within social worlds characterized by privilege and inequities" (p. 104). The consequence of the non-recognition of their own racial locations may have implications for their ability to recognize race as an important factor in how their future students will experience the world. Ladson-Billings (1994) noted that, "If teachers pretend not to see students' racial differences, they really do not see the students at all and are limited in their ability to meet their educational needs" (p. 33). As such, it is essential that teacher education students develop a deeper understanding of the implications of their own social locations so that they might begin to better understand the social locations of their students.

The narratives the candidates write facilitate the development of such multicultural understandings by elucidating the specific multicultural experiences of each candidate. This process encourages the preservice teachers to be self-reflexive about their own racial identity. Engaging in this sort of self-reflexive analysis serves to facilitate greater self-awareness and has the potential to illuminate the unconscious biases teachers hold (Grumet, 1980; Reay, 1996). Shedding light on biases previously unattended to is particularly important considering that research indicates that teachers may unconsciously favor those students whom they perceive to be the most like themselves while being unconsciously closed to those students whom they perceive as different (Rist, 1970). Autobiographical writing can bring about self-reflexive thinking, as illustrated in the following excerpts. One candidate noted that:

> During [my] first semester, I was watching a movie with my roommate and our suitemates. Lying on my bed I realized this was the first movie and "hanging out" session I ever had with someone not White. This made me realize just how bad my diversity in racial background was.

Another candidate reflected that:

> I remember in fifth grade we had a transfer student come in from Milwaukee. She told us of her African-American friends and that her boyfriend used to be Black. Being the naïve suburban White kids that we were, we gave the girl a hard time, saying she would turn Black from hanging out with African-American people. Looking back on this, I am shocked to see how truly sheltered I was to make comments like this! I never had a conversation with anyone but a Caucasian person throughout my early childhood.

Both of these students' autobiographies encourage self-reflexive thinking and serve to inform the methods course instructors use related to the experiences and understandings of each teacher candidate. This personalized information provides the instructor with the necessary information to instructionally differentiate the curriculum to enhance the understanding of each candidate. The need for such differentiation is evident when one considers the significant variation that exists in the prior knowledge held by each candidate. Evidence of the variety of existing understanding can be found in the following reflections. One student wrote:

> My family's ethnic background is primarily English and Cherokee Indian. It is an odd mix because we do not look Native American, so I just grew up feeling White. Just because I technically have minority roots, I have never seen it as such and don't fake that I completely understand how minorities feel today. My white skin has always been a cover for it, so I have never been treated by anyone differently.

This student's writing indicates that he contemplated the social advantages that come from his perceived majority membership and the notion of White privilege—a concept his peers may not have yet considered. Indeed, his classmate was just beginning to consider this idea, as evident in the following selection:

> When I think about the factors of my life that have influenced the person who I am today, ideas about race, ethnicity, culture, and class don't even come to my mind. Upon that realization, I have concluded that those factors are, in fact, the reason that I do not consider them. As a White, Lutheran female raised in an average-size college city, I never faced prejudice regarding my race or ethnicity. Because I never struggled in such a way, I never consider how privileged I really am to have lived such an easy life.

Considering where the teacher candidates' understandings lie allows not only for instruction to be differentiated based on students' individual needs, but also for the students themselves to play an active role in helping develop the understanding of their peers by sharing their stories and experiences. One example of a powerful student story that challenges normative understandings related to race and opportunity is provided in the following narratives:

> Race and ethnicity, even though I don't want to believe it, do play a role in an individual's development. Different races and ethnicities do not get an equal change in developing because some have an easier chance of developing than others. I see it all the time because I come from a biracial family. I see how my biological brothers have an easier chance to [develop] than my siblings who are adopted. Seeing this opened up my eyes, and I realized that some races have to work harder to develop than others do.

Another student wrote:

> As captain of our Cheerleading Squad (which actually became a step team), I learned what "beautiful and Black" meant every day. It means nails done, hair done, lips glossy, clothes tight, and shoes perfect. I learned that the Black culture is not a silent one, and their words are valuable. Black History Month for us meant speakers, dancers, gospel choirs, "I have a dream" speeches, and a true celebration. I've tied my identity to these experiences not as a novelty that "I know Black people," but because I appreciate and understand the differences between 'them' and 'us,' and I don't think it always has to be a bad thing.

These two narratives demonstrate an appreciation for what can be learned and gained by understanding and valuing multicultural experiences.

Awareness of the students' different understandings is also valuable in forming productive discussion groups with members who have diverse understandings and experiences. Asher (2007) noted that:

> When both discourse *and* practice consistently, explicitly, and critically interrogate the historical and present-day intersections of race, culture, gender, and foster a self-reflexive engagement with difference, teachers can open up more meaningful, situated ways of knowing self and other and rethinking extant relations of power. (p. 65)

Knowing the experiences and understandings that preservice teachers hold when they enter methods classrooms can provide teacher educators with the necessary information to differentiate instruction effectively. Furthermore, this gathered information creates an opportunity for the instructor to model how effective teachers assess their students' prior knowledge and utilize the data to plan and deliver lessons that are carefully scaffolded to meet the students where they are.

Awareness and Understanding of Social Class

Social class is rarely defined as an important social location, and it is often overlooked as an important factor in framing a child's experience (Van Galen, 2004). Levine-Rasky (1998) described the lack of attention given to the social class of a child:

> It is prevalent among prospective teachers to persist in interpreting social difference and inequality through the lens of meritocracy in which success is directly related to individual achievement and talent irrespective of environmental or broader social factors such as racial discrimination, poverty, unequal treatment in public institutions, language barriers and other patterns of oppression. The effect of this orientation is justification of patterned, negative judgments and actions against children and their capabilities. (p. 90)

When the students in the current study explicitly situated themselves in the class structure, they were forced to grapple with the realities of power, class, and access to resources. For some, this meant acknowledging hardships they endured as children. For example, one student wrote:

> Along with being the oldest male in the house, my family lived in a one-bedroom apartment. It was my aunt, me, my brother, and my mom. My brother and I slept on the floor. I slept on the floor for about seven years before we moved.

Another student wrote, "When I was a young baby until I was four, I was raised in a one-bedroom apartment by a single mother who sometimes would not eat so that my sister and I could eat." Meanwhile, several students who lived lives of relative comfort addressed the notion of privilege. One wrote, "Along with many of the other families in the community, we were and are still part of the upper/middle class." Another candidate stated, "I never remember once, growing up, my family not having enough money for something that we needed."

In addition to compelling the students to consider their own social class, the autobiographies elucidate the wide-ranging criteria used by the preservice teachers to determine their own class background. For example, one student wrote:

> I still very much identify with being working class; my father practically stocks frozen TV dinners for a living. My mother has lost her job and had to start over at least four times in my life; she currently does administrative assisting. My brother and I work at (a grocery store); I stock produce, and he works as a service clerk.

This student determined his social class based on his parents' occupation. Another student tied the assessment of her own social class to the money her family had in relationship to the others in the community:

> I started comparing myself to other children in my neighborhood at school, and I noticed that I wore a lot of hand-me-downs or garage sale-purchased clothes. I also noticed that my family rarely (if ever) went out to eat, even if it was just to McDonalds. Our furniture wasn't new or expensive-looking, and we waited nearly 6 years to finish our basement because we didn't have the money.

The complexity of the preservice teachers' understandings related to social class is not limited to where and how they placed themselves in the American class structure. Variations also existed within the students' analyses of the relationship among class location, individual talents, and the efforts put forth. For example, the meritocratic assumption that working hard results in monetary success is evident in several students' comments. One student wrote, "My family started at the lower end and my parents' hard work and determination crept us up the social ladder." Another student indicated that, "I would consider our status as being at the very low end of middle class at best. However, my dad is a very hard worker and pushed his way toward the top of his workplace." Concomitantly, a deeper, more complex understanding of the class system is evident in the following student commentary:

> Social class is a huge factor in how people develop because not everyone is afforded the same opportunities that others have the chance to receive. If an individual is raised in a lower class [he or she] will not be able to achieve the same level of development as an individual raised from [a] higher level social class because [the former individuals] do not have the resources needed to achieve that stage of development. I was raised [in] a higher class, and I can say that the opportunities that I have would not have been possible if I [were] in a different class.

Requiring preservice teachers to engage in the articulation of their own social class experiences may help them develop an understanding of how class membership influences their worldview and, in turn, foster greater awareness of social class as an important factor in the lives of their future students. When one understands the multitude of unique experiences that each teacher candidate possesses, the challenge of creating meaningful and relevant experiences to enhance each candidate's capacity for multicultural pedagogy becomes more apparent. Although the diversity of experiences can present challenges, it also provides abundant opportunities, such as providing students who have lived poor and working-class lives with the prospect of using their positionality to challenge the normative assumptions of their peers, whose class experience is of the privileged sort. However, taking advantage of the rich diversity present in a single classroom requires the instructor to be aware of the specifics of that diversity.

Modeling Best Practices: Autobiographies and the Caring Classroom

Effective instruction in the methods of teaching requires more than talk. Telling teacher candidates "how to teach" while modeling "how not to teach" is obviously counterproductive. The autobiography activity discussed in this piece presents an opportunity to show teacher candidates what it looks like to know each student's story and level of understanding. The potential of the autobiography activity for modeling a caring classroom is evident in the students' responses to the activity. For example, one student wrote, "I think your comments were great. I liked this autobiography because I felt you wanted to get to know me and really cared to know me." Another stated:

> I like that thought was put into reading the autobiography. The comments let me know that you actually read what I wrote and thought about it. I have had other teachers assign similar things, only receiving a grade for completing the assignment. This made me think they did not take the time to read it.

Such comments indicate that the autobiography activity can provide methods instructors with the opportunity to model the creation of a caring classroom by developing caring relationships based on the recognition and acknowledgment of the preservice teachers' own stories. The explicit modeling of this approach may encourage the prospective teachers to seek out the stories of their future students, better positioning each candidate to meet the unique needs of every student. The fact that autobiography encourages precisely that sort of reflection is evident in the following student comment:

> I thought it [writing the autobiography] was useful because I learned a lot about how people have affected my life that I never would have known they did. I really had to sit down and consider what made me who I am and how the relationships that I have

formed with people, especially former teachers, have really affected how I think and act.

However, this type of refection may be new to preservice teachers, as evident in several student responses to the assignment. For example, one student wrote, "I never really thought about where I came from and how it relates to my learning." Encouraging students to reflect on their own life experiences is important for developing educators who are sensitive to the life stories of their students (Palmer, 1998). As Pearson and Rooke (1993) explained:

> For teachers to be disposed to care about the flourishing of their students requires that they are able to see the lives of their students in their totality to see the forces that shape the development of their personalities, to understand the social conditions that influence their circumstances in life. (p. 423)

Indeed, the autobiography activity helps preservice teachers think more deeply about the connection between lived experiences and learning. As one teacher candidate wrote, "I think [the autobiography] allows the instructor to see what in the student's life might cause struggle and therefore building [sic] a better relationship of respect between the student and teacher." Another concluded that the activity "lets the teacher understand where her students are coming from and why they act the way they do and what might help them learn better."

Conclusion

The findings from this study indicate that the autobiography activity has the potential to help preservice teachers begin to understand the power of their own social locations and develop an awareness of the importance of understanding the experiences and social locations of their future students. This finding is consistent with the previous work of Grumet (1980), Asher (2007), and Conle (1999). In particular, this study supports the use of autobiography in education methods courses based on the analysis and evidence provided that explicate how the autobiography activity allows for the methods instructor to make pedagogical choices that meet the needs of the teacher candidates. Of equal importance is the finding that the autobiography activity supports the methods instructor's ability to create a caring classroom by providing the opportunity for the instructor to demonstrate sensitivity and appreciation for the lived stories of each candidate as well as the differing levels of understanding and awareness that each teacher candidate holds.

References

Asher, N. (2007). Made in the (multicultural) U.S.A.: Unpacking tensions of race, culture, gender and sexuality in education. *Educational Researcher, 36*(2), 6573.

Banks, J. A. (1998). The lives and values of researchers: Implications for educating citizens in a multicultural society. *Educational Researcher, 27*(7), 417.

Clandinin, D. J., & Connelly, F. M. (2000). *Narrative inquiry: Experiences and story in qualitative research.* San Francisco: Jossey-Bass.

Conle, C. (1999). Why narrative? Which narrative? Struggling with time and place in life and research. *Curriculum Inquiry, 29*(1), 732.

Connelly, F. M., & Clandinin, D. J. (1990). Stories of experience and narrative inquiry. *Educational Researcher, 19*(5), 214.

Creswell, J. (2008). *Educational research.* Jersey City, NJ: Pearson.

Grumet, M. (1980). Autobiography and reconceptualization. *Journal of Curriculum Theorizing, 2*, 155158.

Ladson-Billings, G. (1994). *The dreamkeepers: Successful teachers of African-American children.* San Francisco: Jossey-Bass.

Levine-Rasky, C. (1998). Preservice teacher education and the negotiation of social differences. *British Journal of Sociology of Education, 19*(1), 89112.

Palmer, P. J. (1998). *The courage to teach: Exploring the inner landscape of a teacher's life.* San Francisco: Jossey-Bass.

Pearson, A. T., & Rooke, P. T. (1993). Gender Studies and teacher education: A proposal. *Canadian Journal of Education, 19*(4), 414428.

Reay, D. (1996). Insider perspectives or stealing the words out of women's mouths: Interpretation in the research process. *Feminist Review, 53*, 5571.

Rist, R. (1970). Student social class and teacher expectations: The self-fulfilling prophecy in ghetto education. *Harvard Educational Review, 40*(3), 411451.

Sleeter, C. E. (2001). Epistemological diversity in research on preservice teacher preparation for historically underserved children. *Review of Educational Research, 25*, 209250.

Van Galen, J. (2004). Seeing classes: Toward a broadened research agenda for critical qualitative researchers. *International Journal of Qualitative Studies in Education, 17*(5), 663684.

CHAPTER THREE

Shagging in the South: Using Cultural Autobiographies to Deconstruct Preservice Teachers' Perceptions of Culture

Michele Phillips

At the beginning of the 21st century, the United States is in the midst of the largest influx of immigrants and native-born ethnic minorities in its history (Banks, 2001). Society is becoming increasingly diverse in terms of race, culture, ethnicity, and language and will continue to do so over the next several decades. As a result, today's schools are more diverse than at any other point in history, yet the teaching force is becoming increasingly homogeneous (Darling-Hammond & Bransford, 2005; Nieto, 2005). Currently, African-American and Latino students account for 36% of the student population, with the number expected to rise to more than 40% by the year 2025 (Darling-Hammond & Bransford, 2005; Nieto, 2005) . However, 91% of the teaching force is White, which is projected to increase to 95% by 2025 (Darling-Hammond & Bransford, 2005; Nieto, 2005; Singh, 1996). As a result, a cultural, ethnic, and socioeconomic chasm exists between teacher and student, where teachers trained in traditional methods are working with non-traditional students (Meyer & Patton, 2001)—an issue exacerbated by the fact that White, middle-class teachers and preservice teachers often view themselves as lacking culture (Cochran-Smith, 2004; McIntyre, 1997; Villegas & Lucas, 2002). Thus, teachers must become more familiar with their own cultural backgrounds as well as the cultural backgrounds students bring to school in order to teach students more effectively, interpret behaviors, and find ways to make positive changes in their classrooms in order to increase student success (Meyer & Patton, 2001).

When discussing culture and how it affects students' perceptions in schools, professors and instructors in preservice programs often fail to ask preservice teachers to examine their understanding of their own race, culture, or ethnicity (Cochran-Smith, 2004). However, preservice teachers must be asked to examine their own cultural heritage before they can begin to make sense of or recognize the differences between their own culture and others' cultures. As Kea and Utley (1998) explained, "Teachers lack the awareness of their own ethnocentric views and their limited cultural competence regarding minority and diverse students inhibits use of effective practices with students and families of diverse backgrounds." Preservice teachers must be helped to understand—and, perhaps, unlearn—their own cultural assumptions and beliefs before effective practices can be used in diverse classrooms (Cochran-Smith, 2004).

Preservice teachers are often asked to think about their students' cultures and to teach in ways that will help diverse students learn; however, they are rarely asked to critically examine their own culture and how it affects their perception of teaching and learning (Cochran-Smith, 2004). In addition, college and university professors have often not examined their own beliefs, thus making it impossible to effectively help preservice teachers do so, which results in a further disconnect between theory and practice (Cochran-Smith, 2004; Irvine, 2003). When college and university professors are not fully prepared to discuss and reflect on the influence of their cultural identities on their teaching, they cannot fully support their students with such methods in the classroom. As a result, preservice teachers may perceive cultural identity as unimportant or unnecessary in their own classrooms (Villegas & Lucas, 2002).

To help my preservice teachers—and myself—develop a stronger sense of our own "cultural selves" and explore issues of culture in the classroom, I designed a study emphasizing the use of cultural autobiographies (Cochran-Smith, 2004; Villegas & Lucas, 2002). Preservice teachers enrolled in my course were invited to examine their own views on race, culture, ethnicity, gender, and socioeconomic statuses as well as how these factors influence their beliefs on teaching and learning. Instead of preparing them to teach "other people's children" (Delpit, 1995), the goal was to help the preservice teachers connect with their own cultural beliefs and identities so that they would be better prepared to work with students whose cultures differed from theirs and create meaningful opportunities for these students' success in the social studies classroom.

Framework of the Current Study

The purpose of this study is to understand the value and effectiveness of using cultural autobiographies in a social studies methods course. As research focusing on individual perceptions and beliefs of culture, the study falls within the constructivist paradigm of qualitative research (Crotty, 1998; Schwandt, 1994). Data were collected from one cohort of third-year juniors enrolled in either an elementary or a middle grades teacher education program. The students were asked to write a cultural autobiography, with the following questions provided as a guide:

- Describe your culture.
- Describe one significant event related to culture, race, gender, and social class from your life.
- What is missing related to culture, race, gender, and social class from your life?
- What are the implications of these findings for your own teaching practice?
- What are the implications of these findings for the children with whom you will work?
- What kinds of goals for your own professional growth can you make based on these reflections?

Two forms of data were collected. First, the students' written cultural autobiographies were collected and used to understand their initial thoughts on culture and the resulting influence on their lives and ideas about teaching and learning. Second, anecdotal records were kept on student feedback during classroom discussions and thoughts on culture during the course. Student growth and beliefs can potentially be measured using these two pieces of data, gathered at different points in the semester, with the goal of answering the following research question: Do cultural autobiographies influence students' beliefs and understandings of culture in the classroom? Data were analyzed using Hatch's (2002) inductive data analysis method, in which themes are elicited from the data and generalized to identify the connections within the data. Broad domains were created and the data reread to look for relationships and connections common across the data. These relationships, along with supporting raw data, are reported in this chapter.

Background of the School and Participants

The College of Charleston is a small, public liberal arts and sciences college with a growing master's program. Located in the heart of historic Charleston, South Carolina, many of the college's buildings are antebellum homes, and historic preservation is a core value on campus. The College of Charleston currently enrolls approximately 10,000 undergraduate and 1,500 graduate students. Of the enrolled, full-time, undergraduate students in the fall of 2009, 60% were female and 40% were male; 81% were identified as Caucasian, while less than 5% were identified as African American and less than 1% were international students.

The lack of racial diversity on campus became a core issue in the spring of 2010, when the president of the university, in association with the faculty senate, formed a task force to address minority student concerns about marginalization and disenfranchisement on campus. The task force included local African-American leaders in an effort to improve diversity efforts and develop initiatives to increase diversity on the College of Charleston campus.

Twenty-five students (20 females, 5 males) enrolled in the spring 2010 social studies methods course that is the focus of this study. The course is offered during the second semester of a two-year teacher education program that students begin in their third year of college. All 25 enrollees agreed to participate in the study. Eighteen students self-identified as Caucasian, five as African American, one as Italian, and one as having one parent from Cuba and one of Jewish descent. Twenty-four of the 25 students were between the ages of 20 and 22, with one student being 24 years old. Four of the 25 participants are from states other than the one in which the university is located: One student hailed from the Midwestern United States, one from the Northeast, and two grew up in neighboring Southern states. The majority of the 25 participants view themselves as belonging to the middle socioeconomic class. Thus, participants in this study are demographically similar to the general population of the College of Charleston and of public school teachers nationwide (College of Charleston fact book, 2011; Singh, 1996).

Cultural Autobiographies: Insights from preservice teachers

When I read and analyzed my students' cultural autobiographies, four main themes emerged. First, a majority of students defined their culture primarily through socioeconomic class and religion. Second, students were able to discuss the cultural "others" they had encountered, but only African-American students and students whose parents were from other countries specifically discussed race or ethnicity as a cultural characteristic. Third, students often related their cultural identities to geographic location. Finally, students were able to clearly identify family influences on their beliefs and cultural identities. These four themes were further explored in class discussions and were again revisited in final feedback at the end of the course.

Identifying Culture: "I've never thought of that before!" A number of students specifically mentioned socioeconomic class as a cultural identifier, which was then connected to neighborhood and school. One student wrote that she "came from a peaceful, middle-class family with two married parents and a sister." She did not compare the ideas of marriage and violence to families other than her own, but these were the first words she chose to describe her culture. Another student wrote, "My family is middle class, so we've never really ever had to struggle for anything or see anyone really struggle for anything." She further explained that "everyone I went to school with was pretty much middle class, and, while I am empathetic toward children who struggle, I never saw that when I was growing up." While she could clearly articulate her background and believed she could understand the lives of children whose backgrounds were different from her own, at the end of her paper she stated, "I will have to be careful not to judge my children or their families for things that I may not understand." Another student noted, "While my father's profession allowed me to grow up middle class, I went to school with other children, and this allowed me to see how other people live." Although not specifically addressed, it can be assumed that her reference is to students considered to be of a different socioeconomic status as she repeatedly referred to the idea of class differences during class discussions. This dichotomy between being middle class and potentially teaching children of a lower socioeconomic status was evident in a number of papers, which could perhaps be explained based on the fact that the first semester of the students' program focuses on urban schools and the influence of poverty on education.

The influence of socioeconomic status and religion was evident when students were asked to describe an encounter with someone from a culture different from their own. Of the 25 students in the class, 17 described encountering someone from a different culture either during a vacation to another country or during a church-sponsored mission trip. Descriptions of mission trips were most often accompanied by a description of students' religion and how their religion influenced their beliefs. For example, one student wrote that she "is a good, Southern, Christian woman" whose church formed mission trips "to spread the word of God and help those less fortunate than we are in the United States." A second student explained that her religion had enabled her to "grow up understanding and believing in the importance of morals based on Christian beliefs." A third student explained her encounters with persons of a different culture during a church-sponsored mission trip by noting that she and fellow missionaries, "acting like good Christians . . . took the bottles of shampoo, bars of soap, and rolls of toilet paper out of our hotel rooms every morning and took them to the poor families in the community that needed these supplies."

However, in another example of the influence of church-sponsored mission trips on cultural beliefs, one student explained that, "at the age of 14, when I went on my first mission trip, I first realized that there were people different from me in the world. I had just never had to think about it before." This insight was very powerful for her and her ideas on teaching. She later explained, "I realized that everyone is different and important and valuable, and my job as a teacher is to teach in ways that make students feel important and valuable and smart, even if it takes extra time."

The connection between morality and religion became a topic of class-room discussion, and students were asked to consider whether a person had to be Christian to have good morals. The students thought quietly for a few moments before one female student stated, "I've never thought of that before. Everyone I know is Christian" (personal communication, February 16, 2010). This student assumed that everyone shared her religious beliefs; thus, she had never thought about the morality of those who did not agree with her religious beliefs. A male student quickly added that "of course" a person does not need to be a Christian to have good morals: "All religions have some sort of moral code, so our students will know that" (personal communication, February 16, 2010). Although this statement did open up the idea that other religions will exist in the classroom, students seemed to assume that each person—each student—would have some sort of religious basis for his or her decision making. Religion was a core cultural identifier for the participants in this study; it was so ingrained in their socialization that, even when asked, participants could not conceptualize a future K-12 student who might not hold religious beliefs.

Race and culture. As the scholarly literature often notes, those of the dominant race often do not think about race as a cultural identifier (e.g., Irvine, 2003; McIntosh, 1990; McIntyre, 1997; Tatum, 1997). The autobiographies in this study are consistent with this research. Of the 25 participants, only 7 discussed the importance of race or ethnicity as part of their cultural identity. The five African-American students discussed the role that their race played in their cultural identity. The two students whose parents were from other countries discussed ethnic identity as a family construct, which is explored in the next section. The remaining 18 students mentioned their experiences with people whose race or ethnicity was different from their own, but they never specifically mentioned how their race influenced their cultural identities.

Race was a key cultural identifier for each of the five African-American students in the class, and the sentences in which they identified their race each included a descriptor related to pride, pain, or both. Their stories often painted a vivid picture of the interplay among race, racism, and the class-room. One student stated that being African American was important to him and influenced his beliefs about education:

> This helps me think about education, when I look at history and see the injustice and the mistreatment of a group of people through the loss of culture on a grand scale but to develop their own culture and way of life out of these challenges is amazing. It lets me know as a Black man how important it is to educate and teach not just one group of people but all people. But when you see inconsistency in the system to-wards a group of people, for me at least, I want to see them just get a fair shot.

The role of race in cultural identity and education was also evident in one student's story about a course in which she was enrolled at the College of Charleston: "Because the school I attended before coming to the College of Charleston was predominantly Black, I don't have any scars related to my race." She then cited her first encounter with racism in a course at the College of Charleston. After watching "The Story," a play with predominantly African-American characters that portrays gang violence, a peer in her class complained about having to watch a play "full of Black people." The methods student briefly described her response to her peer, then explained that, "Many people see me at the bottom of the totem pole, and unjustly so, because of my race and gender. But that teacher then told me to be a proud African-American woman who should know the world is my oyster." When she described this scene to the class, the hushed moment of reflection was finally interrupted when someone said, "Just make sure y'all don't ever let that happen in your classroom" (personal communication, February 16, 2010). This student's story resonated with the class, and there was a brief discussion afterward about how many of them believed that such situations could be prevented by encouraging students to get to work together.

Another student wrote that, although he grew up in a predominantly White community, he never felt like "an outsider or somebody who didn't fit in. But I don't feel any unity with my race at this time." He further wrote that:

> As an African-American male college student, I don't represent the norms in today's society. Society today portrays my race very negatively, showing only the negative and hardly ever the positive. Those implications are indicative of today's classroom. Perhaps, if you were to survey a school's most disruptive students, who do you think would be the culprits?

Although his frustration was clear, he noted that he wanted to become a teacher so that he could "serve as a role model and teach his student to have pride and not become a statistic."

These three students' stories stood out as being quite different from the cultural autobiographies of their peers and led to meaningful class discussions on race in the classroom. After hearing these students' stories, many students expressed surprise because such experiences were far from what they had experienced as White students in predominantly White schools. As part of their reflection—and to better understand why they had perhaps not thought about these issues before—I encouraged them to read McIntosh's (1990) article. Some did read this work and specifically addressed it during final reflections at the end of the semester.

Although students other than African Americans mentioned race in their cultural autobiographies, it was in relation to another person, not themselves. For example, one student discussed two childhood friends, one who was African American and one who was Latina. She noted, "I was comfortable with being surrounded by people of other cultures and it helped form my culture; it made me feel at home," yet she still only discussed those different from her without clearly identifying her own racial identity or its influence on her cultural identity. This theme was common in many of the autobiographies, and some students wrote about the importance of learning the cultures of their future students in order to be more effective teachers. However, none mentioned in their autobiographies the importance of learning about their own culture's influence on their teaching. Rather, these ideas had to be slowly teased out during classroom discussions, particularly lessons that focused on behavior, family involvement, and collaborative learning.

The influence of location. The majority of the students enrolled in this course were from South Carolina. Of the 20 from South Carolina, half (10) were from Charleston. The influence of location on cultural identity was clearly defined with these students, as they often waxed poetic on the beauty of being from Charleston and how it had shaped their cultural identity. One student began her autobiography by quoting Rhett Butler from the movie *Gone with the Wind*: "I'm going back to dignity and grace. I'm going back to Charleston, where I belong." This sense of identity and belonging that stemmed from being "born and raised" in Charleston resonated through all 10 autobiographies. These students discussed being rooted in Charleston, with defining characteristics such as having families from Charleston, growing up in only one house, being baptized in the same church as their grandparents, and attending the same schools with the same friends from "kindergarten through college and still today." These students laughed at my shag story because they took shag lessons as children. Although they displayed a clear sense of pride and belonging, some of these students felt that this limited their cultural knowledge and interactions. For example, one student stated that, although she loved Charleston, she "just needs to get out in the world more and see what's out there that's different from what I know." Still, many of these students discussed their plans to graduate and search for jobs in the elementary or middle schools that they had attended.

One student discussed the influence of her hometown, a large city in the Northeastern United States, on her cultural identity. "Being from [the city] defines me. Everything from the way I talk, dress, and even walk are because of where I grew up." She further explained how she often feels like an outsider in Charleston, where she "walks past slow walkers on the sidewalk and often gets accused of speaking too quickly." Although this student clearly perceived her location as a cultural asset, the student from the Midwest viewed "being from [town] as a blessing and a curse." The latter student later explained in her autobiography that she believes her cultural interactions and development were limited: "I never saw an African-American person until I was in the second grade. I knew people of other races existed, but I had never encountered someone whose race was different from my own." She indicated that she never "wants to be a person that isn't tolerant of others and doesn't accept differences. I plan on embracing differences as a way for my classroom to be enriched and unique."

Family and cultural identity. All students discussed the impact of family on cultural identity, but they did so in different ways. As noted earlier, many students related their family's socioeconomic status and religious beliefs as part of their cultural identity. Another group of students clearly identified their race as a rich part of their family heritage that significantly impacted their cultural identities. However, for two students, their cultural identity was deeply rooted in their family's heritage.

One student's cultural autobiography developed around her identity as "just another Italian girl." She noted that, when first asked to write about culture, she "thought it was funny because I can just look at my last name and know that I have a past that will help support me in the future." She further described her cultural experiences growing up in a large Italian family that owned a restaurant: "I had to learn how to cook and work with others. I was never alone, but always part of a community, and this is important to me. I want to make sure my students feel that same sense of family that I did growing up." This student was able to clearly connect the impact of her culture on her beliefs on teaching and learning. She understood why she thinks community and togetherness are important and how such beliefs will be instilled in her classroom.

The other student painted a similar picture when describing her family's heritage on her cultural identity. Her autobiography begins with the sentence, "Culture? Well, we have *plenty* of that in my family." She then told the story of her grandparents' escape from Cuba in the 1960s, "right when Castro was coming to power." She also discussed her Jewish identity and how the two interplay in developing her sense of self and family. She articulated how her cultural identity would impact her classroom:

> My family taught me to hold my heritage and my culture in high regard, which I do. I feel like all of my students should know and love their roots; where they came from and how they got here [to the United States]. I will focus on this at the beginning of every school year. I hope that this will help my students feel included and

welcomed and open *every* student's eyes to their own backgrounds and those of the students sitting right next to them.

Although many students could discuss culture as an abstract concept, these two autobiographies illustrate occasions when students clearly discussed the role of family, heritage, and culture in the classroom.

Changing Ideas and Understanding Culture

After completing the cultural autobiography assignment, students were encouraged to participate in a classroom discussion and share their thoughts and ideas in small groups and then as a whole class group. The class discussions were designed to provide students with the opportunity to compare their experiences with others. Many students stated that the cultural autobiographies were crucial in helping them begin to understand their cultural beliefs and impacts on the classroom, but they noted that classroom discussions were more important in helping them process these new ideas and ways of thinking. Discussions were predominantly student led, with an occasional guiding question from me when a new idea or insight was discussed. Students were excited to share their stories and eagerly compared their autobiographies with those of their classmates. Indeed, when asked whether the discussion during class was beneficial to their learning, one student stated,

> In the paper I was writing about someone I already know, and, after talking to everyone else, I'm finding out all sorts of things I had never thought of before and that's helping me think. I didn't know all this stuff was culture. I just thought it was how things are. (personal communication, February 16, 2010)

Another student stated,

> I feel that my ideas on culture have definitely changed just from seeing things in a new and different perspective. I love the discussion with all of us because I was always really interested in what we were learning even though it was a topic that I thought was so boring but it's not and it matters. (personal communication, February 16, 2010)

As the semester progressed, these students were asked once again to reflect on if and how their thinking had changed during the course. Although some comments were specifically related to social studies, some students spoke of how their thinking on culture had changed as a result of the actions in this course. Most students seemed genuinely surprised that everyone brought a different cultural lens to the classroom. One student stated, "I never thought of myself as being different or that others were that different from me. I need to think about that before I make assumptions in my class-room" (personal communication, February 16, 2010). Another student noted:

> I have always been intrigued by culture. One of the most meaningful things I've learned this semester is that no one person is exactly like another. We are all differ-ent, we come from different experiences, and we all see things through different lenses. Before we judge, we need to think of the situation, and we need to have em-pathy. A great way to engage students is to talk about experiences that pertain to them, and give them the chance to elaborate on their experiences and come to con-clusions about what they have been through. After all, every student is different, and that is what makes classrooms so beautiful. (personal communication, February 16, 2010)

Conclusion

Despite the increasing racial homogeneity of the profession, cultural diver-sity in teaching and in preservice programs exists. A great potential exists for preservice teachers' growth and development in terms of understanding their cultures and the cultures of their students. Cultural autobiographies are one tool that can help preservice teachers better understand how their experi-ences, beliefs, and perceptions impact their teaching. By asking students to reflect on their cultures and how culture shapes their teaching, professors and instructors in teacher education programs can help preservice teachers become reflective practitioners who are better able to negotiate diverse classrooms.

References

Banks, J. A. (2001). *Cultural diversity and education: Foundations, curriculum, and teaching.* Boston: Allyn & Bacon.

Cochran-Smith, M. (2004). *Walking the road: Race, diversity, and social justice in teacher education* (pp. 83-101). New York: Teachers College Press.

College of Charleston fact book.(2011).Retrieved from http://www.cofc.edu/pv_obj_cache/pv_obj_id_7551A716B5BEF927A21E29D44BE1E3 548E7B6900/filename/factbook.pdf.

Crotty, M. (1998). *The foundations of social research: Meaning and perspective in the research process.* Thousand Oaks, CA: Sage Publications.

Darling-Hammond, L., & Bransford, J. (2005). *Preparing teachers for a changing world.* San Francisco: Jossey-Bass.

Delpit, L. (1995). *Other people's children.* New York: New Press.

Hatch, J. A. (2002). *Doing qualitative research in educational settings.* Albany: State University of New York Press.

Irvine, J. J. (2003). *Educating teachers for diversity: Seeing with a cultural eye.* New York: Teachers College Press.

Kea, C., & Utley, C. (1998). To teach me is to know me. *The Journal of Special Education, 32,* 4447.

McIntosh, P. (1990). White privilege: Unpacking the invisible knapsack. *Independent School*, *49*(2), 131138.

McIntyre, A. (1997). *Making meaning of whiteness: Exploring racial identity with white teachers*. Albany: State University of New York Press.

Meyer, G., & Patton, J. (2001). *On the nexus of race, disability, and overrepresentation: What do we know? Where do we go?* Boston, MA: National Institute for Urban School Improvement.

Nieto, S. (2005). *Why we teach*. New York: Teachers College Press.

Schwandt, T. (1994). Constructivist, interpretivist approaches to human inquiry. In N. Denzin & Y. Lincoln (Eds.), *Handbook of qualitative research* (pp. 118137). Thousand Oaks, CA: Sage Publications.

Singh, N. N. (1996). Cultural diversity in the 21st century: Beyond e pluribus unum. *Journal of Child and Family Studies, 5*(2), 121136.

Tatum, B. (1997). *Why are all the black kids sitting together in the cafeteria?* New York: Perseus Books Group.

Villegas, A., & Lucas, T. (2002). *Educating culturally responsive teachers: A coherent approach*. Albany: SUNY Press.

CHAPTER FOUR

"What's a Cultural Memoir?" An Action Research Study of Future Teachers' Understandings of Themselves as Cultural Persons

Edric C. Johnson, Hyun Young Kang, and Laurie Katz

This chapter describes what the researchers learned from using a cultural memoir assignment with preservice teachers in two social studies method courses aimed at teaching social justice. Preservice teachers were asked to complete a case study assignment in which they had to select one student with a different cultural background in their field experience. They developed a cultural memoir with this student during their student teaching placement. The purposes of the assignment were to encourage students to be critically reflective about their cultural backgrounds and beliefs and help the instructors better understand how this assignment influenced their thinking about themselves and their future teaching for social justice. Although many preservice teachers had difficulty examining their own values and attitudes toward people different from themselves, some growth occurred in helping preservice teachers become more aware of their cultural identities.

One of the goals for teacher educators is to prepare preservice teachers to work with children and their families from all different cultural backgrounds, socioeconomic levels, and family structures. As instructors for a social studies methods course, we wondered whether we were making any progress in this area. Standard course evaluations and general reflections about the quality of the course were not providing us this information. Therefore, we engaged in an action research project to study our use of a methods course assignment—namely, a cultural memoir encouraging students to be critically reflective about their own cultural backgrounds and beliefs—and the ways in which this assignment influenced their thinking about themselves and their future pedagogy.

In the artifact project (Allen & Hermann-Wilmarth, 2004), participants were asked to bring in artifacts that would help them think about their cultural backgrounds. They were asked to write, tell stories, and engage in dialogue about their artifacts. In ascribing meanings to their artifacts, the major themes that emerged were family, education, and cultural identity.

Although many preservice teachers were unaware of their values and attitudes toward people different from themselves and even less aware of how they had acquired these values, the data suggest that some initial strides were made toward helping students become more aware of their cultural identities. The study also identifies the limitations and complexity of attempting to dig deeply into these issues, even within a teacher education program focused on social justice.

Examining Cultural Identity in a Self-Study

Two bodies of theory and research informed this study: the work on self-study as an approach to inquiry and critical reflection (Loughran, Hamilton, LaBoskey, & Russell, 2004), along with related work in action and teacher research (Cochran-Smith & Lytle, 1993; Hubbard & Power, 2002; Noffke & Stevenson, 1995), and the theoretical work on cultural identity formation (Holland, 1998; Tatum, 2003) as well as teacher education research related to cultural awareness (Nieto, 2000a; Vavrus, 2002; Yon, 2000; Zeichner & Noffke, 2001).

Based on this research, we asked students in our social studies method courses, through the cultural memoir assignment, to be critically reflective about their own cultural backgrounds and beliefs. We wanted them to look at themselves as multicultural persons with complexly constructed identities. Reflection enables individuals to "see themselves and their relationship to the social and physical environments" (McKenna, 1999, p. 2), which is of critical importance for a teacher because teaching is a process that requires thoughtful awareness along with action.

The heart of the problem is that prospective teachers often struggle with their own identities while working with diverse students (Haberman, 1991). Understanding one's own cultural identity is necessary in order to proceed to cross-cultural understandings (Nieto, 2000b; Zeichner, 1996). Some have argued that we best discover the fact that we have a culture while examining someone else's culture. From the cultural resources available to us in our social experiences, the identity-making process continually occurs (Holland, 1998).

The Cultural Artifact Assignment

The goals for the cultural artifact assignment are twofold: create a cultural memoir representing preservice teachers' culture and create a cultural memoir of one of the students in their field placements. The assignment was described in the syllabus in the following manner:

The purpose of this project is to look at the ways we are multicultural persons with complexly constructed identities that will influence us as teachers. You should collect three to six significant objects, photographs, writings, etc., to help you think about your own cultural background. You will do some reflective journal writing that addresses the following questions, as appropriate and in ways that are meaningful to you. You may substitute other questions if you choose.

- What do the objects in your memoir signify to you in terms of cultural values?
- What have you learned from others in your social context about who you are, what is important to you, what values you hold, how you think about education and yourself as a student and a teacher?
- What life experiences (e.g., cross-cultural experiences, travel, friends who are different from you) have helped you make what is invisible more visible related to your cultural values?
- What are the connections with the things that you learned about yourself during this assignment and the expectations you have for students in your classroom?
- How have your values and perspectives shaped how you think about others? About difference? About social justice in schools and society?

The students discussed their artifacts during the quarter and wrote a final reflective paper. They also discussed their memoir project and created one with a student in their field placement, writing about what they learned. Near the end of their teacher education program, a follow-up survey was administered to probe which parts of the assignment and their learning were influential in their student teaching.

Methodology

Participants. The three researchers for this project taught two sections of a social studies methods course: one section in an early childhood M.Ed. licensure program and the second in a middle childhood M.Ed. licensure program. Sixty-two students were enrolled in the two sections; the majority were White middle-class women. Diversity was inherent within this seemingly homogenous group, which included seven men, one African-American woman, four women whose families were from other countries (Italy, Lebanon, Slovakia, and the Philippines) in the middle childhood cohort as well as two males and five women whose families were from other countries (Mexico, Pakistan, Asian countries, Greece, and Macedonia) in the early childhood cohort. The M.Ed. licensure program is a five-quarter program in which students are placed in classrooms within their program—namely, early childhood preservice teachers are placed in pre-K-3 grade classrooms and middle childhood preservice teachers are placed in fourth- through ninth-grade classrooms.

Design sources and analysis. The triangulated data for this artifact project included the cultural memoir project and final reflective papers about their project (early and middle childhood cohort), audiotaped records of memoir sharing with peers (middle cohort), and a survey administered seven months later. The data analysis for this part of the research project involved categorizing the artifacts in the cultural memoir project as well as coding the written reflective papers and focus group discussions for emergent themes (Patton, 2002) to capture the meanings that students attached to their cultural memoir artifacts. Follow-up surveys administered seven months later were also coded according to emergent themes.

The themes and coding of the data from the early and middle childhood methods courses were developed separately and then negotiated within the research group. The data were then recoded to consistent themes and compared to assess similarities and differences between the two cohorts. Table 4.1 presents a summary of the coding categories that emerged from the analysis of the cultural memoir project, including the reflective papers and focus group discussions. The table indicates the percentage of students from the early childhood and middle childhood cohorts who, in writing and/or discussions, ascribed specific meanings to their artifacts. Appendix A includes tables of the subcodes and examples within each of the categories, including percentages for each of the subcodes for each cohort.

Table 4.1
Meanings Ascribed to Artifacts

	Family	Education	Cultural Identity	Relation-ships &	Social Group	Free-Time Activity	Teaching	Reflection on Difference	Sexuality
Early Childhood Cohort	61%	16%	8%	6%	4%	3%	2%	0%	0%
Middle Childhood Cohort	38%	19%	15%	2%	8%	3%	11%	3%	3%

In writing and conversations with others, the students described what each of the artifacts in their memoir project meant to them and why they included it. The major themes that emerged from the coding—family, education, and cultural identity—are elaborated here.

Theme 1: Family. In both the early and middle childhood cohorts, the most predominant category was related to families. Significant writing and discussion emerged about the importance of families and the values individuals acquired from their families. For example, by using family and wedding pictures, they wrote and talked about values they learned from their families ("Marriage is very important to my family"). Many of them used photographic artifacts to identify family as a significant influence on their cultural identity ("My family made me feel very pleased to be Italian"). Others brought in recipes, passport information, and blankets from members of their families.

A difference emerged between the two cohorts regarding the amount of positive and critical attitudes they described related to their families. The early childhood students tended to describe or view their family as having made positive contributions to their identity. Sixty-one percent of the students discussed family as a significant influence on their views of themselves and the world.

The middle childhood students mentioned their families somewhat less frequently (38%), and a number of them were critical of their upbringing. They described learning prejudices, biases, and stereotypes ("My family is very racist"). One student stated: "I disagree with my parents' view on homosexuality." Another declared, "My mother is an alcoholic, she's a loser and I don't even talk to her." Some were able to examine the enculturation from their families critically, including at times the limitations of using that frame of reference to describe their cultural identity. For example, one student said, "I am realizing that talking about my family does not really address my racial and ethnic identity." Such comments may indicate an emerging awareness of separate identities. For a few, the cultural memoir project had exacerbated relations with their family ("This memoir project helped me see the ways I have grown away from my family's attitudes. This has caused a problem in talking with my parents sometimes"). Critical comments were also apparent in discussions related to topics of identity, social groups, teaching, sexuality, and reflections on differences.

Like Allen and Hermann-Wilmarth (2004), we wanted students "to look beyond the personal relationships of their lives into more deeply rooted, yet more challenging, issues of race, class, and gender in their explorations of culture" (p. 7). Although this occurred for some students in the middle childhood cohort, it was not evident in the data from the early childhood cohort. The differences here may stem from the fact that the middle childhood cohort finished the quarter by sharing their memoir projects with each other in small focus group discussions. These conversations—more than their written reflections—raised these more complex reflections.

Differences in the students' attention to family may have been related to the focus of their programs. A large percentage of the students in the early childhood program had undergraduate degrees in family and human development studies. The early childhood program as well as the social studies method course emphasized family, communities, and consideration of the whole child in the context of families within larger communities. In contrast, the middle childhood social studies methods course focused more on subject matter content and examined social issues, diversity in education, controversial issues, and multiple perspectives of these. Thus, the orientations of the courses may have influenced the emphasis on family in the early childhood cohort.

Theme 2: Education. A second theme that emerged in relation to the memoir project artifacts in both early and middle cohorts was education. Students in both courses included similar kinds of artifacts and explanations. Pictures of educated family members, university clothes and items, copies of diplomas, and graduation memorabilia and pictures were common. Several students discussed their parents' influence and attitudes toward higher education. "Going to college was not an option," said one student. Many students described completing their education as an important accomplishment: "This outstanding achievement medal represents my strong efforts in math, science, and English." Another student explained what he gained socially from his education: "My college education has allowed me to learn from so many diverse people." This emphasis on the importance of education is not surprising for students who chose teaching as their future profession.

Theme 3: Cultural awareness and identity. Another theme found in the data was related to cultural awareness and identity. As one student wrote early in the quarter, "I'm not sure about my culture of being White. All I think is that my family came over on the *Mayflower* and settled here." Several students had not really recognized how they had been constructed within their own cultural contexts or that this process was similar to how other students had grown to be cultured in other ways. The data suggested that a change occurred for some students during the semester. For example, the same student who mentioned the *Mayflower* described the meaning behind her artifact (a shopping bag) as a symbol of her family's value of dressing well and properly, but she also came to see this artifact as marking her own White privilege. Preservice students are able to acknowledge their own complicity in maintaining inequitable power systems and relationships (Leland & Harste, 2005). However, Gloria Ladson-Billings (1994) reminds us that many White teachers are uneasy when it comes to addressing their own privileges and their students' differences, especially racial differences.

Another identified difference occurred in responses between White students raised in small homogenous neighborhoods and students who had immediate family members from other countries/cultures or had significant cross-cultural experiences. Students with more significant contact with persons from other cultures and racial groups typically had less difficulty articulating their values and identifying the influences that formed these values. For example, one student commented on a photographic artifact from her trip to Austria: "I discovered what it's like to be a foreigner."

Evidence suggested that significant learning took place related to understanding that they were "not just American." They came to more explicit understandings of how their values had been constituted within their own particular social context. Nevertheless, many of these students were still struggling with their definition of "culture" (e.g., the difference between culture and ethnicity). Yon (2000) asserted the need to reexamine questions of culture, race, and identity as we experience an increase in globalization, diaspora, and difference in schooling.

Follow-Up Survey

Near the end of the teacher education program and seven months after the conclusion of the methods course, we asked students in both the early childhood and middle childhood cohorts to provide written responses to two questions in a follow-up survey. The questions were:

- Can you identify ways in which the memoir assignment helped you become more aware of your stereotypes, prejudices, and other cultural assumptions?
- Can you identify anything from the project that you learned that "stuck" with you and/or influenced your teaching?

Themes were developed from the responses, and the data were coded to reflect these themes. The findings are presented as a combination of both questions due to the significant overlap that occurred between the responses to the two questions. The students described changes in how they perceived themselves as cultural beings and attributed this change to the cultural project, the classes and sociocultural orientation of the teacher education program, the field placements, personal experiences (e.g., travel and service learning), and friends and university classmates.

The two themes derived from the data in both graduate and undergraduate courses related to their "teacher" identity and their "self"-identity. The teacher identity theme captured discourse related to talking about themselves as teachers and assumptions they had about students. The self-identity theme included more personally oriented values and assumptions.

Survey Data Theme 1: Teacher identity. One category within the first theme, teacher identity, demonstrated an increase in the students' awareness of the stereotypes and assumptions they held about specific ethnic groups, family structures, and socioeconomic backgrounds. For example, some of the participants expected to get little, if any, information about a child's culture if they were from a lower socioeconomic background. Yet they were surprised when they were unsuccessful in obtaining information about a child from an upper class family. One preservice teacher wrote that she had assumed that "All students' parents from affluent [sic] are highly involved and will support their children." Other preservice teachers held assumptions such as "All mothers are primary caretakers" and "Every child has their own room or bed." The project allowed some students to see the contradictions in their assumptions and stereotypical beliefs.

Another category addressed the concept of developing a classroom community. The idea of sharing information about one's culture was an important process in building classroom community. The preservice teachers found that students enjoyed bringing in artifacts from their home and sharing them with their classmates and teachers. One preservice teacher wrote that "Children sharing their culture helps them to open up and be proud of their culture." Furthermore, they noted that having students share aspects of their culture with other students helped them learn about each other's uniqueness as well as similarities. In addition, the preservice teachers found that sharing their culture with the students strengthened their relationships with their students: "After you have gathered some information about your students, you have stronger relationships with them and can build a stronger classroom community." Another preservice teacher wrote that "Getting to know each other better is one way to support the development of relationships and build a stronger classroom community." Prospective teachers must expand their role by examining diversity and equity issues that involve community organizing, students' family and home practices, and the socialization that takes place in schools (Nieto, 2000b).

The students described the importance of implementing something similar to the cultural memoir project in their own classrooms because it was important to learn about their students' cultural backgrounds. Learning about their cultures helped them develop culturally relevant activities and lessons while strengthening their relationships with the students.

Survey Data Theme 2: Self-identity. The second theme related to the preservice teachers' self-identity. Similar to the first theme, the evidence indicated that some of them became more aware of the stereotypes and assumptions they held about students. They also acknowledged a need to reexamine their own values and beliefs: "I must look to examine my own cultural awareness." The data suggested that the cultural memoir project provided preservice teachers with opportunities to reflect on themselves as cultural beings, which clarified their beliefs and values about their culture. They also began to recognize that their own culture heavily influenced their identities. They perceived their own identities to include more of their culture. Many expanded their definition of culture, which had previously been limited to a person's ethnic background (e.g., food, dress). Others noted that "Culture is complex and you must look deeper." As human beings, we possess multiple identities; sometimes these identities affirm or contradict the community in which we live. According to Yon (2000), interrogating our own culture is a highly contested space, especially if it starts to question the shared characteristics or power structures within systems of schools and society. Differences that exist within a defined culture could potentially be viewed as disruptive.

Conclusion

This study of a cultural memoir assignment in both early and middle child-hood cohorts led to some helpful discussions with and knowledge for our students. For some preservice teachers, this project helped them begin building awareness and critical introspection about the origins of their cultural values. Some had never thought explicitly about their values or where they came from. The case study portion of this assignment enabled them to see how understanding their students individually and culturally helped them respond in more sensitive and relevant ways as a teacher. The project activities revealed aspects of their students that were not available to them within the usual interactions between teacher and student. In supporting diverse students, teachers can begin to relate to their families and communities and envision students as constructive participants in a multicultural democracy (Sleeter, 2008).

Our motivation for including this cultural artifact project in our methods courses stemmed from our concern that many of our students seem unaware of their own cultural attitudes and stereotypes. Knowing from others' research that it is difficult to change students' attitudes and stereotypes, we saw the cultural memoir project as a way to directly address issues related to cultural and social differences. Data, including results from both follow-up surveys, demonstrated that—for some preservice teachers—the cultural memoir helped them learn more about themselves and their students, which subsequently led to a better understanding of why it is important for teachers to learn about their students' cultural identities. Investigating their own cultural situatedness helped some of them see the value of helping their students become aware of and feel acknowledged for their cultural backgrounds. For the preservice students, this was a time not only to reflect, but also to begin to think critically about why they had particular attitudes and whether they wanted to change some of the perceptions they garnered from their families and their social world. Thus, these preservice teachers were working toward becoming critically literate for social action (Leland & Harste, 2005).

This type of assignment requires preservice teachers to take some risks, not only to think about their cultural learning and development, but also to share this with others. For some, it appeared to be a low-risk assignment. The memoir project provided a vehicle to affirm the values of their family and show how they were connected with their family culture. For others, this personal reflection and investigation raised new perspectives and deeper issues. In the middle childhood cohort, a few preservice teachers were close to tears as they recounted particular stories or touched on issues that were difficult to handle. Changing one's perspective on the world is not easy, and asking hard questions about one's situatedness and the consequence of prior perspectives can be humbling. Changing teachers' perspectives toward diversity persons is a long process; indeed, Gomez (1996) concluded that it takes two or more semesters (32 weeks or more) before substantial reconsideration of diverse learners takes place among preservice teachers.

As instructors at the University of Wisconsin–Whitewater, we continue to have preservice students carry out a case study with their students. Whether located in an urban or a rural teacher education program, having students do case studies in their field placement served as an eye-opening assignment for many of the preservice teachers. Many were surprised by the openness of students to share their lives—often including quite private or unique aspects of themselves. Most of their case study students thoroughly enjoyed the assignment because someone was really paying attention to them and the things that were important to them. Some of the preservice teachers did the assignment with the whole class because their case study student was so enthusiastic that everyone wanted to do a cultural memoir. Many of the preservice teachers were surprised by what they learned and recognized the value of building student's in-depth understanding more for their future social studies teaching. Some did a cultural memoir at the beginning of their student teaching; many planned to do it at the beginning of the year when they were teaching. It was our perspective as social studies instructors that preservice students must be secure and informed about their own values and the situated nature of these values if they are to practice culturally relevant pedagogy and be culturally sensitive teachers.

References

Allen, J. B., & Hermann-Wilmarth, J. (2004). Cultural construction zones. *Journal of Teacher Education, 55*(3), 214–226.

Cochran-Smith, M., & Lytle, S. (1993). *Inside/outside: Teacher research and knowledge.* New York: Teachers College Press.

Gomez, M. L. (1996). Prospective teachers' perspectives on teaching "other people's children." In K. Zeichner, S. Melnick, & M. L. Gomez (Eds.), *Currents of reform in pre-service teacher education* (pp. 109132). New York: Teachers College Press.

Haberman, M. (1991). Can cultural awareness be taught in teacher education programs? *Teacher Education, 4*(1), 25–32.

Holland, D. (1998). *Identity and agency in cultural worlds.* Cambridge, MA: Harvard University Press.

Hubbard, R., & Power, B. (2002). *Living the questions: A guide for teacher-researchers.* Portsmouth, NH: Heinemann.

Ladson-Billings, G. (1994). *The dreamkeepers: Successful teachers of African American children.* San Francisco: Jossey-Bass Publishers.

Leland, C. H., & Harste, J. C. (2005). Doing what we want to become: Preparing new urban teachers. *Urban Education, 40*(1), 60–77.

Loughran, J., Hamilton, M. L., LaBoskey, V., & Russell, T. (Eds.). (2004). *The international handbook of self-study of teaching and teacher education practices.* Dordrecht, The Netherlands: Kluwer Academic Publishers.

McKenna, H. (1999, February). *A pedagogy of reflection: Pathfinding in a time of change.* Paper presented at the annual meeting of the American Association of Colleges for Teacher Education, Washington, DC.

Nieto, S. (2000a). *Affirming diversity: The sociopolitical context of multicultural education.* New York: Addison Wesley Longman.

Nieto, S. (2000b). Placing equity front and center: Some thoughts on transforming teacher education for a new century. *Journal of Teacher Education, 51*(3), 180–187.

Noffke, S. E., & Stevenson, R. B. (1995). *Educational action research: Becoming practically critical.* New York: Teachers College Press.

Patton, M. Q. (2002). *Qualitative research and evaluation methods.* Thousand Oaks, CA: Sage Publications.

Sleeter, C. (2008). An invitation to support diverse students through teacher education. *Journal of Teacher Education, 59*(3), 212–219.

Tatum, B. (2003). *Why are all the black kids sitting together in the cafeteria? and other conversations about race: A psychologist explains the development of racial identity.* New York: Basic Books.

Vavrus, M. (2002). *Transforming the multicultural education of teachers: Theory, research, and practice.* New York: Teachers College Press.

Yon, D. A. (2000). *Elusive culture: Schooling, race, and identity in global times.* Albany: State University of New York Press.

Zeichner, K. (1996). Teachers as reflective practitioners and the democratization of school reform. In K. Zeichner, S. Melnick, & M. L. Gomez (Eds.), *Currents of reform in teacher education* (pp. 199–214). New York: Teachers College Press.

Zeichner, K., & Noffke, S. E. (2001). Practitioner research. In V. Richardson (Ed.), *Handbook of research on teaching* (pp. 298–332). Washington, DC: American Educational Research Association.

CHAPTER FIVE

Making the Uncomfortable Comfortable: How Deliberate Conversation and Interaction among Education Majors Can Bring about More Profound Awareness of the Self with Regard to Diversity

Catherine Gatewood and Kenneth Hall

This study came about as a result of questions that arose from preliminary research that set out to determine freshmen education majors' beliefs about diversity. Preliminary findings resulted in the present study, which focuses more deliberately on the utilization of disruptive movement theory on the beliefs and practices of preservice teachers at a small, rural, and seemingly homogenous university. Both beginning education majors enrolled in a freshman seminar and seniors in their last methods course the semester prior to student teaching participated in the study. Both groups of participants completed targeted assignments and experiences that offered a variety of opportunities to address and react to issues related to diversity. The analysis emphasized participants' initial personal ideas with regard to diversity issues as well as their espoused beliefs about diversity and sought to determine whether change occurred over the course of the teacher education program. Of particular note is participants' movement from feeling uncomfortable discussing and/or dealing with diversity issues toward instructors' perspectives that preservice teachers exhibit a greater willingness to talk about and/or engage with K-12 diversity.

Past attempts to integrate diversity into a secondary preservice teacher education program at the small university motivated a discussion of one example of successful strategies. We believe the use of targeted classroom experiences and assignments can benefit education majors, especially those from middle-class, largely White, homogenous settings. We encouraged our teacher candidates to step safely beyond their own comfort zones, consider a broader definition of diversity, and recognize their often unconscious or unchallenged bias.

Based on earlier findings and frustrations with various approaches, we were determined to reconceptualize our secondary teacher education program's entire coverage of diversity by utilizing Milner's (2010) theory of disruptive movement. Milner suggests "a theory of disruptive movement in teacher education has some promise, especially as teacher educators' work to expose self-consumed interests that do not have equity at the center" (p. 121). We saw great promise in this approach.

Although Geneva Gay's (2000, 2010) body of work centers on students of color and their mainly Euro-American teachers, her work is still extremely useful for framing an approach with regard to all aspects of diversity teachers will encounter in today's classrooms. In addition, in their editorial for the *Journal of Teacher Education*, Wang, Spalding, Odell, Klecka, and Lin (2010) pointed out that preservice candidates must become fully aware of their own bias and cultural distance from their much more diverse students in order to prepare for culturally responsive teaching. These multicultural education experts and others call for a much more conscious and transparent approach to designing curriculum and programs that prepare future teachers in order to help better prepare them for the culturally diverse classrooms in which they will teach (Brown, 2004; Galman, Pica-Smith, & Rosenberger, 2010; Wenger & Dinsmore, 2005).

Bergen (1989) extolled the need for radical change in the approach to teacher education. Other multicultural education experts have pointed out the often ethnocentric nature of Americans in general that makes it even less likely that they would be prepared as teachers able to meet the needs of the current classrooms (Villegas & Lucas, 2002). Although Bergen suggests that all teacher candidates should spend at least one semester abroad, his point implies that educators must be more creative in helping teacher candidates uncover unconscious beliefs or bias that could potentially stand in the way of their ability to teach to all students.

It was necessary and critical to begin making changes in our secondary teacher education program by first finding that space in preservice teacher candidates' lives in which they can begin a deep and meaningful conversation that would benefit everyone concerned. Our preservice teachers must not only enlarge their view of diversity to create a focus on what is different and to feel comfort in that, but they must also move beyond celebrating difference to celebrating what is similar. To accomplish this, it was necessary first to disrupt the dominant, but often unspoken, ideologies that are often far too familiar in college classrooms. As Milner (2010, p. 122) pointed out, "Starting with teachers' conceptual repertoires of diversity is the most appropriate place to begin a discussion because teachers' thinking plays such a critical role in their curriculum practices and pedagogical decision making." In other words, to have meaningful discussions on diversity issues such as race, gender, socioeconomic status, sexual identity, and differing abilities that will impact future instruction, it is important to change the often internally held notions that these concepts or issues simply have no relevance or meaning to future teachers because they do not see them as their reality (Pohan, 1996; Wenger & Dinsmore, 2005).

It could be argued that now is just the time to capitalize on and offer purposeful and targeted discussions on current issues that saturate the media as these movements naturally disrupt what one believes to be true and allows for the opportunity to view concepts, ideas, or ideologies in a different light and perhaps naturally move toward changing the status quo. In addition, it offers the opportunity to see commonalities among seemingly disparate groups. In their international online training program on intractable conflict, the Conflict Research Consortium (1998) posited that "conflicts cannot be transformed, and people united in well-functioning societies, unless they are tied together with some sense of unity and commonality." In other words, if brought to the classroom, conflicts that lay beneath the surface must be exposed and dealt with openly in order to effect change.

A conundrum often faced when attempting to affect change in new college students is that the majority who arrive in the fall and hope to be future teachers are still acting in the same manner they did during high school. In fact, many find the transition to college extremely difficult and off putting. They have yet to develop adequate skills and habits of mind that allow for quality study, time management, or organizational skills and simply wade through the higher education arena. Therefore, we believe that it is the college faculty's obligation to help students proceed through the process by providing scaffolding to learn these skills and adjust pedagogy accordingly. In this manner, as students mature through the teacher education program, they are at least exposed to the fact that K-12 schools in the United States are increasingly more diverse. Therefore, faculty members working with these future teachers have an obligation to help their preservice teachers prepare for the classes they will teach.

The Teacher Education Program's Social, Cultural, and Geographic Contexts

The institution where this research took place has an enrollment of just over 5,000 and, like many other smaller regional institutions, is distinctly homogenous. Eighty-eight percent of the student population identifies as White, and 90% of the college's enrollees are residents of the state of Pennsylvania. In fact, the majority of students live within a 50-mile radius of the campus, which is located in a small town/rural area. Nearly the same percentage of preservice teachers enrolled in the school's courses indicates that they are from small towns that also have a homogenous population in their high schools. Nearly 100% of our participants identified themselves as Christian.

This year-long project involved two sections of a fall freshman seminar course specifically designed for entering social studies majors who met for one hour once a week. The two sections included 34 students: 20 male and 14 female. The project also included one section of an advanced methods course (i.e., Methods II) that preservice teachers complete during the semester prior to student teaching. The Methods II course included 18 students: 14 male and 4 female.

Freshman Seminar

In the freshman seminar course, a series of prompts derived from a survey used in the preliminary study were modified slightly. These prompts offered discussion items of interest and established a pattern whereby the students knew they would have a space in which to talk freely and respectfully about difference. This approach proved exceedingly helpful to entering freshman. Often the conversations throughout the semester related back to many "new" college-type encounters with which they were dealing that would begin to be shared in the classroom.

Sample of Prompts Used with Freshman Seminar Students

- Will accepting many different ways of life in America strengthen us as a nation?
- Is it true that the reason people live in poverty is that they lack motivation to get themselves out of poverty?
- Should poor people have the same opportunities to get an excellent education and obtain good medical care as wealthy people?
- In general, do you believe certain groups in society place a higher value on education?
- Should teachers be expected to adapt their lessons to accommodate for students' disabilities, or is this too much work and too difficult for already overworked teachers?
- Do you think large numbers of certain groups of students are placed in special education classes more so than other groups?
- Should same-sex couples be allowed to raise children?
- Should society become more accepting of gay/lesbian couples, and should they be allowed to teach in public schools?
- Would you be able to develop meaningful friendships without caring about the other person's skin color, gender, sexual orientation, or abilities?

The prompts utilized for discussion began by asking the students to describe the size and student body of their high school and share any travel experiences they may have had the opportunity to enjoy. These questions were followed up with a number of questions such as whether they felt teachers tend to expect fewer students from certain groups and why such numbers may be limited. They were also asked a variety of more pointed questions with regard to certain identified groups in society and their rights.

After the prompts were used to elicit conversation, a series of seven articles were divided up and read. Groups were required to share a brief synopsis of the article with the whole class, indicating what struck them as a new concept, idea, or way of thinking and connecting it back to the original conversation based on the previous prompts. They were also asked to pose two original questions to the class. This highly structured sharing of ideas and discussion took two class periods and ended with the students writing an individualized reflection paper to address the following statement: Did the articles you read within your group and discuss in class challenge what you thought of as diversity and how would you respond to someone who said to you that talking about diversity was no big deal and not necessary for future teachers?

Articles Read by Students in Freshman Seminar

- Anger, E. J. (2005, January/February). Okay, I'm now a feminist: Confessions of one man's journey. About Campus, pp. 2628.
- Dillon, N. (2005, December). Loss of diversity: Changing demographic patterns in many cities result in racial isolation. American School Board Journal, pp. 3438.
- Deutsch, B. (2006). The male privilege checklist: An unabashed imitation of an article by Peggy McIntosh. Retrieved from http://www.amptoons.com/blog/the-male-privilege
- McIntosh, P. (1990). White privilege: Unpacking the invisible knapsack. Retrieved from http://www.case.edu/president/aaction/UnpackingTheKnapsack.pdf
- McIntosh, P. (2002). Unpacking the invisible knapsack II sexual orientation: Daily effects of straight privilege. Retrieved from http://www.cs.earlham.edu/~hyrax/personal/files/student_res/straightprivilege.htm.
- Pace, N. (2007). I've completely changed: The transforming impact of the Matthew Shepard scholarship. Journal of Advanced Academics, 18(3), 344371.
- Smith, G. P. (1997). Who shall have the moral courage to heal racism in America? Keynote address at the 7th annual NAME Conference, Albuquerque, NM.

One young man responded in his paper with regard to introducing diversity topics in the classroom that "I feel that the timing of 'dealing with it' should be early on so that younger students realize that there's nothing wrong with people just because they are not the same as them." Another mentioned, after reading Peggy McIntosh's article on White privilege, that it, "really opened my eyes and made me realize the distinct advantages some White people have." Finally, a young man who attended a predominantly White private Catholic school stated that, if people would simply be more honest and talk openly about diversity, they "would realize that we are really not so different and that a lot of people from different backgrounds and cultures share the same likes, wants, and needs." Two weeks after the reflective assignment was handed back with feedback, the campus Director of Human and Cultural Diversity, Mr. Kenneth Hall, attended each class section as a guest to further the conversation and push the concept of diversity just a bit further in order to reach consensus on a new definition of diversity, especially as it pertains to future teachers and to them as college students, encouraging them to discuss what various identified groups might have in common with other groups despite their diversity. After eliciting many freely given comments from a now vocal group becoming slightly more comfortable with the uncomfortable, in both class sections the conversation became a highly energized and structured discussion. Among the points that Mr. Hall emphasized during these sessions was that no universal rules or solutions exist for responding to sexual orientation, ethnicity, gender, or cultural diversity in the classroom (Green, 1989). In fact, Mr. Hall emphasized that the topic of diversity can be complicated, confusing, and challenging; for some teachers it is full of uneasiness, difficulty, and discomfort. The information presented in these classes was intended to help increase awareness of matters that both teachers and students find to be particularly sensitive when addressing the topic of diversity in the classroom.

Each presentation—for both the freshman and more advanced students—explored the advantages of employing commonalities or common ground when introducing the topic of diversity. Ignorance can often be transformed and people united when they are tied together with some sense of unity and commonality. Commonalities can help bridge the gulf that can be created when fear and apprehension are introduced by the ignorance of people and situations. Most problems affect all students, but they may be exacerbated by ethnic, gender, sexual orientation, and cultural differences between teachers and their students as well as between students and their peers. Finding commonalities that all parties share can be an excellent bridge for building an appreciation for the true value of diversity.

In both presentations, Mr. Hall and the students also explored the connection between diversity and relationships. During this point in the presentations, the concept of moving students from encountering diversity to engaging it was introduced. It was stressed that diversity is a prerequisite for truly vibrant relationships. If everyone has the same perspective, it would give way to relatively flat synergy. However, if there are diverse views, if those differences are allowed to flourish, and if there is good communication, then those differences can inspire an emergence of ideas that no one considered before they entered the conversation. In this way, the whole becomes greater than the sum of its parts (Gurin, Peng, Lopez, & Nagda, 1999).

At least two students in each section spoke up in continued support of a fairly narrow concept of acceptance that initially made other students in the class extremely uncomfortable. Under the director's guidance, Mr. Hall and the students directly addressed the comments with empathy, concern, humor, and reality. In fact, in one instance, the director questioned whether he had actually "reached" one of the students and pursued a substantial conversation with the student after the class ended. The end result in both sections was a powerful and inclusive description of what diversity can encompass and many comments with regard to what students had found in common thus far in college with people toward whom they normally would feel no affinity.

At the conclusion of the semester, the students in the freshman seminar completed a take-home final examination. The exam included the following:

> The course prerequisites listed on the syllabus were:
> - A desire to be successful and excel in all areas of academic life
> - A willingness and desire to make a positive contribution to the academic community
> - Attitudes open to critical self-exploration
> - An aspiration for leading a principle-centered life
> - In a paragraph or two, reflect on where you were when you entered the course with regard to the above. Then in another paragraph or two, explain to what extent you feel that you have grown or made progress in those prerequisites this semester.

It is interesting to note that, although not explicitly stated, more than 70% of the students responding to the prompt discussed diversity and their own personal growth in their response. One student in particular stated:

> Diversity can really affect things in our society and how it manifests in the classroom. You can't just say, "Oh, everyone is diverse." But, I hadn't realized the magnitude of what that meant to me in the classroom. What my students will bring in with them to the classroom is something I have to learn to handle, and it will all be different. We are facing diverse cultural and societal issues that can be overwhelming to students and teachers alike. We must learn how to reach these kids to affect them positively.

Another student noted,

> As an education major, you must develop a deep sense of what diversity is. A lot of people have the misconception that diversity is based on the color of one's skin, beliefs and culture. Diversity is so much more than just the apparent qualities that separate people; it is the inner person in every one of us that makes you different

from the next individual. As a future teacher, you should not just want to be accepting or tolerant of diversity, but to embrace and celebrate diversity.

Overall, as freshman, they did indeed confront their own attitudes, thoughts, and beliefs; they also did the same for their classmates. The discussions were lively, engaging, and filled with empathy as well as a growing sense of a larger world than the one they had known to date. They were very much becoming more comfortable with the uncomfortable.

Methods II

All teacher candidates entering this advanced methods course participated in the original study's pre-/post-survey model with group-generated feedback and individual reflections (Marks, 2008). Therefore, they were prepared for—or at least not surprised by—the discussion related to diversity in its many forms that was also part of this course. In addition, extremely valuable to our conversations were the two individuals in the course who had taken one or two special education courses. One student had also traveled abroad in China, two students were nontraditional male students, and one student was an openly gay male. Therefore, as a collective group, these teacher candidates were already dealing with trying to be more comfortable with the uncomfortable.

A major assignment component of this course was the introduction to the Teacher Work Sample (TWS) the students would be expected to create during student teaching. The first four parts of the TWS were introduced, assigned, and prepared based on the semester's class work and field experiences during the methods course. Part 1 of the TWS is referred to as "contextual factors" and requires students to understand how individuals learn, comprehend child and adolescent development, demonstrate knowledge of individual differences, and apply contextual factors to develop instructional strategies for all learners. In other words, they needed to thoroughly know the community in which they would teach, the school in which they would teach, and the students who would fill their classes. Therefore, during their field experiences, they gathered information for that school district and their classrooms to write up fact-based reflective pieces similar to those they would be required to write during their student teaching. Furthermore, they were to identify and describe in detail at least two subgroups that would require them to adapt their general instructional materials. This assignment provided them with valuable experiences in identifying information about the learning–teaching context, students' individual differences, and the ability to begin to consider implications for instruction and assessment.

Similar to the freshman seminar, students in the Methods II course were grouped and assigned to read a series of articles that they subsequently shared and discussed with the rest of the class. Their articles included a few that the freshman read as well as others that were more in depth. One other difference with this group was that all students were required to read all articles. However, groups were responsible for sharing a more detailed critique of two articles and were required to pose questions to the entire class to extend beyond what was written and examine what they had witnessed in the classrooms to which they were assigned for Methods I or II during their day trip to two inner-city schools or to life experience. All were required to describe how or whether they were getting a sense of the connections that may exist in the classrooms they had observed with regard to how teachers perceive their students and what may be missed if those same teachers do not have a more holistic concept of diversity and how it plays a role in instruction.

Articles Read by Students in Methods II

- Anger, E. J. (2005, January/February). Okay, I'm now a feminist: Confessions of one man's journey. *About Campus*, pp. 2628.

- Bennett, M. (2008). Understanding the students we teach: Poverty in the classroom. *The Clearing House*, 251-256.

- Deutsch, B. (2006). *The male privilege checklist: An unabashed imitation of an article by Peggy McIntosh.* Retrieved from http://www.amptoons.com/blog/the-male-privilege

- Dillon, N. (2005, December). Loss of diversity: Changing demographic patterns in many cities result in racial isolation. *American School Board Journal*, pp. 3438.

- Jackson, C. (2006). E-bully. *Teaching Tolerance, 29.* Retrieved from http://www.tolerance

- James, D., Lawlor, M., Courtney, P., Flynn, A., Henry, B., & Murphy, N. (2008). Bullying behaviour in secondary schools: What roles do teachers play? *Child Abuse Review, 17*, 160173. Retrieved from www.interscience.wiley.com

- Markow, D. (2008a). *From teasing to torment: School climate in America a survey of students and teachers. The Gay, Lesbian and Straight Education Network (GLSEN).* Retrieved from http://www.glsen.org/binary-data/GLSEN_ATTACHMENTS/file/499-1.pdf

- Markow, D. (2008b). *The principal's perspective: School safety, bullying and harassment a survey of public school principals. The Gay, Lesbian and Straight Education Network (GLSEN).* Retrieved from http://www.glsen.org/binary-data/GLSEN_ATTACHMENTS/file/000/001/1167-2.pdf

- McIntosh, P. (1990). *White privilege: Unpacking the invisible knapsack.* Retrieved from http://www.case.edu/president/aaction/UnpackingTheKnapsack.pdf

- McIntosh, P. (2002). *Unpacking the invisible knapsack II sexual orientation: Daily effects of straight privilege.* Retrieved from http://www.cs.earlham.edu/~hyrax/personal/files/student_res/straightprivilege.htm

- Niehuis, S. (2005). Helping white students explore white privilege outside the classroom. *North American Journal of Psychology*, 7(3), 481492.
- Olweus, D. (1993). *Bullying at school*. Oxford, UK: Blackwell.
- Pace, N. (2007). I've completely changed: The transforming impact of the Matthew Shepard Scholarship. *Journal of Advanced Academics*, 18(3), 344371.
- Schen, M., & Gilmore, B. (2009). Lighting the moral imagination: Through the facing history and ourselves approach, students learn not only history, but also the skills needed for citizenship in a democracy. *Educational Leadership*, 59-63.
- Smith, G. P. (1997, October 31). *Who shall have the moral courage to heal racism in America?* Keynote address at the 7th annual NAME Conference, Albuquerque, NM.
- Solomona, R., Portellib, J., Daniel, B., & Campbella, A. (2005, July). The discourse of denial: How white teacher candidates construct race, racism and "white privilege." *Race Ethnicity and Education*, 8(2), 147-169.

The conversations in this class stretched over three class meetings, spanning two and a half weeks (interrupted by a week in the field). This class was not assigned a reflective piece immediately. It is interesting to note an exchange that took place during the class discussion on the articles. One of the male nontraditional students who came from a privileged upper middle-class background declared during the conversation, "Why do we have to keep going on and on about diversity and why are we forced to constantly discuss who is different because they are Black or gay or disabled?" (personal communication, March 14, 2007). He then followed this statement with the following comment: "This stuff about equity is just talk to make some people feel better anyway. Even if I ever have any of 'those' students, I will be fine. I won't treat them any differently than I would any other student." (personal communication, March 14, 2007). Needless to say, this caused a great commotion among the students for some time and resulted in one of the most frank conversations in which students had engaged on the topic of diversity.

After this fairly dynamic and disruptive conversation, the teacher candidates went out into the field. The following week, when we were to complete the discussion on the readings, the same candidate could not wait to share an experience he had on his first day while teaching. He was assigned to an all-White, rural school about 10 miles from the affluent community in which he lived. At this school, more than 80% qualify for free or reduced lunch. The candidate was doing a lesson on the right to vote and asked this class of juniors whether any of them intended to vote when old enough. Several hands went up; one student was especially eager to respond. The candidate called on his enthusiastic student, stating, "You seem quite eager to respond and must feel strongly about this." The student he called on practically yelled, "You bet I am going to vote." At this point the candidate asked, "Why do you feel so strongly about voting?" The teacher candidate admitted he was quite excited internally as he felt he had engaged the class and thought he was doing a great job of eliciting student response; he could not wait to hear why this student was so eager. However, the student's response left him nearly speechless. The student adamantly proclaimed that he could not wait to vote because "he sure as [expletive removed] didn't want another [racist expletive also removed] Obama in the White House."

As this teacher candidate shared this interchange in the Methods II classroom, he was still clearly very shaken up about the exchange, and his peers looked at him in silence, initially not hiding their "we told you so" looks. The teacher candidate quietly offered a thank you to the class and this instructor and emphatically stated,

> I would have had no idea how to handle that situation if you had not prepared me by talking about these hard subjects and how very much they are real in the classroom and must be understood and confronted on a regular basis. (personal communication, March 14, 2007).

No amount of instruction was further needed. This future teacher truly saw the value of having his own unspoken ideologies disrupted and confronted.

It was simply pure luck of timing that this interchange discussion occurred just prior to Mr. Hall coming to this class for the conversation on diversity. Because Mr. Hall was aware that these students had been introduced to this topic in previous courses, he was prepared to share at a more intimate and concrete level with this group. He had five topics he wanted to share and discuss with this group. He began with a discussion on how to identify biases or stereotypes that individuals may bring into the classroom. Many students in the class admitted to growing up in homogenous environments that were filled with biases and stereotypes based on gender, culture, race, sexual orientation, and religious beliefs. The point was made that, if teachers are aware of their biases, they can monitor and attempt to improve their attitudes before these viewpoints can be expressed through behavior. This process can include paying attention to language, body language, and the stigma being felt by diverse groups. It was also suggested that a change in behavior can help modify beliefs and attitudes.

The second topic covered correct language and examples that may offend or demean any group. It was suggested that teachers try to refer to all students with terms of equal weight (e.g., a teacher should consider using he and she interchangeably in classroom discussions and examples). Other points that were mentioned included recognizing that students may come from different socioeconomic backgrounds; not making assumptions about students' experiences and (or) backgrounds; not making comments about the status of a student's family (e.g., "Did your dad get arrested last week?") remembering that not all students are heterosexual; and making an effort to use case studies, examples, and anecdotes from a number of different cultural and social situations.

The third topic covered discussed how to treat students as individuals and respect them for who they are. Mr. Hall encouraged them to be careful not to project their experiences with, feelings about, or expectations of an entire group onto one student. They discussed that, as teachers, they must keep in mind that group identity can be important for some students and that their class may be their students' first opportunity to experience affirmation of their national, ethnic, racial, or cultural identity; they may feel both empowered and encouraged by the support they find in their classroom.

The teacher candidates also discussed how to encourage students to express their feelings regarding the cultural climate in the classroom and how teachers could communicate to students that they should share whether any aspect of the class makes them uncomfortable. It was suggested that students could be invited to write the teacher a note or see him or her after class. Mr. Hall offered several examples of how to give specific types of feedback the teacher may be seeking, such as: Do I treat all students equally? Are all students comfortable participating in my classroom? What might be making it easy or difficult for a student in my classroom? Do any students feel their ethnicity, race, or gender affect my interactions with them or with fellow students?

Finally, this group spoke about how to encourage discussions on diversity at school-wide and departmental meetings. Mr. Hall stressed how it is important that the conversation regarding diversity be extended beyond the walls of the classroom. A teacher should be able to ask that the agenda of department meetings, and if appropriate school-wide meetings, include topics such as classroom climate, course content, and course requirements.

The interchange of ideas and discussion between Mr. Hall and students in this class was far different from that which he had with the freshmen. These teacher candidates wanted to talk, share ideas, expose their own ingrained ideologies, and be validated that they were growing in their knowledge and abilities to meet the needs of their future students. In fact, this conversation was slated to last 1 hour and 45 minutes, but it ended up lasting two and half hours. Clearly, teacher candidates—whether in the freshman-level or advanced classes—are more than ready to tackle these challenging concepts that make them uncomfortable; it is imperative to disrupt what they believe in order to establish a place from which to start conversations to become more comfortable.

After Mr. Hall's visit, students in the methods course were assigned an individualized reflection paper in which they were to address the following statement: Has what I have observed in my field placements, read in the articles, or discussed in class changed or challenged my concept of myself as "teacher" in any way, and do I see these conversations as valuable for a future teacher? The students were more than able to describe ways in which to engage all levels of learners without hesitation in their classroom interactions, in their reflective pieces, and when creating their lessons and assessments for the rest of the TWS on which they worked for the final project in this course. These students' descriptions of adaptations, differentiated instruction, and abilities far exceeded those of past sections of this course. In one of the reflective papers, a teacher candidate echoed something that many others did in one way or another in their papers:

> I believe, as an educator, it is my responsibility to create a society of understanding, not just tolerance. Tolerance is a great idea, but if one truly thinks about the word "tolerance," they would see that it means that group isn't being accepted or included, they are being tolerated.

This group of teacher candidates articulated at a much higher level of understanding what it means to truly celebrate sameness and difference, which made the instructors confident that these students were heading out to the classroom prepared to at least consider differences and similarities from a position of comfort instead of discomfort.

Conclusion

Past experiences in classes with preservice students resulted in repeated stilted attempts to integrate practical and in-depth discussion or meaningful results from assignments centered on various aspects of diversity within the secondary social studies education program. These courses are taught to education majors who are overwhelmingly from middle-class, White, homogenous groupings that need to find a way to safely step beyond their personal comfort zones, consider a broader definition of diversity, and recognize their often unconscious or unchallenged bias. By rethinking the entire approach in these courses, a successful approach was found using targeted classroom experiences and assignments utilizing Milner's (2010) theory of disruptive movement. Milner's suggestion that "a theory of disruptive movement in teacher education has some promise, especially as teacher educators' work to expose self-consumed interests that do not have equity at the center" was exactly what was needed to be considered in these courses, thereby discovering great promise in this new approach.

Although it will take time to really know whether what took place in these courses has long-term and significant bearing on the realities of these future teachers, especially in their classrooms, there is reason for optimism. Prior approaches seemed to solicit the "right" responses but did not translate into their classroom work and become part of the fabric of these class sessions until this semester. However, 18 of these students are now finishing their student teaching experience, and all have continued to include much more in-depth coverage and discussion with regard to addressing the needs of all students in their classes. In addition, several of the students in the freshman seminar have sought out the instructors just to discuss issues that made them uncomfortable on campus. or they have become much more involved in groups and activities they themselves readily admit they would never have considered prior to this course. Thus, these students seem much more comfortable than uncomfortable with themselves and others.

References

Bergen, Jr., T. (1989). Needed: A radical design for teacher education. *Journal of Teacher Education, 16*(1), 7379.

Brown, E. (2004). What precipitates change in cultural diversity awareness during a multicultural course: The message or the method? *Journal of Teacher Education, 55*(4), 325340.

Conflict Research Consortium, University of Colorado: International Online Training Program on Intractable Conflict. (1998). *Commonality to balance diversity.* Retrieved from http://www.colorado.edu/conflict/peace/treatment/commony.htm

Galman, S., Pica-Smith, C., & Rosenberger, C. (2010). Aggressive and tender navigations: Teacher educators confront whiteness in their practice. *Journal of Teacher Education, 61*(3), 225236.

Gay, G. (2000). *Culturally responsive teaching: Theory, research, and practice.* New York: Teachers College Press.

Gay, G. (2010). Acting on beliefs in teacher education for cultural diversity. *Journal of Teacher Education, 61*(2), 143152.

Green, M. F. (Ed.). (1989). *Minorities on campus: A handbook for enriching diversity.* Washington, DC: American Council on Education.

Gurin, P., Peng, T., Lopez, G., & Nagda, B. A. (1999). Context, identity, and intergroup relations. In D. Prentice & D. Miller (Eds.), *Cultural divides: Understanding and overcoming group conflict* (pp. 133172). New York: Russell Sage.

Marks, M. (2008). *Preservice teachers' beliefs and application of multicultural education in an elementary social studies methods course.* (Unpublished doctoral dissertation). The University of Pittsburgh, Pittsburgh, PA.

Milner, H. R. (2010). What does teacher education have to do with teaching? Implications for diversity studies. *Journal of Teacher Education, 61*(2), 118131.

Pohan, C. (1996). Preservice teachers' beliefs about diversity: Uncovering factors leading to multicultural responsiveness. *Equity & Excellence in Education, 29,* 6269.

Villegas, A. M., & Lucas, T. (2002). Preparing culturally responsive teachers: Rethinking the curriculum. *Journal of Teacher Education, 53*(1), 2033.

Wang, J., Spalding, E., Odell, S., Klecka, C., & Lin, E. (2010). Bold ideas for improving teacher education and teaching: What we see, hear, and think. *Journal of Teacher Education, 61*(2), 315.

Wenger, K., & Dinsmore, J. (2005). Preparing rural preservice teachers for diversity. *Journal of Research in Rural Education, 20*(10), 115.

CHAPTER SIX

Examination of White Racial Identity in the Context of an Elementary Social Studies Methods Course

Brian Lanahan

Many scholars have noted the need for White, middle-class preservice teachers to reflect on their racial identities (e.g., Banks, 2006; Ladson-Billings, 2001; McIntosh, 1988). However, simply having preservice teachers express their thoughts is insufficient for change; preservice teachers need a structure that will enable them to reflect effectively. Moreover, although significant research exists on racial identity, such research is abstract and intangible for most White preservice teachers. The current chapter seeks to utilize structured reflection in combination with Helms' (1990) racial identity model in order to assist White preservice teachers in assessing their racial identities. However, the use of the Helms model proved problematic for two reasons—namely, the students had difficulty understanding the model and/or they were too naïve or ethnocentric to fully utilize the model. The study suggests that the Helms model, as well as other models (e.g., Atkinson, Morten, & Sue, 1989), may require substantial long-term scaffolding to enable most White, middle-class preservice teachers to utilize it.

> I think looking at these stages opened my eyes up to how much more I have to think about this [my racial identity] and how much more I need to grow before I get in a class with non-White kids.

> I am not sure what level I am at in this system, but I know I am sick of hearing how bad White people are.

As these quotes demonstrate, the need to have White preservice teachers reflect on their racial identities is obvious; these beliefs about racial identity must be examined to prepare teachers properly (Nespor, 1987). Nonetheless, simply having preservice teachers express their thoughts is insufficient for change (Hargreaves, 1995). Preservice teachers require a structure for effective reflection, and many researchers believe that the examination of beliefs should be integrated throughout the teacher education curriculum (e.g., Bollin & Finkel, 1995).

Conceptual Framework

This study is based on the concept of 'Practitioner Research' which can be defined as a methodical form of investigation that is communal, reflective, self-critical, and performed by participant(s) involved in the practices under investigation (McCutcheon and Jung, 1990). In Donald Schön's seminal work '*The Reflective Practitioner*' (1983) Schön advocated for systematic reflection to be at the center of creating and transmitting professional knowledge. Schön espoused an epistemology of practice in which, "the knowledge inherent in practice is to be understood as artful doing" (Usher, Bryant & Johnston, 1997, p. 143). According to Schön this research aims to interrogate the researcher's existing beliefs:

> The practitioner allows himself to experience surprise, puzzlement, or confusion in a situation which he finds uncertain or unique. He reflects on the phenomenon before him, and on the prior understandings which have been implicit in his behaviour. He carries out an experiment which serves to generate both a new understanding of the phenomenon and a change in the situation." (Schön, 1983, p. 68).

This form of research refutes that the "technical-rationality" positivist epistemology of practice should be the sole basis for creating and verifying professional knowledge (Schön, 1983). Noting the weakness of "technical-rationality" Usher, Bryant & Johnston noted, "the dominant paradigm which has failed to resolve the dilemma of rigour versus relevance confronting professionals" (1997, p. 143).

In the following decades Schön notion of "Practitioner Research" was adopted by teacher education researchers. In 1995 Hamilton called on teacher educators for more research that was "self-reflective, inquiry-based study of practice" (p. 81). Others suggested that, "Practical inquiry should be considered as an essential element of the work of individual and groups of faculty members and other teacher educators in understanding and improving their teaching and programs" (Richardson, 1996, p. 727). By the end of the 1990s Zeichner provided a review of this "new scholarship" of teacher education in which he found "teacher educators studying their own prac-tices" (1999, p. 11). In 2003 Dinkleman provided a five-part rationale for self-study:

- the congruence of reflection with the activity of teaching;
- the potential of self-study for knowledge production, of value for both local contexts and the broader teacher education research community;
- opportunities to model reflective practice;
- value of self-study participation for preservice students;

- possibilities for programmatic change (p. 8).

Brown (2007) provided an additional rationale for teacher education researchers, "Self-study is grounded in Dewey's democratic tradition and commitment to social consciousness" (p. 548). Acknowledging the use of "Practitioner Research" in other professional fields Cochran-Smith & Lytle, (2009) noted that "self-study" in teacher education had become a new genre of "Practitioner Research." Despite the success of "self-study" in teacher education social studies, researchers have lagged behind:

> Over the past two decades, self-study has secured its place on the map of approaches to better understanding teacher education. Self-study has attracted interest from researchers and teacher educators representing diverse content areas. Curiously, however, social studies has remained largely on the sidelines as an under-represented participant in the growth of this new genre of educational research (Crowe, & Dinkelman, 2010, p. 1).

This study will utilize self-study, as conceptualized above, to analyze the examination of White racial identity in the context of an elementary social studies methods course.

Relevant Literature

Students often find it difficult to analyze their identities. In particular, they have difficulty recognizing it as anything but normal. "Whiteness is the universal standard by which diverse others are measured" (Ortiz & Rhoads, 2000, p. 83). This blindness is often instilled early in life and reinforced in school and media; "whites are taught to think of their lives as morally neutral, normative, and average, and also ideal" (McIntosh, 1988, p. 96). This put students in a hegemonic cloud where "[t]o be white is to be everywhere and nothing at all at once—privileged by a veil of color that provides not cultural identity, but power and opportunity by pretending not to be anything at all" (Fowler, 1998, p. 1). Moreover, students are further challenged to acknowledge "White privilege" (McIntosh, 1988). The resistance to acknowledging "White privilege" may be a form of self-protection; once students have acknowledged it, they must ask themselves "what will I do to lessen or end it?" (McIntosh, 1988, p. 95).

Although significant research has explored students' examination of their White racial identity (for a review, see Ortiz & Rhoads, 2000), much of the research on White identity analysis is published in formats difficult to implement practically in teacher education programs. Despite being abstract and difficult to grasp, this scholarship does offer a variety of racial identity models that hold promise for assisting preservice teachers in examining and

assessing their own racial identities. This chapter chronicles the use of the
Helms (1990) model to assist three White preservice teachers in assessing
their racial identities.

The Helms (1990) model of White racial identity describes six stages
along a continuum of development: (a) contact, marked by a color-blind
viewpoint and a general unawareness of one's own race; (b) disintegration,
during which one's own Whiteness becomes the prominent focus and confusion between morals and societal norms is confronted; (c) reintegration, which
is characterized by stereotypical thinking, feelings of fear and anger, and belief
in White superiority and inferiority of other racial groups; (d) pseudo-
independence, which involves forming a positive White identity among people
of other racial groups; (e) immersion-emersion, when the objective is to define
one's self as nonracist; and (f) autonomy, acceptance, and appreciation for
people of other racial groups. Individuals' movement among these stages
flows from "a superficial and inconsistent awareness of being White" (Helms,
1990, p. 55) to a consciousness characterized by an awareness of White
privilege and a pledge to pursue social change. Helms and Piper (1994)
subsequently explained that these stages could be better understood as
"statuses" that are not linear; individuals may move up and down the continuum based on their experiences with particular issues and individuals.

Research Question

This study seeks to answer the following research question: Can structured
reflection along with the use of Helms (1990) "White Racial Identity" model
be used to enhance the development of a positive racial identity for White
preservice elementary teachers?

Participants and Setting

The study took place at a liberal arts teaching college situated on an urban
campus in the southeastern United States. Twenty-one preservice elementary
teachers seeking certification in K-3 grades and enrolled in a social studies
methods course participated in the study. All but three were under the age of
25, and all participants were female; 18 identified their families economically as middle class or upper-middle class, while the remaining 3 identified
their families as working class. In addition, 19 identified themselves as
White/European American; the other two identified themselves as
Black/African American. This class was chosen using Patton's (1990)
"Typical Case" sampling rationale because the class represented the typical
mixture of ethnic and socioeconomic statuses of preservice elementary
teachers (Walker-Dalhouse & Dalhouse, 2006). All 21 students who took the

course completed a critical autobiography, participated in a classroom discussion about the assignment, and filled out a post-assignment and discussion reflection. These participants were chosen because they represented the three general categories that students fall into with regard to pragmatic open-mindedness, naïve ethnocentrism, and open resistance.

Data Collection

Multiple data sources were used for this qualitative inquiry (Patton, 1990; Yin, 1994). The primary data sources for this study consisted of (a) a critical autobiography (b) classroom observations, and (c) a post-assignment and discussion reflection.

Critical Autobiography

Students were assigned to complete a critical autobiography as part of the social studies methods course. In the first part of this assignment, students were required to create a visual map to illustrate their ethnicity, race, regional identity, experiences in other cultures, religion, gender, disabilities, social class, and family structure. In the second part of the assignment, students were required to respond to the following prompts:

- Describe one significant event related to culture, race, gender, and social class from your life.
- Describe a time when you felt you were treated unfairly because of your race.
- Do you have any close personal friends from a different social and/or ethnic group? If so, explain this relationship.
- What is missing related to culture, race, gender, and social class from your life—in short, what experiences are you lacking?
- As a teacher, how will you relate to children from different social and/or ethnic groups? Provide concrete examples.
- What are the implications of these findings for your own teaching practice?
- What kinds of goals for your own professional growth can you make based on these reflections?

Classroom Session

The second data source came from participant observations during the classroom session in which the students' critical autobiographies were discussed. During the class session, students were challenged to think critically about their own experiences related to these issues and how their experiences differ from those of the children they will teach. In addition, students were presented with the Helms (1990) model of White racial identity; each of the model's levels was discussed to promote reflection. Although the critical autobiography assignment and debriefing class occurs every semester, field notes were taken during this class session to capture students' comments. These comments provided the background for comparing and contrasting what was written in the critical autobiography assignment and post-assignment reflection. Finally, during the classroom session, participants of interest were identified for future analysis.

Post-Assignment and Discussion Reflection

The final and richest data source proved to be the post-assignment reflections completed after the critical autobiography and debriefing class session. The goal of this assignment was to give students a chance to reflect upon the assignments and how, if at all, it changed their perspective. For the reflection, students were required to respond to the following questions:

- Did you find the critical autobiography useful for reflecting on your racial identity?
- Did you learn anything about yourself from the critical autobiography that surprised you?
- Based on what you learned about yourself from the critical autobiography, what, if any, plans do you have to improve your knowledge and abilities related to race, class, and ethnicity?
- What changes would you make to the assignment to make it a more useful tool for students to reflect on their racial identities?
- What did you think about Helms "White Racial Identity" model?
- At what status do you believe you are currently located in the Helms model?
- Why do you believe you are at the _____ status?
- How do you think the Helms model could be best used to help students reflect on their racial identities?

Data Analysis

Data reduction was used to "make sense of massive amounts of data, reduce the volume of information, and identify significant patterns" (Patton, 1990, p. 371). Data analysis occurred within and across cases and was "aimed at ensuring (a) high-quality, accessible data; (b) documentation of just what analyses were carried out; and (c) retention of data and associated analysis after the study is complete" (Miles & Huberman, 1994, p. 27). The analysis was based on Miles and Huberman's (1994) assertions that analysis should produce information specifically about the research questions.

Findings

The findings are organized according to participants and include their thoughts about racial issues, the critical autobiography, and the use of the Helms model.

Alice: Pragmatic open-mindedness. Alice is a nontraditional student in her late 20s. After a brief career in the banking industry, Alice returned to school to complete a degree in education. She describes herself "as a small-town girl with an open mind." Alice was chosen for analysis because she typified the pragmatic open-mindedness approach that many White students take toward racial issues in the classroom. Students who adhere to this approach deal with racial issues from a pragmatic perspective and are open to new information and interpretations of racial events and issues. This approach is best represented by the following quote from Alice:

> If I ended up in a school with Mexican kids, I would learn some Spanish so I could work with the families, but I would not speak it in the classroom. We really need to make sure those kids learn English.

Alice took great care in completing her critical autobiography, providing lengthy responses to each question. In response to the questions about close personal friends from a different social and/or ethnic group, she wrote:

> I worked with two Black women while I was working [processing mortgages]. We all got along, and for the most part we did not talk about race issues, but they mostly stayed to themselves. I guess it was weird for them because there were 15 processors and two supervisors, and everyone was White except them.

When describing what was missing from her life related to culture, race, gender, and social class, Alice explained:

> I have never been out of the U.S. except on vacation. Students these days are from all over the world; for example, in my first field there were Haitians and Russians. I had to look on a map to see were Haiti was.

Particularly interesting was her response to the question about a significant life event related to culture, race, gender, and social class. The following response indicates that Alice has experiences being the "Other":

> When applying for jobs I really began to see how important it was to have an education. I applied for a lot of office manager jobs because I had experience working in my dad's office. I got very few call backs, and in the few interviews I did get the interviewers tried to steer me toward lower paying jobs because I did not have a college degree. It made me feel stupid and embarrassed.

Alice's response to the questions about when she felt she was treated unfairly because of her class further revealed her personal experiences as the "Other":

> I moved before my junior year and had to change schools. I had the same friends for my entire life and had to start over. The kids in my new school were much different. Everybody had more money than we did and I had trouble making friends. I never went to prom at my new school but went [back] to prom both years at my old school.

It appears that Alice's experiences as the "Other" based on her socioeconomic status have given her insights and/or empathy toward children from diverse backgrounds. In her response to the questions about how she will relate to children from different social and/or ethnic groups, Alice noted, "I will really help the 'odd man out' kid and the new kid. I know what it is like to be new and different"

Although it is evident from her written responses that Alice is somewhat aware of issues related to race and class, her comments during the class session were more pragmatic and less inclusive. She was an active participant in all class discussions and often espoused naïve, yet nonetheless practical perspectives on issues of race, ethnicity, and class. During the class session discussing critical autobiographies, Alice voiced her perspective on working with ESOL students, saying, "Those kids need to learn English so they can get jobs" (personal communication, February 12, 2007). While responding to another student's comment about the influx of immigrants into local schools, Alice noted, "I really like working with those [Mexican] kids, but I am worried that if they are here illegally then more will come because of the schools and there will be no space for local kids" (personal communication, February 12, 2007). When the discussion turned to holidays, Alice seemed to strike a balance between pragmatism and inclusion: "I would celebrate all the holidays of the students who are in my class, Christmas, Kwanza, Hanukah, whatever,...but I would not celebrate holidays that are not in my class" (personal communication, February 12, 2007).

In her post-assignment reflection, Alice noted that she enjoyed completing her critical autobiography. "I liked mapping out all of my areas and found myself stumped by some of the questions. Like I have never really been out of the US, except to Cancun." She also noted that she had learned a lot about herself due to the specific structure of some of the questions:

At first I answered some of the questions one way but had to change my answer because I could not provide the specific examples the questions asked for. It made me realize that I might have some more thinking to do.

In response to questions about whether she planned on making any changes based on what she learned by completing the assignment, she noted, "I really need to get out and see the world, especially countries that are really different than us." She also offered suggestions for improving the assignment: "You could also have a place for people to discuss what is special about their culture, not just focus on what you don't know about others."

When responding to the questions about the Helms "White Racial Identity" model, Alice noted some confusion about the nature and purpose of the model, asking, "Is this what professors use to rate their students to see who is ready to be a teacher?" She wrote that she believed she was at the disintegration status because "I am beyond trying to be color blind, and I am still trying to figure out what it means to be White. I also don't think White people are better than other people." Responding to the question about how the model could be best used to help students reflect on their racial identities, Alice noted, "You really need to explain it because it is really kind of tough to understand. If you made it part of the critical autobiography, then people could assess themselves as part of the assignment." With regard to using the Helms model to reflect on racial identity, she noted, "I think looking at these stages opened my eyes up to how much more I have to think about this [my racial identity] and how much more I need to grow before I get in a class with non-White kids." She also noted an unintended benefit of having students self-assess using the model: "Having it laid out like this in steps makes me want to move up the ladder because I know it will make me a better person and a better teacher."

Sam: Naïve ethnocentrism. Sam is a 20-year-old student who describes herself as a "normal girl who is involved in my church and sorority." In many ways, Sam is a typical preservice elementary teacher: White, affluent, and middle class. Sam was chosen for analysis because she typified the naïve ethnocentrism that many students exhibit when addressing racial issues in the classroom. Students in this category approach racial issues with a deficit of knowledge about individuals that are not White, middle-class, and Christian. This approach is best represented by the following quote from Sam:

I'm just real normal. My parents have been married for 23 years. My mom stayed home when we were young, then went back to teaching. My parents made sure we went to church and had good friends who would not get us in trouble.

Sam's written responses to the critical autobiography prompts further revealed her naïveté and lack of experience outside her own culture. In her response to the questions about what was missing from her life related to culture, race, gender, and social class, Sam wrote:

> I feel like I have had a full life. I got to do all the regular kid stuff. There were a few minorities in my classes, but I don't think I missed anything. In fact I think having similar [White, middle-class, and Christian] people was better because we did not have many fights and there were no drugs. The other high school in my town was really mixed, and they had lots of problems with drugs and fights.

While presenting her critical autobiography to the class, she repeatedly mentioned how her life was "normal and boring" (personal communication, February 12, 2007). She also discussed at length her travels with her church group to impoverished countries to provide "physical and spiritual aid" (personal communication, February 12, 2007). The following quote illustrates Sam's perspective:

> We [church group] were in Belize, and I was shocked to see how no one had cars or cell phones. In one village way up in the mountains, I was able to lead bible study with a group of teenagers. After 20 minutes of reading passages and talking about what they mean, one girl asked if Jesus was like a ghost. I did not know what to say. It really hit me then how little these people knew about Christ and the world.

During the class discussion, Sam and Alice engaged in the following exchange, which highlighted how age and life experiences have influenced their worldviews:

> Alice: I think that my experiences in school did not prepare me to work in the real world. I really had no contact with people who were "different" than me.
> Sam: That would not matter if you went back to teach in the school you went to.
> Alice: The elementary school I went to now has lots of Mexicans. It's all different now.
> Sam: My mom still teaches at the school I went to, and it is still kids from all the same families. (personal communication, February 12, 2007).

Unprompted, Sam noted in her reflection, "We have had a lot of racial self-assessments in the program so far, but this one was more useful because we had to think about what we could do to improve our knowledge." When asked about what she learned from the critical autobiography she noted that it "made me realize how fortunate I am to have traveled and how much more experience I have with poor and foreign people". Based on what she learned from the critical autobiography, Sam planned to "[l]earn more about poor people here [in the U.S.] and get to know more Black people." For possible changes that could be made to improve the critical autobiography, she wrote, "We need more time to present about ourselves and our experiences with other cultures".

With regard to the Helms "White Racial Identity" model, Sam seemed somewhat overwhelmed:

> I really had a hard time understanding the model. I do not see how people could move from one level to the next. It seems if you were born around a lot of non-White people, you would be at a higher level.

Concerning her status in the model, Sam again noted her travels: "I think I am at the pseudo-independence level because I have been around other cultures and know there are different ways to live. They might not be as nice as ours, but those are good and nice people." When writing about the future use of the Helms model to help students reflect on their racial identities, Sam stated, "I think the model may be above the average student's understanding. It seems to make people who do not live around Black people look unedu-cated or uncultured or at a lower level." In addition Sam gave an interesting suggestion: "You should have students complete the critical autobiography and then have the other students anonymously read and rate others based on the stages."

Jamie: Open resistance. Jamie is a 19-year-old who, like Sam and Alice, is a typical elementary teacher: White, female, and middle class. Jamie attended an all-girls' private K-12 school located near the college and graduated a year early at the age of 17. Jamie was chosen for analysis because she typified the open resistance approach. Preservice teachers who ascribe to an open resistance approach consistently react negatively to concepts and/or facts that contradict their White middle-class worldview. This approach is best represented by this statement from Jamie: "If we spend time covering every little minority group in America, the kids will never learn about real Americans." Jamie was selected for analysis due to her steadfast resistance to changing her views and her frankness.

Jamie wrote lengthy and forthcoming responses to the questions in her critical autobiography. When describing a significant event in her life related to race, she offered the following:

> When I was in first grade we made little pinwheels for Easter and placed them in the grass on the side of the road in front of my school. In less than an hour kids from the neighborhood (almost exclusively working-class African Americans) rode over them with bikes. I feel like they were just looking for a way to get back at us.

While describing a time when she felt she was treated unfairly because of her race, Jamie offered another illustrative vignette:

> We were not rich, and my parents had to work really hard to send me to private school because the public schools in my area were really bad. I had to pay the full cost of tuition. There were some minorities in my school who were on scholarship and only paid a thousand dollars a year. It made me frustrated because part of my tuition was going to scholarships I could not get.

Jamie's discussion of what was missing from her life with regard to culture, race, gender, and social class indicated more of a Eurocentric worldview:

> My dad builds up lots of miles traveling for his job, so we were able to take a big family vacation every summer. We went to lots of places, but I always liked Europe the best. Everywhere else was dirty and people were begging. Now I take trips with my sister and we go to all the nice European countries.

In response to multiple questions, Jamie noted that she did not want to teach in a public school because she did not feel she would "fit in with the kids." She went on to add that, "I would not be happy because I really just want to teach. I am not really prepared to deal with all of the diversity issues."

At the beginning of the class session, Jamie plainly stated the critical autobiography assignment was "another White guilt project" (personal communication, February 12, 2007). Interestingly, she said little during the discussion. However, she did rationalize her own lack of personal knowledge and experience with minorities and diversity issues by stating that "I went to private school so we did not have many minorities and we did not really talk about this stuff" (personal communication, February 12, 2007).

In the post-assignment reflection, Jamie's responses were by far the lengthiest and at times rambled on. When writing about the usefulness of the critical autobiography, Jamie again noted her skepticism: "It was good for sharing about ourselves but seemed to just be another 'you don't know anything about minorities' project." In response to being asked whether she learned anything from the critical autobiography that surprised her, Jamie wrote "I learned that I have a lily-white life." When writing about whether she planned on making any changes based on this realization, she stated that "I can't change who I am." Her recommendation for improving the assignment was to "leave it out...we did the same thing during 327 [a previous course]."

On the topic of the Helms model, Jamie noted her distrust of "psychobabble" and psychologists who "only want you to be more liberal." Jamie's frustration with the model appeared to climax when stating what status she believed she was at in the Helms model: "I am not sure what level I am at in this system." Finally Jamie discussed how the Helms model could be used to help students reflect on their racial identities: "I think it is a waste of time to do it in an education course but for people who really want to teach in public schools the model could be used to help them really think...."

Discussion

The students' thoughts and feelings about these issues were directly tied to their personal experiences. Although this connection is hardly a new finding (e.g., Calderhead, 1991; Lortie, 1975; Sugrue, 1997; Wideen, Mayer-Smith, & Moon, 1998), it is interesting to note how each individual's particular background produced specific thoughts and feelings. In the case of Alice, it is obvious that her age and work experience made her realize the complexities of the real world and the necessity of addressing diversity issues. For Sam, her very sheltered life experiences led her to a false sense of competency and knowledge of, as she put it, "poor and foreign" people. Finally, Jamie viewed minorities only in negative terms because of her limited and mostly negative experiences with them.

Two of the participants (i.e., Alice and Jamie) demonstrated a disconnect between thoughts and sentiments expressed in the critical autobiography and what they said during the class session. In the critical autobiography, Alice expressed more inclusive and sympathetic views toward diversity issues, whereas during the class session she appeared to draw a harder line on the same issues. Similarly, Jamie's comments on her critical autobiography and post-assignment reflection were very resistant and, at times, combative, but she was almost silent during the class discussion. Both participants appear to have adapted their positions to fit in with the mainstream view during the class discussion.

Many of the students' comments and perspectives agreed with previous findings in the literature. In particular, Jamie's statements that she had no desire to teach in public schools because she would not "fit in with the kids" and "I would not be happy because I really just want to teach" appear to be a self-defense mechanism and concur with McIntosh's (1988) belief that many Whites refuse to acknowledge White privilege in order to shirk responsibility for changing the situation. With Sam's many comments purporting her hyper-normalness (e.g., "I'm just real normal"), she appears to use her White upper-middle class background as the "universal standard" to compare her life to others (Ortiz & Rhoads 2000, p. 83). Moreover Sam's comments also appear to reflect Fowler's notion that "[t]o be white is to be everywhere and nothing at all at once—privileged by a veil of color that provides not cultural identity, but power and opportunity by pretending not to be anything at all" (1998, p. 1). Alice's comments most closely resemble Dewey's (1916) pragmatic approach to education with a focus on doing "what works." In particular, her comments about celebrating holidays illustrates her pragmatic approach (i.e., "If I ended up in a school with Mexican kids, I would learn some Spanish so I could work with the families, but I would not speak it in the classroom. We really need to make sure those kids learn English.").

Conclusion

The use of the Helms model was problematic for two reasons—namely, students had difficulty understanding the levels of the model, and they were either too naïve and/or ethnocentric to assess themselves. In particular, Alice and Sam had difficulty understanding the model and made questionable choices about their status. Alice is more likely to be at the contact status based on her lack of experience with non-Whites. Meanwhile, Sam appeared to be at the disintegration status and still believed in the superiority of White/American culture. All three participants also seemed to be trapped by their own naïve and/or ethnocentric perspectives. In particular, Jamie was very challenged by the mere request to analyze her racial identity. Although Jamie's comments represent a rather extreme level of resistance, they also capture the sentiment of a large number of preservice teachers. These students believe that any attempt to have them analyze their racial identities is a "White guilt" assignment. Future use of the Helms model will require a substantial amount of scaffolding to enable students to truly be able to utilize it. The sequence of instruction and events described herein proved to be ineffective in capitalizing on the potential for using the Helms model. It was obvious that the students need more exposure and practice to be able to effectively use the model.

References

Atkinson, D. R., Morten, G., & Sue, D. W. (1989). A minority identity development model. In Dr. Atkinson, G. Morten, & D. W. Sue (Eds.), *Counseling American minorities* (pp. 35–52). Dubuque, IA: W. C. Brown.

Banks J. (2006). *Race, culture and education: The selected works of James A. Banks*. New York, NY: Routledge.

Bollin, G., & Finkel, J. (1995). White racial identity as a barrier to understanding diversity: A study of preservice teachers. *Equity and Excellence in Education, 28*(1), 25–30.

Brown, E. (2007). The significance of race and social class for self-study and the professional knowledge base of teacher education. In J. J. Loughran, M. L. Hamilton, V. K. LaBoskey, & T. Russell (Eds.), *International handbook of self-study teaching and teacher education practices* (pp. 517–574). Dordrecht: Springer.

Calderhead, J. (1991). The nature and growth of knowledge in student teaching. *Teaching and Teacher Education, 7*, 531–535.

Cochran-Smith, M., & Lytle, S. L. (2009). *Inquiry as stance: Practitioner research for the next generation*. New York: Teachers College Press.

Crowe, A., & Dinkelman, T. (2010). Self-study and social studies: Framing the conversation. In A. Crowe (Ed.), *Advancing social studies education through self-study methodology: The power, promise, and use of self-study in social studies education* (pp. 1-19). New York: Springer.

Dewey, J. (1916). What Pragmatism Means by Practical. In *Essays in experimental logic* (pp. 303–329). Chicago: University of Chicago.

Dinkelman, T. D. (2003). Self-study in teacher education: A means and ends tool for promoting reflective teaching. *Journal of Teacher Education, 54*(1), 6-18.

Fowler, G. (1998). Of nude pantyhose and storybook dreams: A wake up call to white America. *Diversity and Distinction Online, 3 (2), 1–13.*

Hamilton, M.L. (1995). Relevant readings in action research. *Action in Teacher Education XVI* (4), 78-80.

Hargreaves, A. (1995). Development and desire: A postmodern perspective. In T. R. Guskey & M. Huberman (Eds.), *Professional development in education: New paradigms and practices* (pp. 9–34). New York: Teachers College Press.

Helms, J. E. (1990). *Black and White racial identity: Theory, research, and practice*. New York: Greenwood Press.

Helms, J. E., & Piper, R. E. (1994). Implications of racial identity theory for vocational psychology. *Journal of Vocational Behavior, 44,* 124–138.

Ladson-Billings, G. J. (2001). *Crossing over to Canaan: The journey of new teachers in diverse classrooms.* San Francisco, CA: Jossey-Bass

Lortie, D. (1975). *Schoolteacher: A sociological study.* Chicago, IL: University of Chicago Press.

McCutcheon, G. & Jung, B. (1990). Alternative perspectives on action research. *Theory into Practice, 29*(3), 144-151.

McIntosh, P. (1988). White privilege and male privilege: A personal account of coming to see correspondences through work in women's studies. In M. L. Andersen & P. H. Collins (Eds.), *Race, class and gender: An anthology* (3rd ed., pp. 94–105). New York: Wadsworth.

Miles, M., & Huberman, A. (1994). *Qualitative data analysis: An expanded sourcebook.* Thousand Oaks, CA: Sage Publications.

Nespor, J. (1987). The role of beliefs in the practice of teaching. *Journal of Curriculum Studies, 19,* 317–328.

Ortiz, A., & Rhoads, R. (2000). Deconstructing whiteness as part of a multicultural educational framework: From theory to practice. *Journal of College Student Development, 41*(1), 81–93.

Patton, M. (1990). *Qualitative evaluation and research methods* (2nd ed.). Newbury Park, CA: Sage Publications.

Richardson, V. (1996). The case for formal research and practical inquiry in teacher education. In F.B. Murray (Ed.) (1996). *The teacher educator's handbook: Building a knowledge base for the preparation of teachers.* San Francisco, CA: Jossey-Bass Publishers.

Schön, D. A. (1983). The Reflective Practitioner. *How Professionals Think in Action.* London, United Kingdom: Temple Smith.

Sugrue, C. (1997). Student teachers' lay theories and teaching identities: Their implications for professional development. *European Journal of Teacher Education, 20,* 211–225.

Usher, R., Bryant, I. and Johnston, R. (1997). *Adult Education and the Postmodern Challenge.* London: Routledge.

Walker-Dalhouse, D., & Dalhouse, A. D. (2006). Investigating White Preservice Teachers' Beliefs about Teaching in Culturally Diverse Classrooms. *The Negro Educational Review, 57*(1-2), 69–84.

Wideen, M., Mayer-Smith, J., & Moon B. (1998). A critical analysis on the research on learning to teach: Making the case for an ecological perspective on inquiry. *Review of Educational Research, 68*, 130–178.

Yin, R. (1994). *Case study research: Design and methods* (2nd ed.). Thousand Oaks, CA: Sage Publications.

Zeichner, K. (1999). The new scholarship of teacher education. Education Researcher, 28(9), 4–15.

CHAPTER SEVEN

"We Can't Change the World If We Just Keep It to Ourselves": How Do Preservice Teachers See Teaching for Social Justice When They Participate in a National Program Promoting Student Activism?

Russell Binkley

This chapter chronicles the changes in attitudes of 45 elementary and middle-school preservice teachers in a social studies methods class in a predominantly White public university in the mountains of a southern state in the United States. Participants were exposed to various experiences intended to increase the likelihood that they would more clearly see the needs of their diverse students and, consequently, perceive themselves as teachers for social justice. The data revealed that most preservice teachers showed a marked growth in predispositions to teaching social justice. The researcher interviewed six students who had volunteered to mentor in peace education-centered service learning at a local middle school. In these case studies, the preservice teachers revealed more critical stances and firmer commitments to teaching for social justice. The findings confirmed that it is imperative for methods classes to offer students a deliberate, explicit curriculum centered on deep experiences with diversity that include moving outside of individuals' comfort zones, engaging in thoughtful reflections, interacting with classroom speakers, promoting dialogues based on extensive readings, participating in open and safe discussions that confront controversial issues, engaging in meaningful field experiences with progressive teachers, and being active in peace education.

National and state (e.g., North Carolina Standard Course of Study, Social Studies, National Council for the Social Studies Ten Strands/Standards and National Council for the Social Studies Curriculum Guidelines for Multicultural Education) social studies standards plainly call for the teaching of citizenship. As global citizens, we face a plethora of world problems, including discrimination, genocide, environmental degradation, sexism, violence, and war. The predominant factory model that many public schools imitate does little to help our students realize the potential for social change.

Yet the century-old progressive/reconstructionist philosophies of schooling remain unrealized.

My overarching research interest is in teaching for social justice. As I develop my social studies methods syllabus each semester, I tweak the content to feature the teaching of social justice a little more prominently and explicitly. To this end, I examine the following related questions:

- How, if at all, are preservice teachers' conceptions of social justice developed by participating in/teaching the PeaceJam curriculum, among other social justice foci?
- How likely are participants to say they will become teachers whose practices are explicitly directed toward social justice after exposure to this curriculum?

Conceptual Framework

Interacting with and observing practicing social studies teachers is a vital experience for my students. I am especially eager that students have the opportunity to experience classrooms with teachers who prominently feature social justice/peace studies/conflict resolution in their teaching. I use *social justice* in the tradition of John Rawls, who declared that race, sex, and class must not be allowed to determine people's access to fairness (Nussbaum, 2001). Fairness includes equal opportunity and access to education, a peaceful life, and a clean, healthful environment. I approach the topic of teaching for social justice using a graft of feminist pedagogy (Gore, 1993), transformative pedagogy (hooks, 1994), critical race theory (Parker, Deyhle, & Villenas, 1999), and liberatory pedagogy (Freire, 1978). Teaching for social justice incorporates several ideas:

- The teacher must use his or her authority to empower students.
- The teacher fosters a classroom setting where all feel obligated to contribute.
- Students and the teacher may depart from traditional scholarship by telling their stories.
- Teaching is not about domination or the depositing of information.

Methodology

Site. The university, known here as Mountain State, is in a rural setting in the southern United States. Its School of Elementary and Middle Grades Education has approximately 275 students majoring in education. Many are first-generation college students from the surrounding mountain counties. Approximately 130 students graduate each year. At the time of this study, the school employed 13 full-time elementary and middle grades faculty members (5 men and 8 women). Only one faculty member, the "diversity" specialist, was not White. Of the education majors, 91% were female and 9% were male; 89.5% identified themselves as White, 5.5% as African American, 1.5% as Hispanic, 1.1% as Native American, and 0.9% as Asian or Pacific Islander. The majority were Protestant Christians.

Course context. All elementary education (and middle school with social studies concentration) majors are required to complete the social studies methods course. The syllabus unambiguously focuses on social justice content. Assignments directed toward social awareness and action include:

- each preservice teacher investigating her or his master identities;
- ample readings in social justice pedagogies;
- selections of readings, videos, and audio materials presenting alternate histories and viewpoints;
- small- and whole-group discussions;
- direct interactions with others with differing ethnicities, races, religions, sexualities, and social classes followed by written reflections;
- classroom guests and panels presenting viewpoints of often marginalized populations; and
- service learning in a local school in connection with the curriculum of PeaceJam, which is a worldwide organization linking young people (K–20) to the work of Nobel Peace Laureates, demonstrating the possibilities of change through youth-directed projects that actively address local, national, and global problems (for a more comprehensive understanding, see peacejam.org).

Participants. Six preservice teachers enrolled in my social studies methods course participated in interviews. Five were women, and one was a man. Five students were White; one woman was Latina. All the women were traditional students (ages 20–22) and unmarried; the one man was married and in his mid-30s. The students participated in at least 10 hours of service learning (i.e., PeaceJam) in an eighth-grade classroom at a local middle school. PeaceJam was incorporated so these preservice teachers could observe what teaching for social justice looked like in practice rather than having it described through the preaching and testifying of this professor.

Individual interviews with participants lasted for approximately one hour and took place at the end of their semester's experience with social studies methods and PeaceJam. The data collected are presented as bounded case studies (Miles & Huberman, 1994). Cases were built solely from what the interviewees said in response to the following questions:

- What is social justice?
- How do you think your family background framed your understanding of social justice?
- How do you think your own teachers regarded social justice?
- What kind of teacher do you think you will be after this semester's experiences?

The Interviews: Case Studies

One day per week, 10 preservice teachers went to a middle school to mentor 2 sections of eighth-grade social studies students. As part of the team's social studies program, the teacher used the PeaceJam curriculum. The preservice teachers each spent at least 10 hours with the middle school students and taught mini-lessons about issues of justice in the context of the work and lives of 10 Nobel Peace Prize Laureates who are integral to the PeaceJam story. The preservice teachers worked with and advised the small groups as they prepared to implement their global call-to-action projects. They helped small groups of students create oral and visual presentations before the eighth graders went out to solicit funding from local organizations. They also coached students on how to present their final projects at the culminating regional conference.

A simple interview protocol with five open-ended questions was used to interview the six participating preservice teachers:

- What is your definition of social justice?
- Tell me about the place of social justice when you were growing up.
- In your own schooling, how do you think your teachers regarded social justice?
- Discuss your recent experience with PeaceJam.
- How do you see yourself as a teacher?

During the interview, I probed further when something arose that I found interesting. Fortunately, these five questions provided sufficient stimulus and the interviewees were forthcoming enough that I learned a great deal about each preservice teacher. Their responses were extensively narrated so that each story closely paralleled the others in construction.

Narrative Analysis

I read and reread the interview transcripts—a process that Bernard (2000) calls "pawing," during which time the researcher looks for emerging themes; these themes begin to make sense as the researcher lives with the data until patterns "hit you between the eyes" (p. 445). The "pawing" was followed by cutting and sorting using Microsoft Word. Each transcript was saved in a distinctly different color font; when specific codes or themes emerged (Kvale, 1996; Shank, 2006), these contexted passages were copied and pasted under each theme. This process resulted in visually accessible clusters that demonstrated when any substantial similarities in the interviewees' thoughts and experiences existed.

Using the six interview transcripts, I wrote up bounded case studies in which the individual interviewee is at the heart of each study and the case is solely built on what the interviewee chose to share (Miles & Huberman, 1994). No data were collected via classroom observations; data were also not collected via interviews with friends, families, or teachers or participation and interaction in my class.

Findings and Discussion

After a semester in which I flooded students with teacher talk, discussions, and activities with social justice at the core, I was hoping for evidence of profound understandings of the concept. However, my preservice teachers did not seem to consistently articulate the deep comprehension that was the goal of such activities. They struggled to define social justice, and an undertone of ambiguity, uncertainty, and vagueness was evident. McDonald (2008) claims that preservice teachers often have an individualistic notion of social justice rather than a sociopolitical notion of it; this claim was supported in the current study. The preservice teachers' schooling seems to have reinforced explicit messages emphasizing "the great man theory of history" while minimizing "ordinary" citizens' roles in social movements.

Social justice teachers are rare. Based on preservice teachers' reported school backgrounds, addressing social justice in teaching is unfamiliar territory. They have had little opportunity to integrate what they believe into practice or to see social justice teaching in practice. An eighth-grade teacher was one of few they ever saw trying to integrate social justice into practice. Only one preservice teacher recalled her teacher interrupting his subject (math) to address social justice, showing a film about the Rwandan genocide, saying, "This is really important for you to know about."

Social justice teaching requires action. To Heather, one of the preservice teachers, social justice teaching involves active expression. Practicing social justice is a matter of identifying what is wrong and then saying aloud the things in which one believes: "Speaking out for the children who are abused, that's a social injustice. You're going to speak out and help them get the justice they need and get them safe and taken care of" (personal communication, April, 29, 2009).

Knowledge of social injustice results in empathy. Sara's contribution is somewhat passive; she defined social justice as an attitude, a state of mind based on knowledge, not necessarily resulting in following through with any action: "I think social justice is more of understanding where other people are coming from, having the knowledge about differences other than your own" (personal communication, April 22, 2009). Perhaps Sara's definition implies an element of empathy; Jon spoke more explicitly. Being a teacher for social justice means knowledge is coupled with critical thinking. For Jon, the teacher opens "the opportunity to provide students with the balanced assessment of historical events, being able to understand both sides of an event and understand where judgments and biases and other types of imbalance come from" (personal communication, April 20, 2009). I might have preferred that Jon refer to all sides of an event, but his grasp of teaching content and critical analysis indicates someone looking beyond the superficial. He added that laying the academic groundwork will result in "providing students with the ability to empathize" (personal communication, April 20, 2009).

Religion and values. Students often referred to their strong religious faith in our class discussions, while the nonreligious or religious minorities were inclined to keep quiet. Jon asserted that conservative Christianity sometimes stands in the way of a clear path to social justice:

> Unfortunately I think that sometimes that narrow view of faith spills over into the whole idea of social justice. It is so narrow on that line. How are you going to be able to be open when looking at things like homosexuals and minorities as inferior? It just seems like it gets promoted. (personal communication, April 20, 2009)

Because Jon is at least 15 years older than the other preservice teachers, it is possible that his maturity accounted for the introspection he revealed. Is that deeper understanding explained by his being in a different developmental stage, as Haberman (1992) claimed? Jon alluded to the cultural capital (Bourdieu, 1977) of his middle-class background giving him advantages: "Being middle-class, it's something I've always had" (personal communication, April 20, 2009). He reflected on being stopped by the police while driving: He is ready for them with his license and registration; if it is dark, he knows to turn on the car's interior light. "A lot of the lower kids, minorities, don't have that [awareness]" (personal communication, April 20, 2009). He added another example about how he knew that going to an urgent care center costs less than the emergency room and how many of the poor "just don't have that knowledge" (personal communication, April 20, 2009).

Meanwhile, although Sara did not say that her family referred to social justice, she stated that they are proud of her for "trying to do better and make a difference" (personal communication, April 22, 2009). Her grandparents, "backwoods" and "uneducated on a lot of levels...even though they don't understand it," are "actually quite proud" of her (personal communication, April 22, 2009). Sara believed they still respected her, but they had "reservations" about the changes they perceived in her. They asked, "What are they teaching you?" because Sara's opinions sometimes confounded them; for them, "everything has to be White and female" (personal communication, April 22, 2009). She said that she tries not to confront them when they make offensive comments, but she must be "comfortable enough to tell them how I feel "cause we can't change the world if we just keep it to ourselves" (personal communication, April 22, 2009).

When Jon's parents divorced, he was "alienated a little bit" during this time. He felt disequilibrium "that caused me to step away from the idea(s) they were presenting and really question religion, race prejudices, stereotypes, and social and economic differences" (personal communication, April 20, 2009). Looking inward, Jon confronted his attitudes toward race, seeing them as "very ingrained" and influenced by the Whiteness in which he was immersed. Meanwhile, Brenda—unlike the others—grew up in a metropolitan area: "You could hop on the train and be in D.C. in half an hour." She talked about living in a "kind of melting pot" and noted how she "loved the diversity" (personal communication, April 24, 2009).

Carla, a Latina who emigrated from Mexico with her parents, went to elementary and middle school with some other Mexican migrant children who attended seasonally. When the schools pooled into a regional high school, there were more Latino students, but still she was "very much a minority." At first she denied witnessing any overt racism, but she finally admitted that she did experience some. She also found that being away from family has enabled her to examine her parents' values: "Ultimately, what you were raised with should not be what you believe" (personal communication, April 27, 2009). Carla indicated that her Christian family assumes that she will not change her views, but she cannot reveal how she really feels about some things. For example, she had hidden her relationship with her African-American boyfriend from her parents, who believe that "dating outside your race would never come up. Not possible" (personal communication, April 27, 2009).

Jon's tendency to exclude religion as a viable catalyst to social justice differed from those like Heather, who believed that her Christian background nourished and encouraged her inclination toward social justice. When Heather was in kindergarten, her best friend's poverty brought ridicule from peers. Heather's mother told her that supporting the little girl with her friendship may have meant "you might be the one person that helps her get through school" (personal communication, April 29, 2009). Heather credited her home church with her understanding the importance of giving back to the community. Her parents taught their children, "Look at what is going on around you. Look to other people; think about what they're going through and never judge. Be friendly to everyone, speak to everyone, and be respectful to everyone" (personal communication, April 29, 2009). As a result, Heather said that "I always felt I'd been put in the community to help those kids. That's what I need to be doing" (personal communication, April 29, 2009).

School Histories

Preservice teachers who were helped to examine their own schooling were more likely to look at their future teaching using a social justice lens (Frederick, Cave, & Perencivich, 2010). In these interviews, preservice teachers identified unchallenged social conditions, school composition, curriculum, and teachers as factors influencing why social justice was not featured in their own schooling. Specifically, these preservice teachers indicated that social justice received little—if any—attention for several reasons, as indicated in the following paragraphs.

School and community composition. Sara's schooling was consistent with most of the participants; other than economic diversity (which was downplayed), there was little to no ethnic, racial, religious, or sexual diversity or acknowledgment as to why these differences were absent or seemed invisible. Sara believed that one reason her teachers may not have mentioned social justice was because of the lack of racial diversity in her school. "There wasn't much diversity at my school, so we didn't learn a lot about social justice. We learned primarily about ourselves" (personal communication, April 22, 2009).

Jon attended a mostly White "upper-middle-class boarding school of 700 students. It was fairly racially homogenous. I don't think there really was any discussion of [race]" (personal communication, April 20, 2009). He mentioned that he did not see any students with special needs until he began a public high school in his junior year.

Brenda's school experience was an exception from many education majors at Mountain State. She reported: "I grew up with everyone, Latin Americans and just everyone, and so to me, it was normal. I grew up having friends like that and not seeing color boundaries" (personal communication, April 24, 2009). However, Brenda's claims seem contradictory. She celebrated her exposure to diversity as positive and open, but then added that race and ethnic diversity were seldom discussed because "you never knew how people would take it" (personal communication, April 24, 2009). This contradiction was often coupled with a belief that avoiding difficult issues such as racism and homophobia in the classroom will keep these issues from becoming problematic.

Unchallenged social injustices. Emaline took responsibility for not recognizing the need for social justice teaching for much of her school life. Accustomed to seeing "a lot of poverty," she seemed inured to its presence: "I just thought it was how it was" (personal communication, April 27, 2009). Inequity was regarded as natural, inevitable, and unchangeable.

Rigid curriculum. With state testing and mandated texts, many preservice teachers cited an inflexible curriculum as one reason for little social justice content. Emaline explained that social justice was not explicitly taught: "We just really didn't touch on it" (personal communication, April 27, 2009). However, she remembered her high school government teachers taught as if they might care about social justice issues, although they curtailed the students' discussions because they had to focus on the tested curriculum: "We have to get this done and we have to get this done—and you can have your thoughts and those are good, but we've got to move on" (personal communication, April 27, 2009). In Brenda's account, the teachers sounded only half-hearted. They wanted to look as if they welcomed independent thought, but they would rather no one actually express it: "You got shot down. There wasn't much freedom of speech there" (personal communication, April 24, 2009).

Heather did not think that social justice ever came up during her schooling: "The curriculum didn't really go out into the community or talk about things that were going on outside and bring it in to the classroom" (personal communication, April 29, 2009). Her teachers might have mentioned poverty rates, but they stopped short of talking about causes or solutions. According to Heather, social justice teaching was absent not because of teacher ignorance, but because the curriculum was already too full. Sara added that required testing was the reason social justice "was put on the back burner" (personal communication, April 22, 2009).

Teacher knowledge. Some of these preservice teachers believed their teachers were not informed enough to teach about social justice. Sara claimed that her teachers would not have known "how to approach" teaching about social justice issues. Brenda remembered fellow students "naturally questioning things about the world, or something you'd hear in the news," but teachers did not acknowledge the students who brought up these topics (personal communication, April 24, 2009). In fact, Brenda suspected that her teachers just did not know enough about the issues and so they moved on. Emaline (personal communication, April 27, 2009) wondered whether her teachers felt overwhelmed and unable to handle such a heavy load:

> They didn't really know how to address it themselves. They didn't know what to do other than to teach us to the best of their ability and hope we will be educated enough to go out searching on our own.

Teacher discomfort. The participants thought their teachers were compelled to avoid community censure by dodging risk and controversy. This reluctance is not surprising given that fear of administration, parents, and community was repeatedly cited in methods classes when discussing controversial topics. When Carla thought back to middle school, she could not recall any overt social justice content. She attributed this lack to the discomfort that comes with discussing sensitive issues. Brenda's high school teachers also skirted controversial issues. She believed that her teachers were "definitely afraid to speak their minds" because they feared parents would complain to administrators (personal communication, April 27, 2009):

> Don't talk about touchy subjects! Keep it very P.C. We would try and then people would kind of get in heated discussions and the teacher would just come and squash it. They would see that it's going towards a touchy subject—race, religion—definitely big ones.

Teacher hostility. Carla did not remember any explicit social justice agenda in high school. Initially, she noted that teachers were "pretty respectful" concerning issues of diversity, but then she paused to talk about some exceptions, such as teachers who also coached boys' sports "were more inclined to talk...in a negative way, especially about sexual orientation" (personal communication, April 27, 2009). Carla also saw social injustice reinforced with homophobic and sexist jokes. She recalled the boys' soccer coach who taught math. "Some of the students in my classes were soccer players, so he was open...he would...joke [about gays and lesbians]" (personal communication, April 27, 2009).

Teacher indifference. Preservice teachers thought their teachers may have believed that social justice was not a valid educational objective. Jon spoke negatively of both his private and public school teachers for presenting "a basically black and white, lecture-based, standard, traditional view to the class" (personal communication, April 20, 2009). If his teachers in either school talked about social justice at all, he missed it: "Honestly, I don't think that it's anything any of them ever considered. I don't remember doing any kind of service learning project or anything where I was involved in the community" (personal communication, April 20, 2009).

Teachers who address social justice. Only three participants recalled a teacher who addressed social justice explicitly. Emaline had her first exposure to social justice teaching in an 11th-grade U.S. history class. The topic was poverty and people in the world "who didn't have everything" (personal communication, April 27, 2009). Heather's AP math teacher veered off into teaching social justice. They had already covered the curriculum and done the required testing, so the teacher showed the film *Hotel Rwanda.* Her math teacher said, "This is really important for you to know about" (personal communication, April 27, 2009). She thought that this teacher just wanted students "to know what was going on." The class discussed Rwanda and genocide. For Emaline, this marked the time "when I started becoming culturally aware" (personal communication, April 27, 2009). The harsh material touched her, and she questioned why she had not known about these problems earlier. She started to see the rampant poverty and alcoholism in her community. According to Emaline, throughout 11th and 12th grade, "It just started hitting me" (personal communication, April 27, 2009).

Preservice Teachers' Perceptions of Their PeaceJam Involvement

For their service learning assignment, the six preservice teachers invested a minimum of 10 hours in an eighth-grade classroom helping to support the PeaceJam curriculum. Although only the male student (i.e., Jon) intended to seek a middle-school teaching position, the other students expressed surprise that their preconception of middle-school students as "scary" and challenging to teach had been faulty. All reported that the time that they spent in these classrooms was positive.

Student engagement. These preservice teachers seemed to analyze teaching style before they considered teaching effectiveness. As Carla talked of her involvement with PeaceJam in the eighth-grade classroom, she admitted she was initially put off by what she perceived as a chaotic and unstructured classroom environment: "It's really free—in and out, people walking in and moving around the classroom" (personal communication, April, 27, 2009). However, the results soon refuted Carla's prejudgment: "I saw that these kids were really involved in what they were doing. But in the end they really knew what they were talking about, and I think they wanted to do something and then they really did it" (personal communication, April, 27, 2009).

Brenda also initially interpreted the freedom in the classroom to mean that discipline and order were absent: "I'd be a little (more) authoritative" (personal communication, April 24, 2009). She suspected that students were not always attending to the important information the teacher was delivering, but she had to admit there "was very little acting up or out." She remarked on the pleasant and affirming atmosphere in the classroom: "There are posters everywhere of anyone and everyone, not just the typical Caucasians" (personal communication, April 24, 2009). This style may have reflected the teacher's preferences, but it also considered the student: "(There is) just freedom, to get up, move around; if you have a thought you can voice it and not be squelched for it" (personal communication, April 24, 2009).

The eighth graders surprised Carla, who was expecting them to be more passive: "I saw these kids were really involved in what they were doing. In the end they really knew what they were talking about. They wanted to do something and then they really did it" (personal communication, April 27, 2009). Perhaps Brenda entered the PeaceJam experience in the middle-school classroom with the most trepidation. Wanting to teach early elementary grades, she was intimidated by eighth graders. However, after a little time, she found she liked interacting with 13-year-olds:

> I really liked going into middle school. Going in, I thought, they're middle-schoolers; they're not going to really be enthusiastic about it. They really are, and they surely did learn a lot of things. They really shocked me. I remember when I was in eighth grade, I wasn't thinking about stuff like that. I commend them. (personal communication, April 24, 2009)

Handling tough topics. Initially, Emaline was troubled when the eighth-grade teacher spoke so plainly about problems of social injustice, such as starvation, infant mortality, rape, and genocide: "He started telling them all these graphic details, and I was just like 'they're just little kids'!" (personal communication, April 27, 2009). In the end, she had to admit just how skillfully the teacher was able to talk with his students about controversial topics. In addition, this time with PeaceJam in public schools led Jon to see the hard reality of "some of the beliefs and attitudes that are still there" (personal communication, April 20, 2009). Jon referred to the blatant homophobia of some eighth-grade boys when they encountered some openly gay students at the regional PeaceJam conference. "How do we break it?" he wondered. Of course, teacher responses to such dilemmas are made muchmore complex in the context of the conservative politics and strong Christian beliefs in our area.

Participants' reflections on PeaceJam. PeaceJam caused Heather to think about the place of social justice in her own future classroom:

> I think it's great that they are reaching out to these young kids telling them they can make a difference in the world. I like it; it's had a positive impact…. Even if for some reason my school couldn't get involved in it, I think it'd be interesting to have those kinds of projects for kids in the community. (personal communication, April 29, 2009)

Carla taught a lesson on human rights as part of the PeaceJam curriculum: "The whole PeaceJam thing really made a difference" (personal communication, April 27, 2009). Carla was referring to the students' receptivity to her teaching, which seemed especially relevant because she is the daughter of Mexican immigrants:

> I don't know in their classroom, but for me, specifically. I couldn't believe the questions they would ask when I did my presentation. I was surprised how they were into it. We talked about things they were really open about—like what their views were about immigration. I was really amazed that there was actual conversation. There was actual debate. One said, "Well they have families to support." Other people were saying, "Well my opinion is this." They actually happened to think about something. I was really surprised that they were interested and had a viewpoint. (personal communication, April 27, 2009)

It was encouraging when Sara credited her service learning with Peace-Jam with reinforcing the place of social studies as a key part of the curriculum: "[It's] 'not…on the back burner" but "really…one of the core classes" (personal communication, April 22, 2009).

Facing difficult issues. When we work with children, we are still dealing with adolescents whose beliefs are being formed. As previously discussed, the region in which the participants live and work is dominated by strong dispositions toward biblical literalism and social and political conservatism. The PeaceJam ethos emphasizes tolerance and safety for all, so the culture at the larger regional meetings is accepting of minority sexual orientation. Even if PeaceJam did nothing else, it provides the opportunity to dialogue about differences and the right to be "other."

After these eighth-grade students returned from PeaceJam's regional conference, Carla sat in on the debriefing, which their teacher facilitated. She noted how some of these students referred to an openly gay boy they had met when they were grouped with students from other schools. He was likely the only young person they had ever been around who was open about being homosexual. According to Carla, they talked "about that guy who was 'too friendly, friendly in a weird way' they called it. It was funny just to see how they were still not comfortable" (personal communication, April 27, 2009).

Jon, who had gone the extra mile in volunteering as an enthusiastic mentor at the regional PeaceJam conference, helped with that debriefing: "At PeaceJ'am it was okay for that boy to say, 'Hey, I'm gay and I'm proud. I think I said something like, 'Wasn't it brave for him to say that?'" (personal communication, April 20, 2009). Jon wanted to present students with a sort of common ground so these eighth graders could at least notice what courage it took for that boy to be "out." Jon hoped to emphasize how much alike, rather than different, these boys were.

According to Emaline, participation in PeaceJam increased her confidence as a social justice teacher, especially in handling troubling subject matter. In addition, witnessing how the teacher was able to handle debriefing helped diminish her anxiety:

> With the PeaceJam experience, I feel better prepared to talk about it and to approach it, especially learning how to debrief. Through PeaceJam, the middle school students became more aware of what is going on in the world and what they can do to bring justice to all people. (personal communication, April 27, 2009)

At the end of the semester, Brenda stated she was "definitely more tolerant, of just people and their opinions, their way of thinking and looking at the world through their eyes" as the result of exposure to PeaceJam (personal communication, April 24, 2009). The emphasis on the lives of the Peace Laureates—about whom she had not previously known—was invaluable.

How Do These Preservice Teachers See Themselves as Teachers?

After their lifetimes of experience, teacher education, social studies methods, and service learning with PeaceJam, how do these preservice teachers see themselves as teachers?

Addressing controversy. Sara alluded to encouraging students to address controversial and difficult issues: "We need to allow students to be able to talk about it even though there might be differences in the classroom" (personal communication, April 22, 2009). When Brenda was asked how she felt about bringing up controversial topics, she said, "I don't want to offend anyone. That's my biggest thing, but I'm learning now I do want to talk about it and I think it's very healthy to talk about it" (personal communication, April 24, 2009).

Celebrating diversity in the classroom. Some of my own interactions with preservice teachers revealed a duality; in methods classes, I sometimes heard students insist that diversity "should not be a big deal anymore." Some said "we got it already" or "we're sick of that topic" as if there was nothing more to be said. Still, a mass of current literature reveals that many teachers—White, Christian, and middle class (Johnson, 2002)—are confounded by how to make their teaching and curriculum fit their students' needs. Sara discussed this challenge:

> I think that it's very important, especially as a teacher, because you're going to have a lot of students that are different from you. You need to be able to meet them in the middle and make them feel comfortable in the classroom. I don't think that your kids will want to open up to you, you'll have a block and they won't care about anything you say and it doesn't matter if it's a math lesson or if it's actually something that will benefit them in their lives, if you don't respect them by trying to understand where they're coming from. (personal communication, April 22, 2009)

When asked to picture her future classroom, Sara described it as:

> Very inviting. Everyone seems to be comfortable doing what they are doing in the classroom. Friends are sitting by friends, but they are doing their work. They are getting it done, but they still have time to have fun and learn about each other and just know that we're all people and that we all make mistakes and we all do different things and we are all different and we respect that, to do what we need to learn to teach each other about our differences. It will be hard work (personal communication, April 22, 2009)

Sometimes our observations served as a caution. Jon referred to bullying he saw directed at an isolated student (not at the PeaceJam school). He confronted two boys who discounted their bullying of another boy because "he's this gay kid." John explained: "What's so funny is I saw myself in him. The kid had his head shaved. He was wearing black. He was the Goth kid, screaming for attention. 'Hey, I'm different'!" (personal communication, April 20, 2009). When Jon asked teachers about this student, they shrugged off the bullying and said he brought the abuse on himself. While trying to understand the teachers' viewpoint, Jon thought,

> So what? What harm is he doing? Well, because he looks different. What do we as teachers bring to the table that's going to help bring him positive energy? This social justice is definitely something that I think about and look at, 'cause I don't want that. I want those kids to be supported even if they are different and bizarre and out there and wanting the green hair. (personal communication, April 20, 2009)

Jon seemed to be referring to fostering an educational environment that is open to a diversity of viewpoints. Sara concurred:

I think it's good to know each other's opinions and where you stand and why you think the way you do. I think some people—even though it may sound bizarre—they have vital points, too. But I think that's important. People need to be able to stand up for themselves and for what they believe instead of shutting them out. (personal communication, April 22, 2009)

What Place Should Social Justice Have in One's Practice?

Preservice teachers noted that they want to teach for social justice, but they were not yet specific about how they plan to do it. Sara explained:

I just feel like you can't be the best teacher that you want to be if you don't have some kind of social justice in the classroom. This semester, I've learned a lot. It's really opened my eyes to really want to try to do social justice and make it happen in my class. There's just so much that you can do...but mostly just educating the students. (personal communication, April 22, 2009)

Heather asserted that social justice teaching is bringing the community into the classroom so that students will know how to interact with it and "see the need to give back to the community that has given to us." She noted," I think you should teach things that are going on out there so that you are aware and are not just blindsided" (personal communication, April 29, 2009). She argued that children need to have an appropriate amount of information about the injustices in the world. Meanwhile, Carla, who plans to teach early elementary grades, seemed unsure how she can integrate social justice teaching into practice with younger children, anticipating being misunderstood by teaching peers and parents.

Perhaps because of the combination of her experiences at Mountain State, Brenda indicated strong optimism about teaching that may have been previously dormant. According to Brenda, this semester's experiences prompted her to identify where she stands as a teacher and how to present herself to students:

I think you should teach social justice. Even if you don't call it that in elementary school, just teach a form of that. I think it does give me hope that the kids I'm going to be teaching, hopefully that's where they're going. I think that is a good idea that they want to start talking about it. I'm taking time to learn everything and to teach them. It's not a lost cause. Hopefully, it's going to be with them throughout their lives. (personal communication, April 24, 2009)

Emaline indicated that she wants to design a different approach:

I guess authentic teaching. It's something I've been thinking about. It's not just the straight and narrow. I want to use different points of view—documentary films, interviews, and voice recordings, different views coming together and intertwining—so that kids are more aware. I guess this semester has opened my eyes. Curriculum is essential and isn't just something you get from a text or workbook; it's not just something that's on the *Standard Course of Study*. It's given me the tools to bring social justice into the classroom. I feel better prepared to do that. I know where to look for resources. (personal communication, April 27, 2009)

Poverty. Heather stated that she hopes to create lessons to show students a realistic version of the world. Her example of equipping her students to see the world as it is means teaching students about poverty in their community. Perhaps she would have them visit a soup kitchen. Heather pondered how to handle the topic of poverty sensitively, especially if there are students in her class whose families use these services. She does not want her students to think that such social problems only happen for "people...from Africa; I want to make sure that they're seeing this happens right next door" (personal communication, April 29, 2009). Jon also concluded that economic justice should be considered:

Through (thinking about) social justice, I've become more aware of that gap—not only the technological gap, but just that gap that happens between people from low income areas, education level, vocabulary, the discussions at the dinner table, the fact that they're not interested in what's happening in the world, news, newspapers, because it's not important. What is important to them is finding where their meal's coming from—whether or not they're going to make it. (personal communication, April 20, 2009)

Race. Carla concluded that teaching about race will be "easier" because she is a racial minority—namely, a Latina. She explained that students of color may identify with her, which would enabled her to "help them see that their race is not a bad thing" and help them "deal with situations in school" (personal communication, April 27, 2009 Meanwhile, Brenda, who is White, indicated that one element of social justice teaching is to provide a healthy exposure to understanding racial and ethnic differences, especially if the community is not overtly and obviously diverse. If Brenda said what she really meant, such a response is refreshing, as some educators believe teaching for diversity is only relevant when the class includes a multicultural population. Regarding her students and the need to educate them about differences, Brenda noted, "You never know where your life's gonna go, so you need to experience that" (personal communication, April 24, 2009).

Recommendations

PeaceJam was new to all the participants. One reason that it was appealing to these preservice teachers is likely because it is so active. They saw the middle schoolers searching for problems to solve. One eighth-grade teacher's music videos captured student enthusiasm as he taught the students about the Nobel Peace Laureates. Students then took action, collecting money and toiletries, giving speeches, and publicly sharing their work. Based on the themes that emerged in this study, addressing the following issues would likely bolster social justice teaching and increase the infusion of explicit social justice teaching into all methods courses.

We should nurture preservice teachers' active and critical investigations into the presence and absence of diversity in university experiences and school placements. Moreover, given the "apartheid nature" (Swartz, 2003) of U.S. schools, it is imperative to help raise preservice teachers' consciousness regarding the complexity and significance of diversity.

In addition, we need to require substantial and deep reflections on preservice teachers' stances regarding social justice. Perhaps a good place to begin would be with Peterson's (1994) specifications of traditional, progressive, and critical educators. We should continue the exploration by helping preservice teachers identify oppression and privilege in others and themselves, understand cultural capital, and model the interrogation of hegemonic power structures (Milner, Flowers, Moore, Moore, & Flowers, 2003).

We should also seek out and provide professional role models as clinical faculty and supervising teachers in field placements so that preservice teachers can witness and interact with social justice advocates at all grade levels. Preservice teachers should see a wide range of identities among teachers, representing the culture at large, and they should know the work of teachers of color (Gardenhire-Crooks, Collado, Martin, & Castro 2010), sexual minorities (Bishop, Caraway, & Stader, 2010), and caring male teachers in lower grades (Johnson, 2008).

Furthermore, we should develop and support service learning opportunities and acknowledge the intricacy, messiness, and problematic nature of helping (Hui, 2009). We must seek involvement in social justice advocacy in programs such as PeaceJam (Powers, 2009) for schools that actively address real-world problems. We also need to integrate history that centers on the contributions of "ordinary" and organized women and men. Iverson and James (2010) were disappointed to find that participation in a critical service learning project raised the preservice teachers' awareness of the need for individual responsibility, but apparently failed to awaken awareness of the power of collective action. Middle-class students and educators valued the heroic individual, whereas their working-class counterparts were more likely to elevate the ideal of enhanced social consciousness and collective action (Schutz, 2008). Students need an expanded understanding of citizenship beyond the "one person can change the world/make a difference" message (Iverson & James, 2010).

In addition, we should recruit and retain diverse faculty. Such diverse faculty must do more than head diversity initiatives and teach multicultural classes. Existing faculty should have ample opportunities for professional development in cultural competence (Melnick & Zeichner, 1995). Teacher education schools will need to provide a wide range of mentoring for new faculty with diverse racial, gender, and class identities to be recruited and retained (Rodriguez & Sjostrom 2000). Naturally, the success of each new faculty member will help welcome and reassure other diverse faculty (Osajiima, 2009) and students. In addition, we need to recruit and retain a diverse student body of preservice teachers, including addressing the shortage of males in lower grades (Skelton, 2007).

Finally, we must invite activist community members—alone or in panels, online or in person—into methods classrooms to discuss and advocate for their social justice passions. Perhaps some of these guests may be students who have participated in past PeaceJam projects or students of color to discuss their campus and school experiences (Morrell & Collatos, 2002). Furthermore, we should also include those advocating for children, women's rights, and the welfare of the poor as well as those fighting sexual oppression and religious discrimination.

References

Bernard, H. R. (2000). *Social research methods: Qualitative and quantitative approaches.* Thousand Oaks, CA: Sage.

Bishop, H. N., Caraway, C., & Stader, D. L. (2010). A case for legal protection for sexual minority educators. *Clearing House: A Journal of Educational Strategies, Issues, and Ideas, 83*(3), 84–88.

Bourdieu, P. (1977). *Reproduction in education, society, and culture.* Beverly Hills, CA: Sage.

Frederick, R., Cave, A., & Perencevich, K. C. Teacher candidates' transformative thinking on issues of social justice. *Teaching and Teacher Education: An International Journal of Research and Studies, 26*(2), 315–322.

Freire, P. (1978). *Pedagogy of the oppressed.* New York: Continuum.

Gardenhire-Crooks, A., Collado, H., Martin, K., & Castro, A. (2010). *Terms of engagement: Men of color discuss their experiences in community college.* New York: MDRC. (ERIC Document Reproduction Service No. ED508982)

Gore, J. M. (1993). *The struggle for pedagogies: Critical and feminist discourses as regimes of truth.* New York: Routledge.

Haberman, M. (1992). Should college youth be prepared for teaching? *Educational Forum*, *57*(1), 30–36.

hooks, b. (1994). *Teaching to transgress: Education as the practice of freedom*. New York: Routledge.

Hui, S. M. (2009, November–December). Difficult dialogues about service learning: Embrace the messiness. *About Campus*, *14*(5), 22–26.

Iverson, S. V., & James, J. H. (2010, February). Becoming "effective" citizens? Change-oriented service in a teacher education program. *Innovative Higher Education*, *35*(1), 19–35.

Johnson, L. (2002, March–April). "My eyes have been opened": White teachers and racial awareness. *Journal of Teacher Education*, *53*(2), 153–167.

Johnson, S. P. (2008, Winter). The status of males in public education today. *Education Policy Brief*, *6*(4), 1–12.

Kvale, S. (1996). *InterViews: An introduction to qualitative research interviewing*. Thousand Oaks, CA: Sage.

McDonald, M. A. (2008). The pedagogy of assignments in social justice education. *Equity & Excellence in Education*, *41*(2), 151–167.

Melnick, S. L., & Zeichner, K. M. (1995). *Teacher education for cultural diversity: Enhancing the capacity of teacher education institutions to address diversity issues*. East Lansing, MI: National Center for Research on Teacher Learning. (ERIC Document Reproduction Service No. ED392751)

Miles, M. B., & Huberman, A. (1994). *Qualitative data analysis: An expanded sourcebook* (2nd ed.). Thousand Oaks, CA: Sage.

Milner, H. R., Flowers, L. A., Moore, E., Moore, J. L., & Flowers, T. A. (2003, November–December). Preservice teachers' awareness of multicultural and diversity. *High School Journal*, *87*(1), 63–70.

Morrell, E., & Collatos, A. M. (2002). Toward a critical teacher education: High school student sociologists as teacher educators. *Social Justice*, *29*(4), 60–70.

Nussbaum, M. (2001). *The enduring significance of John Rawls*. Retrieved from http://chronicle.com/free/v47/145/45b00701.htm.

Osajiima, K. (2009, December). Telling our stories to one another. *Education Digest: Essential Readings Condensed for Quick Review*, *75*(4), 62–64.

Parker, L., Deyhle, D., & Villenas, S. (Eds.). (1999). *Race is...race isn't: Critical race theory and qualitative studies in education*. Boulder, CO: Westview Press.

Peterson, B. (1994). Teaching for social justice: One teacher's journey. In B. Bigelow, B. Harvey, S. Karp, & L. Miller (Eds.), *Rethinking our classrooms: Teaching for equity and social justice* (pp. 30–36). Milwaukee: Rethinking Schools.

Powers, B. H. (2009). From National History Day to PeaceJam: Research leads to authentic learning. *English Journal*, *98*(5), 48–53.

Rodriguez, Y. E., & Sjostrom, B. R. (2000, February). *Faculty of color in teacher education: A multicultural approach to mentoring for retention, 2000 and beyond*. Paper presented at the 52nd annual meeting of the American Association of Colleges for Teacher Education, Chicago, IL.

Schutz, A. (2008). Gender, policy, and initial teacher education. *Teachers College Record*, *110*(2), 405–442.

Shank, G. (2006). *Qualitative research: A personal skills approach* (2nd ed.). Upper Saddle River, NJ: Pearson.

Skelton, C. (2007, November). Gender, policy, and initial teacher education. *Gender and Education, 19*(6), 677–690.

Swartz, E. (2003). Teaching white preservice teachers: Pedagogy for change. *Urban Education, 38*, 255–280.

Part III
Diversity in Teacher Education Programs: Constructs and Concepts

CHAPTER EIGHT

The Home Visit: Apprehension, Assumptions, Acceptance, and Action

Laura L. Marasco

As the demographics of our public school population continue to change, inservice teachers are being tested in their ability to address not only inclusive classrooms, but also those with students who bring differences in language and culture. This chapter draws on five years of case studies conducted by pre-K–12th grade, middle-class, female, predominately White inservice teachers enrolled in a graduate course entitled Literacy and Diversity. Using critical pedagogy as a theoretical framework, the course explores the relationship between mainstream literacy education and students who are traditionally marginalized by their diverse learning needs. The requirements of the case study assignment for this course dictate that the student for study as chosen by the teacher must come from a culturally and/or linguistically different background from that of the teacher. Although the teachers were apprehensive and sometimes resistant to the additional requirement that they must make a home visit and conduct a parent interview, the author examined the shift—sometimes radical—that occurred after the visit and the resulting effective changes in teachers' cultural and professional responses to their students and their school communities.

The graduate course Literacy and Diversity is intended to engage working professionals to examine learning problems from a contextual perspective rather than isolating them in the individual student. In other words, teachers need to consider personal and environmental factors that affect a student's learning. Too often our assumptions about "at-risk" students, their families, and their ethnic, cultural, and economic backgrounds lead us to believe that they will learn the way we want to teach and interact with them without sufficient regard for—or understanding of—the contextual nature of their difficulties or awareness of our own assumptions and biases.

The primary assignment in this course is for the inservice teachers to conduct a case study project based on a home visit and parent story. The teachers began by selecting a student for their study who had a very different ethnic, linguistic, cultural, and/or socioeconomic background from their own and who met at least one of the following criteria:

- The student is receiving instruction as an English language learner (ELL) and is significantly below grade level in reading ability and/or
- The student is an ELL who has been identified as having a learning disability that significantly affects his or her literacy learning.

The vast majority of graduate students enrolled in this course each fall are White, middle-class females who have little or no experience with home visits, although many have been teaching for at least five years.

Coming from a western region of the country that counted many Native American and immigrant Latino children in the public schools and where home visits are common, the researcher, who was the professor of this course, was unprepared for the graduate students' reaction to the case study/home visit assignment. The researcher thus began to collect writing excerpts from the students' case studies in hopes of assessing how the home visit assignment was perceived, and if it eventually caused a change in the way these teachers' interacted with or on behalf of the students and the families they studied. Over the course of five years, four stages have emerged in common reoccurring themes; these case study stages have been categorized as apprehension, assumption, acceptance, and action.

Apprehension

Landsman (2006) discussed White teachers' willingness to discuss and face their biases about diverse parents and students as long as such a discussion occurs in a nonthreatening environment. During the first few weeks of the course, through various other assignments, the inservice teachers began to talk about their beliefs about diverse learners, reflect on how their own experiences of learning to read—both at home and at school—had affected their professional practice, and describe any of their efforts—successful or not—to establish a relationship with parents from different backgrounds from themselves. When inservice teachers were asked to submit a narration of their prior experiences with home visits and identify barriers or obstacles, including personal doubts, about the parent interview, their apprehension became apparent and vocal.

Although the teachers wholeheartedly endorsed parent–school communication, their idea of how the parent–school connection transpired was embedded in tradition. My graduate students remember their own school years, their parents' participation, observe and experience it now as teachers in their own schools, and believe that parent–school involvement has been, and continues to be, structured around middle-class, U.S.-born, and native English-speaking families. The teachers believed that back-to-school nights, parent–teacher conferences, and PTA meetings were adequate venues in which to engage parents. Home visits were seen as problem-solving endeavors and, as such, the responsibility of the school nurse for medical/health purposes or the vice principal or principal for behavior issues. Even in professional educational literature, (Harry & Klinger, 2006; Middleton, Coleman and Lewis; 2006; Rishel, 2008), reinforce strategies about how to get parents and families to come to school. Little is written about how teachers go to these homes and what happens during the home visits.

A common response of the inservice teachers in defense of not making a home visit was that they did not speak the home language; therefore, it would be difficult to communicate with the parents. They were also worried about going to an unfamiliar neighborhood. The researcher once offered to accompany a teacher on her home visit to translate for her and the family. When asked about her school neighborhood, she said, "I really don't know anything about this area. I just drive to school and then go into my building. When I am done for the day, I leave and go home, which is not near here" (J. Worthington, personal communication, Fall, 2008). Another student stated that her school district did not encourage home visits and that she did not want to go against this policy. One student's narrative reflected the sentiments of a majority of the inservice teachers: "I had never been on a home visit before. I found the prospective of this very overwhelming and intimidating. The thought of going to someone's home and interviewing, this was out of my comfort level" (M. Allen, personal communication, Fall, 2008). Although the teachers shared their discomfort with leaving their comfort zones (i.e., school and classroom) to meet with parents, it did not occur to them at this point to connect their feelings to the possibility that parents might feel the same apprehension coming into school to see them.

Assumptions

Buried in teachers' apprehension about home visits were assumptions they had at both the personal and professional levels. In Quintanar-Sarellana's (1997) study, 127 teachers were placed on a continuum of cultural awareness. The study's statistical analysis demonstrated "that certain characteristics of teachers are important factors in the attitudes they hold about linguistic minority students" (p. 46). Euro-American teachers who had no bilingual classroom experience and who had little Spanish language background were situated on the lowest end of the spectrum. "Their responses to the various items on the questionnaire show that they are largely unaware of the educational value, or cultural capital, that the language and culture of minority students represent" (p. 30).

Although personal assumptions were often masked, they became transparent through inservice teachers' professional assertions about parents. One student wrote, "I thought that progress reports, parent teacher conferences, and the family nights that we have were enough to keep parents involved in their child's education. Another stated,

> I believed that the parents of these children didn't care about their success, so why should I? Most of the parents of diverse learners didn't come into school very often. That made me think that they weren't concerned and that they just sent their children to school because they had to.

Meanwhile, another inservice teacher explained, "Until now, I have been rather naïve in believing that as long as I knew the student very well, the parent perspective was not extremely important." Often the inservice teachers found fault with the parental lack of response:

> Before I had Roel enrolled in the after school program I found fault with his mother for not providing him with the homework support he needed. I wanted her to check his agenda every night and be an active participant. Because I did not see this happening, I thought she did not care enough.

Another assumption thread appeared within the discussion of English language policy and identity. One inservice teacher indicated, "In the beginning, even though I hate to admit it, I was one of those people who believed that if you come to this country to live you should speak English."

Assuming national identity by cultural or linguistic characteristics was another eye-opener for some:

> Most of what I have learned about María is personal information, rather than academic information. Since she is an ELL student, I had always thought that María must have immigrated to the United States recently. In fact, María was born in the United States and is an ELL student because her language at home is primarily Spanish.

One of the frustrations that plagued the classroom teachers, who had not had much or any bilingual or English language acquisition instruction, was their perceived inability to connect with students who spoke little or no English. As one inservice teacher divulged,

> I believed that I could just teach the minimum to these diverse learners, but not make them my main focus. I thought that there would be no need to waste time putting all of my energy or focus into them, when they would be leaving in the middle of the year anyway. I also believed that they weren't retaining anything anyway, and would just sit there all day taking up space, but never really learn anything or understand what was going on.

Meanwhile, a high school teacher wrote, "Because I could not measure academic growth with these students, I was getting frustrated and rationalizing to myself that there was nothing that could be done with them until they were fluent in English." Indeed, ELLs' ability was another issue raised: "I thought all students coming from other countries performed at a low level because of the language gap."

Acceptance

Midway into the semester, the inservice teachers scheduled their home visitations. Despite communication obstacles, such as family work schedules, no home phone, translation issues, school or district policies, and teachers' own reluctance, dates were confirmed for the home interview and parent story. Using Edwards's (1999) Parent Stories Questionnaire as a guide, teachers prepared their own questions based on their current knowledge of their student and family. Some obtained parental permission to record responses, whereas others asked permission to take notes. This process ultimately demonstrated that teaching something in class is not the same thing as students learning it. "Learning happens when students make cognitive transformations, expanding and reorganizing the knowledge in their cerebral filing systems. Only then can they assimilate and act upon ideas" (Fiore & Elsasser, 1987, p. 96).

As the inservice teachers shared their home visit experiences in class, those teachers who had not yet met with their students' families tended to become more confident. Stories of welcoming families who issued invitations to stay for dinner and made the teachers feel special and honored became common threads of discussion. Teachers who arranged and needed translators reported how important that link was to their success with the interview and gaining information they would otherwise have never known.

The inservice teachers' case studies clearly demonstrated a change in thinking after having what Dewey (1933) called an educative experience. The teachers started to realize that the home visit was a critical factor in home–school dialogue and a bridge to cultural understanding and acceptance.

On parents and family. The inservice teachers were treated with respect and welcomed into their students' homes. They learned that home visits provide an opportunity for them to observe interactions among family members and ask questions that they would not have thought to ask in a school setting. They also discovered that not all parents fit the profile that educators often assume equals an involved parent. Through their visits, they were able to assess the amount of time and ability parents have to spend with their children on homework and academic help. The teachers spoke with parents, not just at them, establishing relationships that surface in later interactions and conversations that indicate that their presence in the home made a positive difference. These common themes are illustrated in the following narratives.

> If I would have made no contact with the parents, they probably would have never made an effort to come into school. I now know how intimidating it is entering an atmosphere that you know little about, and everyone treats you like an outcast. I was very nervous to conduct my interview with Mark's family because I knew no Creole and felt like an outcast. Thankfully his family treated me with respect and open hearts.

> After meeting and interviewing his mother and grandfather, I have also developed a positive relationship with the family. This was a very crucial first step to helping Akram to become a better reader. At first, Akram's mother was very intimidated by our school setting and would not visit the school. Now, I feel that she would be more comfortable coming in for a conference and learning about what she can do at home to help Akram. On the other hand, I also feel more comfortable contacting the family for information and other concerns.

> Socially, after meeting Roel's family and watching their interactions with each other and experiencing their interactions with me, I am able to see that his mild, timid personality is a product of his upbringing. His mother and brother had matching characteristics.... Every member of his extended family was very respectful and reserved.

> My White, female, middle-class world is only representative of about one third of the children I teach.... Through the process of learning about Antonio and his background, the most important lesson I've learned is that just because a parent doesn't fit the profile most educators deem as an involved parent doesn't mean that she or he doesn't care or doesn't value education.

> After visiting Randy's home, there is an understanding that his mother has limited abilities that may affect her ability to help him with his assignments as he continues in his later years of schooling. Ms. Smith shared with us that she has a reading disability that was not diagnosed when she attended school. She also stated that she taught herself to read.

A principal taking the course explained,

I feel that I really have gotten to know Gabi. I now have a better understanding of where she comes from and where she is headed. I also think I am more sympathetic to her situation. I find myself really listening in when someone mentions Gabi's name or talks about how she is doing.... I think she is glad that I took a special interest in her. The last time I observed a class that included Gabi, she was sure to participate and to share what she had learned. I cannot be sure it was because I was there, but she did not do that before I met with her and her father.

After interviewing his mother, I was able to learn more about his home life and why he does not get much support from them. I think his parents would like to help him with his school work, but they do not have the time or the confidence in themselves to help him.

I now know that taking a more active approach toward parent participation is necessary for the success of diverse learners. Talking with parents and finding out about the literacy development at home is necessary in order for a teacher to completely understand how instructional practices should change in order for students to achieve better at school.

Since visiting my student...I now think I have more of a connection with her and her family. I found out a lot of personal information about her family and her heritage. I never knew that she was interested in being a dancer. She never shared that information in class.

The home visit was probably my favorite part of this project because I had a chance even less teachers have by visiting the family where it all happens. We have parents who come to school in order to meet about their child. We do not get to see the family in an environment in which they are comfortable. Plus, we do not get the chance to ask a lot of questions about their upbringing because we are more concerned about what their child is doing/not doing in class.

The nature of the assignment has required and encouraged me to focus more directly on María, her cultural heritage, and her literacy.... Although María's parents were not entirely comfortable during our interview and may not have given entirely accurate information at all times, the effort to contact them and know them has had substantial rewards. Since our interview, María tells me that both her parents have asked specifically how she is progressing in my class and have agreed to meet with the school's guidance counselor to discuss higher education options.

Marco has shown more confidence since I visited his home. He heard what I was telling his parents, and he knows that I think he is a very intelligent young man. Marco was excited about my visit to his house, and just my presence at his home helped him know that I care about him and his education.

I realize now how important it was for me to visit with Min and his family at their home. I connected with them on a personal level, and they understood that I was not there to critique them but to learn more about their son and how I could best assist him in my language arts class. They were very appreciative of my visit, and Min has reaped the benefits of the two worlds (teacher and parents) working together and caring about him and his success.

On culture. The inservice teachers developed greater awareness about their students as well as themselves. Through a reflective lens, they began to see things about their own culture that they had previously ignored. Assumptions fell by the wayside as these teachers faced people different from themselves in terms of language, culture, and experience. Viewing their own students from the "other side of the desk," they learned of fears, tensions, joys, dreams, family stories, and cultural practices that were fundamental to the makeup of their individual students not openly demonstrated or shared with them in the classroom. According to Campano (2007),

> many students who have been negatively labeled...are in fact coping with issues such as poverty, memories of war and flight, the death of loved ones, the incarceration of family members, racism, and the ongoing challenges of crossing political borders and cultural boundaries (p. 52).

This proved evident for one student, as reflected in her findings:

> She led a double life. At home Aarya was the way her parents wanted her to be, and at school she became someone else. At school she sometimes felt like an outsider because of her Muslim heritage in a nondiverse place. Adding more pressure to downplay her heritage is the prejudice she faces as a person of Pakistani origin. Her mother even hinted toward this when she pointed at a picture of Osama Bin Laden in the magazine she showed me. She said that he doesn't even speak their language, but people associate him with her family.

Excerpts from other students' reflective writings included:

> I have always believed that all students regardless of ethnicity, religion, gender, and cognitive abilities could achieve at least some level of literacy success. This case study, however, made me realize and value the influence of different cultural backgrounds, including my own. The most enlightening aspect of this experience was learning the parents' story. I found that I really didn't have a full understanding of Tyrone and his background until I spoke with his mother.

> The cultural information I gained from Ansia's mother opened my eyes to the daily tension that Ansia faces due to the mix of female and male students in her school. Each and every day is a battle between being true to her culture and religion versus following the rules set by the school and teacher.

> One of the greatest surprises of this case study was the home visit. If I had not vis-

ited Shir's home, I would not have gotten to interview her father. In the past, I had only exchanged pleasantries with him at school concerts and events. I always had conferences with Shir's mother. I made the assumption that her father did not speak English well and was uncomfortable talking with me. During the home visit, I learned that my assumptions were incredibly wrong! I learned so much from Shir's father. He shared his culture, religion, background, and love of the United States. He spoke comfortably with me, made Israeli tea for me, and was excited to share his experiences and beliefs with me. In fact, he was disappointed that I was not able to stay for dinner on the night of the interview. I promised the family that I would join them for a Sabbath dinner on a Friday night (that they invited me to attend). I felt the parents' passion for their children's education. I never would have gained this information over the telephone or in a school setting.

On language. The most obvious experiential learning that occurred related to language. The inservice teachers demonstrated the same fear and frustration related to trying to speak or be understood as their students did. They came to understand just how difficult communication and learning another language could be. They empathized with children and youth who are shut out of a conversation or lesson in their own classrooms because of language differences. This was especially true for those inservice teachers who were accompanied by adult translators during their home visit. Yet they also realized that, with a little effort, communication could take place and that parents were just as nervous and frustrated as they were. One of the common findings was the surprise that their students and families did not speak English at home. In the graduate course, several inservice teachers stated that they simply assumed everyone spoke "broken English" when communicating with each other. Powerful new learning about home and school language took place in these kitchens and living rooms.

> After visiting Marie's home and talking with her parents, I have a new appreciation for how ELL students feel when they enter a classroom speaking little to no English. I felt awkward and out of place when Mr. and Mrs. St. Pierre spoke to Mme Ford in French. There was an entire conversation that I was not privy to. It was at that moment that I empathized with many of the ELL students.... Allowing a student who doesn't understand the language, either reading or speaking, to sit in the back of the classroom without participating in class is no longer acceptable.

> The language barrier has been knocked down somewhat, as I realized that I am able to communicate with Mrs. Lopez and she is willing to participate in my conversation. It was uplifting to see how determined she was to have the best for her son and how interested she was in the well-being of her children. Often when parents do not show up for parent conferences, the thought will cross your mind that it is due to lack of interest, but that is obviously not the issue in this case.... The language issue also probably made her feel nervous as well as it did me.

Overall, the interview of Ella and her aunt was eye-opening. I have always felt that if I moved to a country where English was not the primary language, the first thing I would do is learn the other language. Now I feel this probably would not be the case. The day-to-day challenges of paying bills, providing a home and food, and spending time with family would take precedence. These challenges are exacerbated by an American culture that has a history of immigration, but does not respect immigrants and the acculturation process all of our ancestors lived through.

I imagined that So Young and her parents spoke an equal amount of Korean and English in their house. Much to my surprise, they never speak English unless they are somewhere in which they have to do so. While they are at home, they speak Korean.

Action

The reflective and critical thinking that occurred in both processing and writing about their findings through the home visit and interview provided the inservice teachers new ways of understanding and solving problems (Dewey, 1933). Teachers were anxious to share their findings with their school improvement teams, colleagues, and principals. Plans were made to meet with curriculum coordinators and guidance counselors. Some set dates to share information during in-staff meetings, including the importance of knowing the cultures being taught and parents' suggestions conveyed during the home visits regarding things such as having vegetarian options on the school meal plan. Others planned inservices or workshops to share what they had learned. Another proposed more opportunities for families of other cultures to share their language and customs at the school. One teacher pledged to get more involved with an English language program for parents of students offered by the translator at her school. She offered that perhaps a class during the day would be helpful because many parents work at night.

According to one inservice teacher,

I now know how important it is to have a translator present for parent conferences when the parent does not fluently speak English. I know that I would never survive in a school in France, and I took five years of French. I can only imagine what these students are going through. Seeing how well Chen's mom responded to my questions through the translator shows me that she felt very comfortable with him there. I want to make my students' parents feel comfortable when they enter my classroom, and if that means having a translator present for all conferences then that is what I will do.

Another plan of action surfaced regarding library books: "Our school library does not contain a single second language book. I will share this information with the principal and encourage home visits for the upcoming school year." One inservice teacher planned to speak to her media specialist and principal about ordering culturally relevant and sensitive materials for students and teachers. Meanwhile, another teacher indicated in her action plan that,

> I am very interested in beginning a library program at my school for next year. I think it is important to get parents involved in the literacy development of their child and perhaps themselves. Parents should not feel intimidated to walk into the building that is responsible for educating their child.

Some of the inservice teachers proposed action on the policy level. The case study required them to look at districts' ELL policies; most teachers were shocked to discover that few to no such policies were in place. Although this information had not been considered relevant to their professional lives prior this course and the home visit/interview, it came to the forefront on their agendas: "Our county currently has no ELL policy. I will push for the Board of Education to adopt an ELL policy"

> I have complimented the ELL teacher and recognized her difficult job. I never realized how heavy her caseload was and how little support she received from the Board of Education and within my school building.... My county does not fund the ELL program as it funds the Special Education programs. In fact, the county states that it offers an ELL program as if it were an elective. I plan to share my findings with my principal, ELL teacher, community, and especially the School Board.

Some teachers planned to invite administrators and educators to rewrite their mission statements to include all parents. Others suggested that the districts should create a parental survey in the necessary languages and then take action on the results. A few teachers suggested contacting the relevant state department of education about the need to require a diversity course for recertification. Other action projects included connecting with more bilingual people in the community; family event, or teacher conference; scheduling children literacy parenting sessions with an interpreter; and creating a modified version of the parent interview for all students in the class. A few teachers acted immediately, even before the end of the semester.

> Already I have contacted her current teachers and shared with them some of the knowledge I gained from the case study so that they may use it to foster an interaction with her family. Most of her other teachers have had little contact with her family due to the language barriers, and by sharing my success with them, I hope to encourage them to make efforts of their own.

Although the home visit inspired the inservice teachers to advocate and take action for their students and families, not all teachers were supported by their administrations.

Unfortunately, our administration remained on the side of caution during the entire experience. I would talk to them about what I was learning by documenting Julio and speaking with his mother, and although they thought that was "lovely," they decided to maintain their position on home visits. I do not think that home visits will be encouraged throughout the duration of my teaching career, but I will continue to visit my students in public areas, outside of school, so that I can get a glimpse of them as people, not just students.

Another inservice teacher, who also encountered resistance from her school district, planned on solving the problem in a different way:

I now realize that not all parents feel comfortable or may not understand the process of coming to school for parent–teacher conferences. Therefore, I need to begin making contact with these parents explaining that process. It is my professional opinion that, due to the home visit I made this semester and the valuable information I gained, I will continue to ask to make home visits. This is a powerful tool to learning more about the family, student, and their culture.

Confronted with powerful experiences, these teachers were challenged to review their prior assumptions—what Mezirow and associates (1990) call "transformative learning":

Now that I have completed this case study, I believe I know my student much better. I am aware of her family background and support received at home, which gives me some insight as to what type of extra support is needed from me. I am aware of her mother's expectations and goals for her daughter and am now motivated to be sure I meet those goals to my best ability.

I will also make more home visits, as I felt that I gained valuable knowledge from my home visit with María's family. Also, I got a sense that her family got to know me better as a person. I think there is a lot of misunderstanding between teachers and families from other cultures.

Taking the time to visit a home could result in a turning point in a child's academic future. I only spent a few hours with Shir's family, yet I believe the time we spent together was immeasurable. We took our relationship and trust to a new level. I cannot help but think of the students' homes that I should have visited in the past and the possible changes I could have made in their lives.

Conclusion

The teachers learned that parents' stories were an opportunity for both parents and teachers to become better acquainted and to help each other with the children's education. According to Bateson (1979), storying is the most basic form of communication and is fundamental to all forms of life. Family stories help us understand differences "if we are willing to look beyond our own accepted view of knowledge, an opportunity to learn from culturally and linguistically diverse families, and a vehicle to reflect on our own stories" (Sánchez, 1999, p. 358).

During the case study process, common misconceptions were put to rest. Teachers no longer assumed that parents' absence from school equated to not caring about their children's education or future. The teachers discovered that families do not always have the same goals for their children that other families or teachers might share. They also began to understand that parental involvement has many faces, and different strategies are necessary for home–school interaction and communication.

Although the case study and data collection was never intended to be scientific research, it did provide documentation on the process of attitudinal and behavioral change that developed over the course of the semester as a result of the home visit and interview. The reflective thinking that occurred during the course through the requirements of the case study led these teachers to a new place in their personal and professional practice. The teachers created action plans as they now saw their role as advocates for their chosen student and family, as well as for the larger diverse school community. Their awareness and thinking about sociocultural, political, and economic issues expanded to view themselves and their diverse students and families differently. They were now able to see curriculum in the context of community. Freire (1970) defined this development of critical consciousness as "learning to perceive social, political and economic contradictions and to take action against oppressive elements of reality" (p. 19).

Teachers' assumptions were challenged by their experiences with these diverse families, which led to informed action on their parts that had not been considered previously. One of the most immediate results of this case study assignment was a department change in the scheduling of this course, which had previously been scheduled for each spring semester. The teachers petitioned the graduate department to change the rotation to each fall semester because they wanted future students to be able to have the second half of the year to act upon their new bonds with families and use information obtained in the home visit to better support the students in their classrooms.

As we move into the next decade of the 21st century, our teachers will less and less mirror the diversity of students who enter their classrooms. It is critical that institutions of higher education provide instruction and opportunities to enable preservice and inservice teachers to explore their own identities as well as those different from themselves. Teaching and learning must be transformed by validating identity, experience, story, and culture of all students and families. Using the home visit to address such issues is not a new idea in education, but such activity has declined in recent years. We declare that every child is important and we know that parental participation is an important component in the academic success of a student; however, if we are dedicated to that belief, then we must use all the tools in our power to build the bridges from knowledge to action. The home visit can serve as such a bridge.

References

Bateson, G. (1979). *Mind and nature: A necessary unity.* New York: Dutton.

Campano, G. (2007). *Immigrant students and literacy: Reading, writing and remembering.* New York: Teachers College Press.

Dewey, J. (1933). *How we think.* Boston: Heath.

Edwards, P. (1999). *A path to follow: Learning to listen to parents.* Portsmouth, NH: Heinemann.

Fiore, K., & Elsasser, N. (1987). Strangers no more: A liberatory literacy curriculum. In I. Shor (Ed.), *Freire for the classroom: A sourcebook for liberatory teaching* (pp.115128). Portsmouth, NH: Heinemann.

Freire, P. (1970). *Pedagogy of the oppressed.* New York: Herder & Herder.

Harry, B. & Klinger, J. (2006). *Why are so many minority students in special education: Understanding race & disability in schools.* New York: Teachers College Press.

Landsman, L. (2006). Being white: Invisible privileges of a New England prep school girl. In J. Landsman & C. Lewis (Eds.), *White teachers/diverse classrooms* (pp. 13–26). Sterling, VA: Stylus.

Mezirow, J., & Associates. (1990). *Fostering critical reflection in adulthood.* San Francisco: Jossey-Bass.

Middleton, V., Coleman, K., & Lewis, C. (2006). Black/African American family: Coming of age in predominately White communities. In J. Landsman and C.W. Lewis (Eds.), *White teachers/diverse classrooms: A guide to building inclusive schools, promoting high expectations, and eliminating racism* (pp. 162181). Sterling, VA: Stylus.

Quintanar-Sarellana, R. (1997). Culturally relevant teacher preparation and teachers' perceptions of the language and culture of linguistic minority students. In J. King, E. Hollins, & W. Hayman (Eds.), *Preparing teachers for cultural diversity* (pp. 40–52). New York: Teachers College Press.

Rishel, T.J. (2008). From the principal's desk: Making the school environment more inclusive. In T. Turner-Vorbeck and M. Miller Marsh (Eds.), Other kinds of families: Embracing diversity in schools (pp. 4663). New York: Teachers College Press.

Sánchez, S. (1999). Learning from the stories of culturally and linguistically diverse families and communities: A sociohistorical lens. *Remedial and Special Education, 20*(6), 351–359.

CHAPTER NINE

How a Multicultural Literature Survey Altered the Pedagogical Methods and Curriculum Content for Two University Professors

Bethany Hill-Anderson and Darryn Diuguid

Many researchers who have studied multicultural literature have noted that it provides students with many benefits. One such benefit is seeing the similarities that exist between cultures (Levin, 2007). Researchers have further noted that children are able to see themselves in the literature, which provides a reflection of themselves (Mendoza & Reese, 2001). Multicultural literature is more prevalent than ever before, making it necessary for teachers to address diverse students' various needs in the classroom. Johnson (2009) stated that, "although the numbers of multicultural books recently published has declined slightly, the overall number of books published in the last decade far exceeds that of any previous decade" (p. 318). However, adults (e.g., teachers) maintain control over children's literature, including what is published, reviewed, awarded, purchased (Davila & Patrick, 2010), and essentially read in the classroom. The current chapter highlights a project focused on cooperating teachers' responses to multicultural materials in the classroom. The researchers explain the project, methodology, results, and suggestions for altering teaching to meet the needs of all students.

Purpose of Study

Given the increasing number of multicultural reading materials in print, it is critical to ensure that libraries are stocked with these important books. The American Library Association and the Council on Interracial Books for Children have led the way in increasing published literature dedicated to meeting the needs of diverse populations (Johnson, 2009). Norton (2009) described how multicultural literature is beneficial in the classroom as it can "help readers identify cultural heritages, understand sociological change, respect the values of minority groups, raise aspirations, and expand imagination and creativity" (p. 2). According to Roser (2010), "we (educators) should cling tightly to three essential practices (in the classroom). That is, to

ensure that our children read more, read better, and read more widely" (p. 211). It is the "read more widely" part of this statement that sparked the interest of the current researchers in this study. Not only is it important to see what is available in the classroom, but it is also essential to gauge educators' views and use of the materials.

Growing Disparities in the Teacher–Student Relationship

As more K-12 students are coming from diverse backgrounds, including race, ethnicity, and social class, teachers are challenged to work with demographics with which they are not familiar (Banks & Banks, 2007; Davis, Brown, Liedel-Rice & Soeder, 2005; Easter, Shultz, Neyhart, & Reck, 1999). In fact, many question the teaching abilities of preservice teachers simply because of the growing disparity between teachers' and students' backgrounds (Easter et al., 1999; Garmon, 2003). Sleeter (2001) described the situation as a "cultural gap" that is large and growing. Society is faced with "tomorrow's teachers," who are mostly White, female, and middle class with little intercultural background (Banks & Banks, 2007; Davis et al., 2005). Sadker, Sadker, and Zittleman (2008) detailed the disparities: 84% of new teachers are White, whereas 69% of students are White; only 16% of teachers are minorities while 31% of students are minorities. African-American students make up 17% of the student population; African-American teachers make up only 8% of educators. For the Hispanic population, these percentages are 19% and 6%, respectively. Grant and Gillette (2006) demonstrated that teacher educator demographics have not changed in the last 20 years: "the prospective teaching force and the majority of teacher educators are predominately white" (p. 292). This is one of the many reasons that multicultural literature is important for connecting with K-12 students.

Difficulties with Incorporating Multicultural Materials

Considering that many of our new teachers are not connected to students, they often do not know how or when to use such multicultural materials. Davis et al. (2005) pointed out that it is difficult to prepare teacher candidates to work with diverse populations because they have had "limited experiences with diverse populations and may perceive diversity in a negative way" (p. 176). Furthermore, many of these teachers do not understand the need for students to "see" or "hear" about others in their classroom materials (Gayle-Evans, 2004). It appears that these teachers believe that students only need to understand their peers in the classroom and not others in the worldwide community. However, other researchers have reported that teachers are awkward or sensitive to misuses of cultures in which they are not familiar. Controversial issues may also play a role in why teachers do not use such materials; many multicultural books deal with "divorce, death, abuse, and homelessness (and) are highly praised by critics and popular with children" (Johnson, 2009, p. 16) while often being dismissed by parents and teachers. These books do not make it into the curriculum due to their controversial topics (Johnson, 2009); furthermore, teachers are sensitive to objections by colleagues, administrators, and parents. According to Gayle-Evans (2004), "Whether a classroom is monocultural or not, it is imperative that teachers provide multicultural materials and activities and allow students to be active participants in these activities" (p. 2). In addition, teachers are the most important factor in many students' lives (at times, even more so than peers and parents), and it is "what teachers say and how they say it, what they include, and what they leave out (that) all have an impact on students' perceptions of what is right and how things should be" (Landt, 2007, p. 20).

Use in the Classroom

Multicultural materials need to be used at regular times throughout the day and year. These materials are often isolated from the traditional classroom and regulated to the awareness months, which are dedicated to specific cultures. However, when multicultural characters and stories are regulated to certain times of the year, these subjects are reinforced as "atypical, different, or unusual" (Landt, 2007, p. 20). Landt (2007) explained that "a solution entails effectively melding literature featuring non-mainstream individuals with content area curriculum" and "(it is important to) represent various perspectives throughout your teaching" (p. 20).

Research Questions

According to the literature, the need exists to determine whether K-12 educators are meeting the needs of students with their classroom materials. In addition, these authors/researchers continue to fine-tune their university courses which requires a continuous redesign of the curriculum along with a thoughtful reflection on pedagogical methods. Three overarching research questions assisted the researchers in formulating the current study:

- What are teachers' opinions about incorporating multicultural education?
- What is the availability of multicultural materials in the classroom?
- What multicultural materials would teachers like to have in their classroom?

Participants

A sample of 24 cooperating teachers (elementary level) who were also university students participated in this study. These university teacher candidates were selected due to their enrollment in the Methods of Teaching Social Sciences, a required course in the elementary education certification program at a small Midwestern university. Of the 22 enrolled students in the course, 19 cooperating teachers agreed to participate in the study. In return for their participation, each cooperating teacher received a literacy bag containing the book *A School Like Mine*, along with a variety of literature response activities. Funding for the literacy bag was provided by a Phi Kappa Phi grant that the researchers received during the previous semester. To obtain additional surveys, the researchers surveyed an additional five cooperating teachers who were working with student teachers during the same semester. Cooperating teachers and university students had no advance notice of the research project because the pairings occurred randomly by a university staff member. Cooperating teachers volunteered to accept teacher candidates who observe in their classroom for 48 hours. The cooperating teachers came from a wide variety of school settings, including urban, suburban, and rural areas. Their K-12 students were multicultural in terms of race, socioeconomic backgrounds, gender, ethnicities, disabilities, and giftedness.

Instrumentation

The researchers developed a two-part survey that consisted of 10 open-ended and 3 closed-ended survey questions during the fall semester in 2009. In the closed-ended section of the survey, teachers were able to select answers from a Likert-type scale: strongly agree, agree, somewhat agree, somewhat disagree, disagree, or strongly disagree. The open-ended questions dealt with the overarching questions of the survey.

On the reverse side of the survey, cooperating teachers were asked to answer six questions dealing with basic demographic information: gender, grade currently teaching, content area of concentration, years of experience as a teacher, age, ethnicity, family's annual total income, and religion or faith tradition (if applicable).

Researchers gathered the surveys and ran statistical analysis software (SPSS) to determine whether significant differences occurred in gender, ethnicity, income level, and religion. The Pearson correlation coefficient was calculated for relationships among all variables. The data indicated significant relationships between several of the variables at both the 0.01 and 0.05 levels (two-tailed). Coding of the open-ended questions was conducted to determine whether any significant themes emerged.

Procedure

Cooperating teacher participation letters and surveys were sent with the teacher candidates during one of their first visits to their field experience. The researchers followed up with the teacher candidates during the next few weeks to determine whether their cooperating teachers were willing to participate. All surveys were anonymous, and the researchers reminded participants not to include identifying names or schools on the documents. Completed surveys were returned via a self-addressed stamped envelope, which was delivered to the school along with the signed participation letter. The survey data were analyzed collectively to maintain the privacy and confidentially of the participants.

Results

Teachers' opinions and incorporation of multicultural education. The quantitative data suggested major themes. First, teachers in the higher elementary grades tended to have more variety of materials in their classrooms than teachers in lower elementary grades. Second, teachers who stated that they incorporate multicultural materials within their curriculum were also committed to multicultural education in their classrooms. Moreover, these teachers did not tend to believe that either time or standardized testing limited their inclusion of other cultures. Third, teachers who were committed to incorporating multicultural materials during classroom instruction tended to believe they are not limited by school funding, time in the classroom, or standardized testing. The data further showed that these teachers also believe that parents' views would not conflict with incorporating multicultural education.

However, significant relationships emerged between teachers who believed that the limitations put upon them in turn limited their use of multicultural materials in their classrooms. Teachers who stated that time limits the inclusion of multicultural education also believed that they were limited by school funds, standardized testing, and parents' views. Teachers who stated that standardized testing limits the amount of time they spend on including other cultures also believed that school funds limited their ability to infuse multicultural education. Teachers who stated that school funds limit their ability to infuse multicultural education also believed that parents' views would conflict with incorporating multicultural education, but they also believed that parents should play a leading role in exposing their children to diverse cultures.

Materials teachers are using. The qualitative data indicated that teachers use a limited variety of materials. Nineteen teachers listed "books" and "literature," and 10 teachers listed some type of curriculum, such as reading or social studies textbooks. Seven teachers included "posters" as part of their materials, but they did not elaborate on how they may have been used as part of the instruction. Although four teachers referred to incorporating Spanish, no details were provided beyond "lessons once a month" and "English/Spanish dictionary." Four teachers also listed "units" as well as computers and/or technology. The only specific unit that was mentioned was "Hanukkah (created when I had a Jewish student)"; no specific computer programs or technology sources were provided. Three teachers stated specific holidays, including Hanukkah, Christmas, Cinco de Mayo, and Kwanzaa. Two teachers cited Black History Month as well as videos/movies, speakers, and toys/games. Several items and events were listed one time each—namely, the Internet, concerts, field trips, worksheets and activities, Chinese New Year, and St. Patrick's Day. In addition to holidays, one teacher identified Native Americans and heroes as themes that were part of the curriculum.

Expanding the horizon. Teachers were also asked what they would like to see in a multicultural education curriculum. The most common theme was more exposure to a wider variety of cultures. The most frequent resource listed was books (four teachers), followed by guest speakers and videos (three teachers each). Positive role models, presentations, monthly featured culture, drama/plays, and photographs were each identified by one teacher. Another common theme was that teachers wanted more specific information on individual cultures, including music (three teachers); art and foods (two teachers); and clothing, customs and traditions, books, and activities (one teacher). Finally, a third theme emerged: more time for planned curriculum (two teachers) and professional development in the form of technology and dealing with controversial issues and parents. Five teachers simply stated "more resources." Teachers were also asked to provide any additional comments not addressed in the survey. One teacher stated that she uses much of her own money; another teacher indicated that—although kindergarten does not endure standardized testing—reading intervention minutes have "cut time."

Discussion

Based on these data, it can be concluded that certain variables affect teachers' ability and/or opportunity to effectively infuse multicultural educational materials into their classrooms on a routine basis. The data suggest that these teachers lack depth of understanding and methods for easily incorporating a variety of cultures, which clearly leads to an absence of multicultural infusion beyond holidays and Native Americans. Teachers who stated that they are committed to actively incorporating multicultural materials in their classrooms do not cite limitations commonly attributed to standardized testing, funding, time in the classroom, or parents' views. Therefore, it is imperative that those responsible for educating future teachers must foster students' true commitment to multicultural education. Furthermore, teachers who believe they are limited by one factor also tend to believe they are limited by several additional factors. These teachers are also inclined to believe that parents should be responsible for cultural diversity. It is imperative to enable preservice teachers to build their own access to easily available and affordable resources. By fostering preservice teachers' commitment to incorporating multicultural materials in their lesson plans, they will not feel that they are limited by external factors when they get into their own classrooms.

Methods of Teaching Elementary Social Studies

The social sciences course in the current study incorporates multicultural materials through both direct and indirect instruction. During direct instruction, the objectives are clearly stated and students know the purpose, which is to introduce them to and model the use of multicultural materials. To indirectly teach teacher candidates about multicultural materials and concepts, world music (often CDs produced by Putumayo) is played every morning as they arrive in class as well as during the 15-minute breaks, elementary students are referred to using non-Anglo names (e.g., Juan, Guadeloupe), and in-class learning activities are assigned using a wide range of resources featuring culturally diverse children and families. Based on the researchers' commitment to multicultural education, connections were made between social studies and multiculturalism throughout the course.

One of the resources used on a regular basis is Teaching Tolerance, which provides an abundance of materials, lesson ideas, and links through its website TeachingTolerance.org. "Starting Small" is a video with an accompanying book featuring teachers across the country who incorporate a variety of diversities in their early childhood and elementary classrooms. On the first day of class, the video clip "Everybody's Story" (Seattle, WA, Happy Medium Primary School) is played; this video shows children discovering each other's skin colors. In this class, there are no "White" children or "Black" children, but more accurately matched colors, such as cinnamon and peach. After viewing and discussing the video, preservice teachers make their own faces using multicultural construction paper, a variety of materials for hair (e.g., ribbon, yarn), as well as markers and googly eyes to complete their look. After a brief discussion about how they felt about the process and possible scenarios in their future elementary classrooms, the faces were put together to create the class. During the history of the course, no preservice teacher has ever not been interested in creating him or herself out of these materials; indeed, they have often replicated this same activity with elementary students the following semester.

Another learning activity created for the course enables preservice teachers to develop a better understanding of how diverse our world truly is. First, an original quiz is administered based on *If the World Were a Village: A Book about the World's People* (Smith & Armstrong, 2002). The preservice teachers initially work in pairs to agree on global statistics based on a village of 100 people. Then, two video clips are shown to provide the correct answers. The first video is more informative and was chosen to provide additional background knowledge. Throughout this video clip, stimulating and thought-provoking photographs accompany statistics such as religions practiced and languages spoken as well as more sobering facts such as access to clean water, electricity, and education (DHODHOTT, 2007). The second video clip is a delightful cartoon that could be used as a visual representation of the information in an elementary classroom (Jibreelk, 2007). Preservice teachers are most often stunned at what they do not know. Finally, the use of a variety of books published by Dorling Kindersley that feature stunning photographs and engaging text about the daily lives of children from around the world is discussed (Buller, 2005; Kindersley & Kindersley, 1997; Kindersley & Kindersley, 1995; Smith, 2007; UNICEF, 2006).

This project has significantly affected the researchers' perspective on the use of multicultural educational materials in the social studies methods course. The researchers sought to guide preservice teachers to a deeper understanding of and appreciation for their own diversity. Preservice teachers created individual cultural collages to acquire deeper self-awareness and demonstrate diversity among those who may "look" very similar but are, in fact, quite diverse. As their own cultural heritages emerged, they compared and contrasted the difficulties their ancestors experienced to a variety of cultures often overlooked or stereotyped. The goal was for preservice teachers to develop an awareness of the importance of expanding their elementary students' perspectives on diverse peoples and give them the resources to make it possible for them to routinely infuse multiculturalism into their pedagogy.

Children's Literature Course

A need to incorporate additional assignments. As the first few surveys detailing cooperating teachers' uses and commitment to multicultural issues started to arrive, the researcher decided it was time for the Children's Literature class (a cross-listed course) to see new assignments, including a graduate research project that was a discourse analysis of a culture within children's literature books. For example, graduate students delved into the Native-American, single-parent, autistic, African-American, and Cajun cultures via an assignment in which they read an additional 15 to 20 books. The students designed three research questions along with qualitative data (discourse within the books) to support the research. Many students discovered that it was difficult to locate any books on the specific culture and were dismayed by this fact. In reality, the students were able to determine whether the culture was fairly represented in literature. In the conclusion section of the discourse research project, graduate students were required to make suggestions for current classroom teachers; many noted the strong need for teachers to use the materials throughout the curriculum.

Providing resources for university students. Before the actual survey, much of the focus in the course was on Caldecott and Newbery medal winners, creating a need for students to review the Coretta Scott King and Pura Belpre awards for outstanding children's literature dedicated to the African-American and Latino cultures. Students were able to explore these new resources as they completed an in-class assignment that required them to go to the American Library Association website and identify/summarize the winners from the previous five years. In addition, as students completed literature logs (a major project of the course), they were required to identify whether the books were award winners (Caldecott, Newberry, Coretta Scott King, or Pura Belpre) as this activity was expected to deepen their understanding of the awards.

After receiving the surveys and reading professional articles concerning the lack of diversity in Scholastic Book Clubs, the researchers began to think of other ways to provide resources for the preservice teachers. One such need identified in the course was to assist students in preparing a balanced classroom library. Like many other teachers, they had succumbed to the Scholastic Book Club "illness." McNair (2008) explained that

> Scholastic Book Clubs operate by making low-cost books, mainly paperbacks, available each month for purchase. Teachers distribute order forms to their students, and when the students and their parents order books, teachers earn bonus points good for additional books and other educational materials. (p. 193)

McNair found that, over a one-year period, 600 White authors and illustrators were featured; only 34 people of color were mentioned. Thus, although the goal had been to do something great for the teacher candidates by assisting them in building their own classroom libraries, in fact the activity had reinforced the dominance of White Euro-American authors and illustrators in classrooms. The graduate course continues to change the ways in which it assists our teacher candidates by providing alternative means to build a diverse classroom library that truly reflects the K-12 student population.

Building a Classroom Community

Knowing that many K-12 educators are encountering and will encounter more multicultural environments, the researchers decided that it was best to replicate building a classroom community, as many researchers recommend. First, the class was brought together in grand conversations to begin the process of building a successful learning community (Tompkins, 2010). Second, book groups were established in which individuals feel less threatened, such as a "female only" or groups for non-native English speakers (texts would be in their first language) (Lin, 2002). Third, students and teachers should take joint ownership of their classroom, including responsibility for their assignments and for working together while the teacher models the expected behavior (David & Capraro, 2001). Finally, when future teachers provide a routine and consistent environment, students feel safe and are more likely to be successful (Tompkins, 2010).

Conclusion

The purpose of this study was twofold. First, it investigated the use of multicultural educational materials among a diverse group of local elementary teachers. The data analysis suggested that teachers often lacked easily accessible materials, but if they were committed to incorporating such materials, they did not feel limited by additional issues. Most importantly, teachers who did not feel committed to incorporating multicultural materials often believed that extraneous limitations prevented them from routinely incorporating multicultural educational materials in their classrooms.

Thus, the second component of this project was to efficiently guide preservice teachers to better understand the importance of multicultural education and present them with the appropriate tools for use in diverse elementary settings. The researchers aim to inspire students to effectively infuse multicultural educational instruction and materials into their course lesson plans and, of course, their future classrooms. Through this process, it may be possible to successfully guide School of Education graduates in developing a personal and professional enthusiasm and commitment to sharing the adventure, wonderment, and lifelong experience of learning about those who may be quite different from ourselves.

References

Banks, J. A., & Banks, C. A. (2007). *Multicultural education: Issues and perspectives* (5th ed.). Hoboken, NJ: Wiley.

Buller, L. (2005). *Children just like me.* London: Dorling Kindersley.

David, H. L., & Capraro, R. M. (2001). Strategies for teaching in heterogeneous environments while building a classroom community. *Education, 122*(1), 80–87.

Davila, D., & Patrick, L. (2010). Asking the experts: What children have to say about their reading preferences. *Language Arts, 87*(3), 199–210.

Davis, K. L., Brown, B. G., Liedel-Rice, A., & Soeder, P. (2005). Experiencing diversity through children's multicultural literature. *Kappa Delta Pi Record, 41,* 176–179.

DHODHOTT. (Producer). (2007, April 23). *If the world were a village of 100 people.* Available from http://www.youtube.com/watch?v=1v9xJPiIlQU

Easter, L., Shultz, E., Neyhart, K., & Reck, U. M. (1999). Weighty perceptions: A study of the attitudes and beliefs of preservice teacher education students regarding diversity and urban education. *The Urban Review, 31*(2), 205–220.

Garmon, M. A. (2003). Six key factors for changing preservice teachers' attitudes/beliefs about diversity. *Educational Studies, 38*(3), 275–286.

Gayle-Evans, G. (2004). It is never too soon: A study of kindergarten teachers' implementation of multicultural education in Florida's classrooms. *The Professional Educator, 26*(2), 1–15.

Grant, C., & Gillette, M. (2006). A candid talk to teacher educators about effectively preparing teachers who can teach everyone's children. *Journal of Teacher Education, 57*(3), 292–299.

Jibreelk. (Producer). (2007, July 10). *If the world were a village.* Available from http://www.youtube.com/watch?v=oumVHSj6AE8&feature=related

Johnson, D. (2009). *The joy of children's literature.* Boston: Houghton Mifflin Harcourt Publishing Company.

Kindersley, A. & Kindersley, B. (1997). *Children just like me: Celebrations.* London: Dorling Kindersley.

Kindersley, A., & Kindersley, B. (1995). *Children just like me.* London: Dorling Kindersley.

Landt, S. M. (2007). Weaving multicultural literature into middle school curricula. *Middle School Journal, 39*(2), 19–24.

Levin, F. (2007). Encouraging ethical respect through multicultural literature. *The Reading Teacher, 61*(1), 101–104.

Lin, C.-H. (2002). *Literature circles.* Bloomington, IN: ERIC Clearinghouse on Reading English and Communication.

McNair, J. (2008). The representation of authors and illustrators of color in school-based book clubs. *Language Arts, 85*(3), 193–201.

Mendoza, J., & Reese, D. (2001). Examining multicultural picture books for...possibilities and pitfalls. *Early Childhood Research & Practice, 3*(2), 1–38.

Norton, D. (2009). *Through the eyes of a child: An introduction to children's literature.* New York: Norton and Co.

Roser, N. (2010). Policies can follow practices. *Language Arts, 87*(3), 211–214.

Sadker, D. M., Sadker, M. P., & Zittleman, K. (2008). *Teachers, school, and society.* Boston: McGraw-Hill.

Sleeter, C. (2001). Preparing teachers for culturally diverse schools: Research and the overwhelming presence of whiteness. *Journal of Teacher Education, 52*(2), 94–106.

Smith, D., & Armstrong, S. (2002). *If the world were a village: A book about the world's people*. Tonawanda, NY: Kids Can Press.

Smith, P. (2007). *A school like mine*. London: Dorling Kindersley.

Tompkins, G. (2010). *Language arts: Patterns of practice*. Upper Saddle River, NJ: Pearson.

UNICEF. (2006). *A life like mine*. London: Dorling Kindersley.

CHAPTER TEN

Multicultural Technology Project: A Strategy for Introducing Preservice Teachers to Culturally Responsive Teaching Methods

Janie Hubbard

The sheer numbers of CLD students entering public schools in the United States have created the need to better prepare preservice teachers to serve these students. To understand how such population increases affect class-rooms, it is important to consider the steady growth over the last several years. For example, the Hispanic population in the United States increased from around 9 million in 1970 to 45.5 million in 2007 and is projected to reach 59.7 million by 2020 (U.S. Census Bureau, 2010). Likewise, the school-age population is estimated to grow by 25% within the next decade (Payne, 2005). By 2020, CLD students will comprise approximately half of the U.S. public school population (Cho & DeCastro-Ambrosetti, 2005–2006). Students of color will make up approximately one half of the nation's school-age population by the year 2010, and one in four will be Hispanic (Davis & Yang, 2006; LaDuke, 2009).

Paradoxically, although the population of White, non-Hispanic students is steadily declining, most American teachers are White, middle-class women (Banks & Banks, 2001; U.S. Census Bureau, 2010). As the nation moves toward a non-White majority, teachers—especially those in suburban schools—accustomed to mainly White students from middle- and upper-class income households need new tools to create school environments that demonstrate respect for diversity and pedagogies that scaffold the under-standings that children bring from outside the classroom (Gay, 2000; Lee, 2002). Explanations and examples that seemed relevant and interesting in the past may be meaningless to students from diverse backgrounds. Growing demands for effectiveness and change, without proper support in understand-ing and dealing with the needs of diverse students, leave some teachers overwhelmed and inclined to leave the profession (Banks, 2009; Ferguson, 2007). In addition, research suggests that teachers have lower expectations and fewer interactions with minority students, further prompting the need to endorse efforts that support teachers in working with culturally diverse students using culturally proficient teaching methods (Tucker et al., 2005; Villegas & Lucas, 2007).

Cultural Proficiency

At the center of culturally proficient teaching is a commitment to educational equity and a belief that all students can learn. *Cultural proficiency*, in this case, is defined as the values and behaviors of an individual that enable him or her to interact effectively in a diverse environment (Guerra & Nelson, 2007; Robins, Lindsey, Lindsey, & Terrell, 2002). Within the framework of social constructivism, teachers have an opportunity to examine and address CLD learners in the mainstreamed classroom, reflecting on practices that give both students and teachers the tools needed to interact effectively in a diverse academic setting. In a classroom that reflects a social constructivist philosophy, students explore similarities and, through conversations with each other, come to construct meaning. Such a classroom builds on the prior experiences of the participants as students share different interpretations of phenomena in their world and relate these experiences to new ideas. The social constructivist classroom is one in which CLD students should thrive for several reasons—namely, (a) prior knowledge, even that which is cultural in nature, is valued as a foundation for learning; (b) the classroom environment is one of respect for all, no matter the student's culture or stage of language development; (c) discourse is encouraged and expected, thus practice with English language is embedded within the class; (d) curricula are delivered through student-centered methods and include differentiation as needed while teachers help students connect their conceptual understandings to real life and refrain from the transmission of facts; and (e) working with others within collaborative groupings improves academic achievement and social skills.

Preservice Teachers and Diversity

As an elementary social studies methods instructor and intern supervisor, the author has completed hundreds of observations of preservice teachers in their K-6 practicum and internship placements. One of the most striking issues noted has been the lack of understanding and confidence in working with linguistically and culturally diverse students. These children were often left alone to look at a book or sit at a computer, and the author seldom observed teachers or other students interacting with them.

Students entering teacher education programs usually have an awareness of diversity issues, either through their own school experiences or popular media; however, problems emerge with regard to conceptualizing what diversity is and anticipating or understanding problems surrounding issues of diversity (Alsheikh, Elhoweris, & Parameswaran, 2004; Lee, 2002; Phillion, Malewski, & Richardson, 2006). Few preservice teachers have considered that another's worldview, especially those of children in schools, could be so profoundly different from their own (LaDuke, 2009). Hence, teacher educators, working primarily with White, middle-class preservice teachers, often face preservice teachers' resistance to multicultural education (Carpenter-LaGattuta, 2002; LaDuke, 2009; Phillion, Malewski, & Richardson, 2004; Wells, 2008). Preservice teachers may question the relevance of multicultural education or consider it a new type of bias favoring minorities (Alsheikh et al., 2004; Carpenter-LaGattuta, 2002; LaDuke, 2009; Phillion et al., 2004). Expectations for teaching these young students may also be inherently low because of a "deficit view" (Alsheikh et al., 2004; Davis & Yang, 2006), which occurs when teachers interpret a child's uniqueness as a flaw rather than simply a different set of background experiences.

Preservice teachers often have preconceived notions about what various groups of people do, their values, and how they act, sometimes seeing them as inferior or un-American (Wells, 2008). Expectations are lowered because of the belief that the child is less teachable, especially if the parents are poor or not as well educated as the teacher or other parents. For example, in a 2009 study of preservice teachers' reactions to multicultural education, LaDuke determined that there were missionary overtones in preservice teachers' thinking about teaching in multicultural areas; the preservice teachers wanted to create classrooms to serve as "safe havens" for children from what the teachers perceived to be unstable families. To overcome these stereotypic tendencies, teachers need to know about their students' lives to engage them in meaningful learning and interaction with classmates, including the family makeup, immigration history, favorite activities, concerns, strengths, prior knowledge of different school subjects, and even day-to-day challenges in living in the United States. However, learning generic information unrelated to students' real lives leads to stereotypical thinking about cultures and social groups (Villegas & Lucas, 2007).

Multicultural Education and Global Education

Teachers must be prepared to understand the sensitive socio-cultural learning environment that they control, recognizing that they are responsible for providing all students with an equitable and quality learning experience. What is at stake is not limited to a certain school or area; our democracy and the futures of those disadvantaged by race, ethnicity, class, and first language are at risk (Brown & Kraehe, 2010; Phillion et al., 2006).

Thus, creating a culturally responsive classroom may necessitate a blend of multicultural and global education. Although theoretically and historically these fields of study—in their purest forms—are distinct, the relationship between them is similar in several ways. They advance justice, equity, and peace; they address diversity at every level; and they explain interconnectedness among people (Wells, 2008). Wells suggested that teacher educators use global perspectives from outside the U.S. context, rather than other more immediate and connected multicultural topics, to enable teachers in training to examine fundamental issues in a less threatening way. Using global examples may overcome resistance and defensiveness while opening dialogue about multicultural issues and concepts. A second reason to infuse global perspectives within classes is that teacher education programs cannot predict where or whom their graduates will teach; thus, the development of sensitivity as well as methods and techniques should be applicable to a variety of cultures (Saracho & Martinez-Hancock, 2007). A third rationale for developing a global perspective within teacher education is to overcome the misrepresentation of multiculturalism shared by many teachers and schools.

James Banks (1999) developed a widely recognized model asserting four approaches to multicultural curriculum reform. The first approach, contributions, reflects a superficial level and the least amount of teacher and student involvement. Teaching using this approach focuses primarily on ethnic heroes, holidays, foods, and other elements isolated from the regular curriculum. Taking one month out of the year to teach students about a particular ethnic group is an example of the contributions approach. In the additive approach, content, concepts, themes, and perspectives are added to the curriculum without changing it; however, this approach does not necessarily change thinking. The transformation approach involves consideration of diversity as a basic premise and encourages students to view concepts, issues, themes, and problems from several ethnic points of view. The fourth, social action approach, combines the transformation approach with activities to encourage students to actually contribute to social change.

If not properly addressed in the classroom, multicultural education themes may be perceived as receiving shallow treatment. Global education themes, like multicultural education themes, can also be challenging for teachers to implement effectively. Teachers' use of isolated examples from particular groups can seem sensational and lead to exotica; thus, time is needed in order for P-12 students to scaffold a deep understanding of the culture being studied. Viewing a culture from an inescapable Western lens may also create a naïve presentation or—even worse—perpetuate a stereo-type. One way that teachers might address young students' lack of knowl-edge about diverse ethnic groups and/or cultural biases is to invite people of differing ethnic and cultural subgroups into the P-12 classroom, including recent immigrants to the United States, in an effort to provide global perspec-tives (Wells, 2008).

Introducing a Multicultural Technology Project to Preservice Teachers

Bringing different cultural voices into the classroom can be an added challenge. However, technology can serve as a vehicle for connecting people of different cultures, transporting various perspectives into the classroom, and cultivating sensitivities. Using digital storytelling as the medium, the author initiated a social studies methods class project to accomplish three primary goals. First, it would give preservice teachers a strategy for developing greater understanding and empathy for their future culturally and linguistically diverse students. The preservice teachers in the author's social studies methods class were primarily rural, first-generation college students from working-class homes. They knew about cultures but did not appear to understand the extent to which our state demographics had changed over the last few years, especially with regard to a rapidly growing Hispanic student population. Although this particular course did allow enough time to deeply examine profound issues such as "White privilege" and power struggles within the United States, our discussions and their in-school observations did produce a realization of the disparity of educational opportunities that exists within our schools. The hope was that the awareness and support they received in this course would help these novice teachers acquire the self-efficacy needed to create their own culturally responsive classrooms in the future. Second, this project would showcase a strategy using Microsoft's Photo Story 3 to implement technology in their present and future lessons. Digital storytelling is a method that could be used in preservice teachers' future classrooms to create historical documentaries, personal narratives, and fictional stories as well as explain abstract concepts (Rudnicki et al., 2010); they could also teach their own young students the process of digital storytelling for presentation purposes. Third, the project was designed to satisfy state curriculum standards requiring multicultural awareness in higher education teaching.

A number of studies have suggested that technology integration, en-twining learning and technology in a single context, is an effective teaching and learning experience. For example, Phillion et al. (2004) created diverse field experiences for preservice teachers using videoconferencing and found that, overall, virtual field experiences can "provide meaningful, practical opportunities to inform future teachers on how to educate an increasingly diverse citizenry" (p. 11). In another study, DeGennaro (2010) used digital stories as a pedagogical tool for preservice teachers to demonstrate their understanding of learning theories by creating digital stories. After the project, students stated that they were more personally connected to their learning, and the multimedia representations were essential to their understanding of the concepts and overall involvement in the learning process. Likewise, Rudnicki et al. (2010) successfully used digital storytelling with students across the curriculum within their university's college of education. Products of this ongoing commitment to technology integration include a website of student-constructed digital stories, professional development seminars, and a digital storytelling festival that is being planned for the future.

Project Steps

Table 10.1 highlights the step-by-step instructions for teacher educators to guide students through a multicultural technology project. The first step of the current project was designed to give preservice teachers knowledge of the diverse populations that currently exist in elementary schools within their state. To this end, they researched and wrote a short introduction paper citing current statistics and included a written discussion about how they believed the cultural differences and language barriers might affect students and teachers in local classrooms. A class discussion highlighting the characteristics of a culturally responsive classroom followed, and preservice teachers shared examples of when cultural responsiveness was or was not evident to them during their previous classroom placements. Second, the preservice teachers received classroom instruction on an important research technique: interviewing. They then interviewed a foreign-born individual who had moved to the United States as a child or adult, obtaining written permission from the interviewee to use the information as well as photos for the project. The preservice teachers frequently interviewed people working in restaurants, nail salons, and other businesses. If they could not find a foreign-born person to interview, international students enrolled at the university were more than willing to help. In addition, preservice teachers checked out digital cameras from the university media center and took photos of the interviewee and personal artifacts that were culturally important to that person (e.g., art, dishes, family photos, furniture, documents).

Table 10.1.
Steps for Implementing a Multicultural Technology Project

Step 1 – **Awareness**	• Begin a class discussion including students' prior knowledge of current population shifts in the United States. • Direct students to write a short research paper that includes population statistics in their state or local area and how they believe this affects public school teachers and students. • Provide written directions and a scoring rubric with criteria for expectations.
Step 2 – **Contact**	• Teach students appropriate interviewing techniques (a research strategy that they can teach their future students). • Direct students to interview a foreign-born individual. • Make prior arrangements, with foreign-born friends or university students, for students who cannot locate a foreign-born individual to interview. • Direct students to obtain written permission from the interviewees to use their information and digital photos. • Provide written tips and instructions for interviewing protocols (see Table 2).
Step 3 – **Presentation**	• Teach students to create a digital story of the immigrant's life using the interview data and digital photos. • Provide written directions, a scoring rubric, computer microphones, and computer lab time, if possible. • Note: Some newer computers have built-in microphones and speakers.
Step 4 – **Reflection**	• Provide time to view the digital stories and discuss the results. • Facilitate a class discussion and suggest or introduce other strategies that support the creation of a culturally responsive classroom.

The third step in the process was teaching preservice teachers techniques for creating a photo story using Microsoft Photo Story 3, a free downloadable computer program. In the computer lab, the preservice teachers downloaded the digital photos they had taken during the interview and combined them with others retrieved from the Internet that related to the interviewees' home countries. These supplementary photos included images of food, traditional clothing, language, traditions, celebrations, religion, homes, geography, recreation, sports, and so on. With guidance, preservice teachers learned the simple process of blending photos, narration (using computer microphones), and music to create a photo story of the interviewee's life. One requirement was to include information about the interviewee's reasons for coming to the United States, his or her experiences or his or her children's experiences in public school here (if any), and challenges as well as positive experiences of living in the United States as a foreign-born individual.

Tips for Conducting Successful Interviews: A Resource for Preservice Teachers

Before the Interview
- Contact the person you want to interview and ask for an appointment.
- Clearly express the purpose of the interview.
- Tell the person approximately how much time you will need for the interview (keep it short).
- Write a list of questions.
- Reduce questions that give responses of yes and no. Prompt the interview with clarifying questions.
- Some people may want a list of the questions before your meeting so that they can think about the answers before the interview.
- Limit each question to only one idea to avoid confusion.

During the Interview
- Arrive on time and prepared.
- Take notes so that you remember exactly what the person said.
- If you want to audiotape the interview, you must ask the interviewee for permission to do so.
- Watch the clock.
- If you do not understand a response, you may ask the person to repeat or clarify the answer.

After the Interview
- Summarize the points that you recorded and ask the person whether the summary is correct.
- Thank the person.

From the beginning of the interview to end, always approach the interview with common sense and courtesy (Freedman, 2004; Thomas & Thomas, 2006)

Results

The outcomes of the project were significant. Because the photo stories were only a few minutes in length, the preservice teachers viewed each one in class. The projects examined the lives of a truly international assortment of people with unusual backgrounds. The preservice teachers were excited and proud of their work, and many went above and beyond the requirements. For example, several students asked the interviewees to narrate parts of the photo story in their native language, thereby enabling viewers to hear the interviewees' voices. Throughout the discussions, most of the preservice teachers validated the project by saying that they had gained new insights by personally getting to know a foreign-born individual as well as empathy for people, especially children, in the United States dealing with cultural and linguistic challenges. In this case, familiarity led to greater understanding.

In addition, at the end of the semester, when these particular students were in their elementary practicum placements, the author observed their efforts to include these children in all classroom activities, indicating that preservice teachers had developed some degree of self-efficacy in working with culturally and linguistically challenged students. Likewise, several of the preservice teachers crafted photo stories to supplement their lessons, and lessons dealing with cultures were less superficial than might sometimes be found in an elementary classroom. For example, one cooperating teacher asked her assigned preservice teacher to create and teach lessons on the topic "Christmas around the World." Instead of showing conventional, ready-made videos that frequently lead to stereotypical perceptions, the preservice teacher created a photo story that included personal accounts of this and related international holidays by people who have actually celebrated them in other countries. The personal interpretations were authentic, credible, and interesting to the young students. One preservice teacher commented:

> When our multicultural Photo Story project was assigned, I was apprehensive. I couldn't understand how such a project could possibly be useful. I thoroughly enjoyed interviewing my subject and gathering pictures of her family, however. I have been teaching three years now and have used my Photo Story several times to increase my students' appreciation for individuals and cultures different from their own. The part my students always enjoy the most is hearing my subject's voice during the Photo Story. They also like the pictures of her home country of Thailand. I was wrong about the project. The finished product was definitely worth the time and effort. (Scott, S.B., personal communication, December 7, 2010)

The second year of the project was even more successful. The university decided that applied technology for teacher education might be more effectively learned in context; thus, the administration gave the author the opportunity to collaborate and team-teach the project with the technology instructor. The technology instructor taught the preservice teachers technological strategies to make their photo stories more polished, and they received a grade for those in her senior-level Applied Technology course. By not teaching technology, the author had more time to concentrate on the interviewing techniques and multicultural portions of the presentation. At the end of the semester, three of the preservice teachers traveled to the state capitol and presented their projects at the state social studies conference. This project ultimately became a benchmark assignment for preservice teachers' electronic portfolios, which the university uses for teacher certification and accreditation purposes.

In extending the project, the author recently traveled to an international school in Brazil to teach social studies methods to a group of teachers working on their master's degrees. These teachers taught high school English, English as a second language (ESL), Montessori preschool, and various other preschool, elementary, middle, and high school grades and disciplines. This international school, like others, has a perpetual influx of "third culture kids" (TCKs) who live abroad for at least a portion of their formative years, away from their passport countries, because of their parents' life choices (Kidd & Lankenau, 2009; Stultz, 2002; Useem & Downie, 1994). Knowing that the inservice teachers in Brazil would need strategies for integrating CLD students into the school's American and Brazilian culture, the author adapted the multicultural education project and assigned it as an optional task.

The teachers embraced the project and adapted it in many ways to fit their needs. For example, many digital stories were used by classroom teachers and the school counselor to spotlight students and their cultures and help them "fit in." Teachers said that by showing photos of their former homes and lifestyles, the interviewed students could gain power. Other ESL teachers interviewed CLD students about common games in each of their cultures, thereby providing a non-threatening, yet interesting way for students to investigate similarities. Others interviewed CLD students who narrated their experiences of being new to the school; this particular digital story is being used as an orientation tool for newcomers.

Conclusion

Teachers must have encouragement to change existing attitudes, behaviors, or cultural expectations, which may be barriers to connecting with all students. Even more, support should help teachers learn culturally responsive teaching methods and select relevant materials to promote the achievement and social success of students from diverse cultures and increase self-efficacy in teaching them (Tucker et al., 2005). Teacher education programs can be instrumental in giving preservice and inservice teachers the strategies and confidence to create their own culturally responsive classrooms in which culturally and linguistically diverse students receive attention and respect for who they are and what they bring to the class.

References

Alsheikh, N., Elhoweris, H., & Parameswaran, G. (2004). College students' myths about diversity and what college faculty can do. *Multicultural Education, 12*(2), 13–18.

Banks, J. A. (1999). *An introduction to multicultural education* (2nd ed.). Boston: Allyn and Bacon.

Banks, J. A. (2009). Human rights, diversity, and citizenship education. *Educational Forum, 73*(2), 100–110.

Banks, J. A., & Banks, C. A. (2001). *Multicultural education: Issues and perspectives* (4th ed.). New York: Wiley.

Brown, K. D., & Kraehe, A. M. (2010). The complexities of teaching the complex: Examining how future educators construct understandings of sociocultural knowledge and schooling. *Educational Studies, 46*(1), 91–115.

Carpenter-LaGattuta, A. (2002, July). Challenges in multicultural teacher education. *Multicultural Education.* Retrieved from http://findarticles.com/p/articles/mi_qa3935/is_200207/?tag=content;col1

Cho, G., & DeCastro-Ambrosetti, D. (2005–2006). Is ignorance bliss? Preservice teachers' attitudes toward multicultural education. *The High School Journal, 89*(2), 24–28.

Davis, C., & Yang, A. (2006, April). Welcoming families of different cultures. *Responsive Classroom Newsletter, 18*(2). Retrieved from Northeast Foundation for Children, Inc., at responsiveclassroom.org

DeGennaro, D. (2010). Grounded theory: Immersing preservice teachers in technology-mediated learning. *Contemporary Issues in Technology and Teacher Education, 10*(3). Retrieved from http://www.citejournal.org/vol10/iss3/currentpractice/article1.cfm

Ferguson, R. F. (2007, Summer). Become more sophisticated about diversity. *National Staff Development Council, 28*(3), 33–34.

Freedman, D. (2004). *Chatting them up: Tips for a successful interview.* Retrieved from http://www.Underdown.org/interview_tech.htm

Gay, G. (2000). *Culturally responsive teaching: Theory, research, and practice.* New York: Teachers College Press.

Guerra, P. L., & Nelson, S. W. (2007, Summer). Assessment is the first step to creating a school that educates everybody. *National Staff Development Council, 28*(3), 59–60.

Kidd, J. K., & Lankenau, L. L. (2009). *Third culture kids: Returning to their passport country.* Washington, DC: U.S. Department of State, Bureau of Public Affairs. Retrieved from http://www.state.gov/m/dghr/flo/c22473.htm

LaDuke, A. E. (2009). Resistance and renegotiation: Preservice teacher interactions with and reactions to multicultural education course content. *Multicultural Education, 16*(3), 37–44.

Lee, G. (2002). Realities and challenges facing multicultural education. *Early Childhood Education, 31*(1), 1–8.

Payne, R. (2005). *A framework for understanding poverty* (4th ed.). Highlands, TX: aha! Process, Inc.

Phillion, J., Malewski, E., & Richardson, J. (2004). Personalizing technology to interrupt the resistance of preservice teachers to multicultural education. *Journal of Special Education Technology, 19*(3), 34–45.

Phillion, J., Malewski, E., & Richardson, J. (2006). Personalizing technology to interrupt the resistance of pre-service teachers to multicultural education. *Electronic Magazine of Multicultural Education, 8*(2), 1–14. Retrieved from http://www.eastern.edu/publications/ emme/2006fall/phillion_et_al.pdf

Robins, N. K., Lindsey, R. B., Lindsey, D. B., & Terrell, R. D. (2002). *Culturally proficient instruction: A guide for people who teach.* Thousand Oaks, CA: Corwin Press, Inc.

Rudnicki, A., Cozart, A., Ganesh, A., Markello, C., Marsh, S., McNeil, S. et al. (2010). *The buzz continues... The diffusion of digital storytelling across disciplines and colleges at the University of Houston.* Retrieved from http://www.coe.uh.edu/documents/Buzz.pdf

Saracho, O. N., & Martinez-Hancock, F. (2007). The culture of Mexican-Americans: Its importance for early childhood educators. *Multicultural Perspectives, 9*(2), 43–50.

Stultz, W. (2002). Global and domestic nomads or third culture kids: Who they are and what the university needs to know. *SAHE Journal of Student Affairs, 12.*

Thomas, M., & Thomas, M. J. (2006). *Tips for effective research interviews.* Retrieved from http://www.dinf.ne.jp/doc/english/asia/resource/apdrj/z13fm0300/z13fm0313.html

Tucker, C. M., Porter, T., Reinke, W. M., Herman, K. C., Ivery, P. D., Mack, C. E., & Jackson, E. S. (2005). Promoting teacher efficacy for working with culturally diverse students. *Preventing School Failure, 50*(1), 29–34.

U.S. Census Bureau. (2010). *Hispanic population of the United States.* Retrieved from http://www.census.gov/population/www/socdemo/hispanic/hispanic_pop_presentation.ht ml

Useem, R. H., & Downie, R. D. (1994). Third culture kids. In K.C. McClusky (Ed.), *Notes from a traveling childhood: Readings for internationally mobile parents and children* (pp. 65–71). Washington, DC: Foreign Service Youth Foundation.

Villegas, A. M., & Lucas, T. (2007). The culturally responsive teacher. *Educational Leadership, 64*(6), 28–33.

Wells, R. (2008). The global and the multicultural: Opportunities, challenges, and suggestions for teacher education. *Multicultural Perspectives, 10*(3), 142–149.

CHAPTER ELEVEN

Infusing Civic Engagement into the Teacher Education Program: Authentic Experiences in Addressing Diversity

James K. Daly

A diverse setting and a diverse university do not guarantee a teacher education program that addresses diversity well. One teacher education program decided to explore diversity within a civic focus. This chapter describes the consequences of that decision on both traditional coursework and the infusion of authentic experiences for students. The program includes a traditional required course focused on multicultural education and provides field settings that allow students to examine various aspects of diversity. In a different required course, students explore hate sites and engage in readings and simulations designed to increase awareness of prejudice, stereotyping, and discrimination.

National and international programs have been infused into program requirements, with the active involvement of the university students. At the sophomore and junior levels, students are trained in Project Citizen (The Center for Civic Education) and work in area urban middle schools (electronically and in the classroom) to assist with project preparation. Sophomore students are trained in the Deliberating in a Democracy (DID) program. They work with a local school involved in the DID project, where they observe and then lead deliberations. They also work on DID with students at the Kyiv Pedagogical University in Ukraine. In the 2010–2011 academic year, DID work began with the Vilnius Pedagogical University in Lithuania as well. Finally, social studies methods students (juniors and seniors) during the previous year worked with both an urban diverse high school and University of North Dakota students to explore issues related to teaching and learning in diverse settings, culminating in two video conferences.

The Setting

The university discussed in this chapter is located in the New York metropolitan area, a region rich in diversity of every conceivable kind. The university is proud of its commitment to diversity. However, the department and the program studied are much less diverse. The program faculty includes all Euro-Americans and is primarily male. The faculty in the department is also overwhelmingly Euro-American but largely female. The students are mostly the same with respect to background, and a majority of the students are female, especially in the elementary education program of the college within which the program is housed. The program's NCATE report, addressing standard 4, indicates that 68% of all students are classified as White, 10% are Hispanic or Latino, and 6% are African American.

Although the region is diverse, many of the communities are not. Communities that can be categorized as primarily White exist alongside communities that are primarily Black. Class also plays a role, with wealthy communities often bordering middle- or lower-class towns. Ethnic groups tend to cluster together as well, with large representations in some communities and little in others. The majority of the program's students are from within the state, which is home to a range of diversities that are geographic in nature. Entire counties tend to be dominated by particular groups and characteristics, including wealth and educational achievement. The result is that, although they live in a diverse state, many students do not come from schools that reflect that diversity. Over the past three decades, the communities from which they come have increasingly become what Bishop and Cushing (2008) referred to as communities of sameness, with residents experiencing similar ways of life, beliefs, and politics. They suggested that, in these settings, the ability to understand perspectives and views held by others is almost impossible, and the intolerance for differences is growing. Preparing students to deal with the challenges of diversity given such a context is daunting.

Program Characteristics

Students preparing to teach social studies work with the same advisor for the entire duration of their time at the university, as do students preparing to teach in other areas. Advisors and advisees meet twice a year for registration and are regularly available for advisement and discussions, both academic and otherwise. With five full-time faculty members, students are in faculty members' courses two or more times during the program. Faculty members work with students in their field experiences as formal supervisors and observers. As a result, faculty and students know one another fairly well. Program meetings routinely include the discussion of specific students, addressing problems and achievements.

Assessment of students, both formal and informal, is often no more than a matter of agreeing to do so, which supplements a detailed and robust assessment system that monitors student progress each semester from various perspectives, including field supervisory reports and in-class products. Change is a relatively easy process, with agreement relying on consensus and a common commitment to ongoing systemic improvement driven by both anecdotal and quantitative data. In this context, the program makes use of existing university requirements and experiences to prepare teacher education candidates with the knowledge and skill to address diversity.

Relying on the University as a Foundation for Addressing Diversity

The challenges presented by the characteristics of the program's state and students as well as their prior schooling are significant, as are the opportunities. In this program, such challenges are addressed in a variety of ways, and in all of these a significant benefit is the size of the program. However, many of the approaches described may be of value to larger institutions as well. Undoubtedly, a three-credit methods course cannot thoroughly prepare preservice teachers to address diversity when they become teachers of social studies. Indeed, the program faculty has acted on the contention that it is the totality of the experiences provided for students throughout their time that meets the requirement. Thus, the nature and consequences of diversity are examined across courses, experiences, and different components of the university. Even larger programs may need to plan on ways to consciously use and build on the existing university resources and common student experiences.

The program uses as a foundation for exploring diversity the required university core program, consisting of three courses completed during students' first three years. Several program faculty regularly teach in these university core courses, primarily the one for all incoming freshmen. The first-year course provides a common experience for all students to better understand the nature of diversity. This course is designed to examine a range of philosophical and spiritual perspectives from diverse sources. The readings provide an opportunity for students to explore alternative views on the meaning of life and how to live well. The religious traditions of the Catholic Church, Christianity, Judaism, Hinduism, and Buddhism are explored, and students complete readings in philosophy. A film series accompanies the class, focusing on experiences from diverse historic, geographic, cultural, ethnic, and religious traditions. In class discussions, readings, and film, students address the human condition across time and experiences. Students learn to explore controversial topics from various perspectives and worldviews, and it is expected that they develop or reinforce tolerance for and an understanding of differences in all of the areas addressed in the course.

Discussions among the program faculty teaching the course result in shared materials and approaches. The common knowledge and experience that all of our students bring to their education classes are valuable. In their education classes, it is possible to remind them of prior readings, require that they reflect on their prior discussions addressing diversity, and apply them to the context of the classrooms in which they are preparing to teach.

The Challenge of Fieldwork

Like many institutions, the program faculty anticipates that placing students in diverse field experience settings helps prepare them for planning, teaching, and assessing in such settings. However, faculty members' experience has been that the opportunities students have to plan, teach, and assess their work in such traditionally assigned fieldwork are too often both random and limited. Many end up in classrooms where they do little more than observe. Some are actively working with mentors who themselves may not be skillful in dealing with the diversity in those settings. Ongoing efforts to improve and systematize the process continue, but program faculty members recognize that a field placement or two seems unlikely to provide the knowledge, skills, and dispositions needed for successfully addressing diverse students and communities.

Relying on Multiple Education Courses and Experiences to Address Diversity

An effort has been made to provide a systematic and developmental approach to focusing on elements of diversity throughout the students' coursework while in the program. Students take at least one education class during each semester over the course of four years. Through discussion and consensus, faculty members have identified in these courses across all semesters themes, concepts, knowledge, and skills that are foundations for the work done to prepare candidates for dealing with diversity. The first-year students in the program take in their second semester a required course that addresses the interplay of culture, schools, and communities. Readings and discussion focus on the impact of race, gender, and class on schools and how communities and schools seek to navigate the issues and procedures that often separate them. Faculty teaching this course have routinely had students interact with a variety of on-campus groups, including English language learners (ELLs) in the university's English as a second language (ESL) program.

During their second year, all program candidates are required to spend a year tutoring students at an area middle school. Once a week they meet with a group of two to three or more students who need assistance; students are selected by the middle-school teachers. The middle-school students include classified students, students with primary languages other than English, and students whose academic performance and behaviors are perceived as likely to improve from systematic interaction and support from a college tutor. The program students get firsthand experience helping middle-school students from different ethnic, racial, and social class groups succeed.

As the program students continue tutoring as a field experience, the fall education class requires them to examine the challenges that come with diversity. They consider the contention that slogans do not bring people with significant differences together. Although the program faculty would agree that diversity is a strength, they lead the students in an examination of the challenges it brings. Using a continuum, program students are asked to take a stand with respect to the importance of addressing diversity in the classrooms in which they will be teaching. This usually results in a robust exploration of a wide range of views. Program students then begin to analyze the nature of stereotyping, prejudice, and discrimination.

They are subsequently brought into a university computer lab where they are divided up into pairs and directed to one of many hate websites. The sites are updated every year and portray a variety of racial, ethnic, and religious perspectives. The students are required to identify the purposes for which the site exists. Discussion boards and the website log of the number of hits provide a sense of how many users visit the site and a sense of the topics those users are addressing. Students must consider the influence of the technological sophistication of the site as well as its effectiveness in present- ing the views the group maintains. The students reflect on claims made at the site and prepare responses to a series of instructor-generated questions in an online classroom discussion board. Class discussion follows the computer sessions. Students are then directed to a simulation of a school board that implements a policy designed to identify and punish hateful speech and actions. The questions and discussion that flow from this activity address constitutional considerations, an examination of zero tolerance policies, and whether as well as how individual teachers and their students consider historic and current injustices.

This course also examines moral development; thus, another activity makes use of a moral dilemma designed to engage the students in consider- ing dealing with diverse learners in their future classrooms. The dilemma requires that students imagine themselves living in Germany in the late 1930s. They must make a decision that puts the lives of people at risk and that threatens their own and their families' well-being. As the debriefing of the dilemma concludes, students are asked how to conduct an examination of difficult decisions infused with prejudices and stereotyping from the safety of examining them in the past to the issues and challenges facing classrooms and schools today.

Relying on Established Programs and Materials to Address Diversity

Working with students different from one's own experiences can be challenging. Americans are increasingly living in communities populated with people holding similar views, experiences, and expectations. It is reported that they do not read perspectives that differ from their own or watch television news broadcasts or listen to radio programs that convey other views. To the extent that such a phenomenon is correct, people have little practical experience in confronting the robust range of perspectives that characterize issues of importance. This creates a condition ripe with potential conflict for teacher education candidates as they enter into diverse school settings, either during their preparation period or as they begin their careers. In addition to the work already described, program faculty have adopted and modified national and international programs and infused them into existing coursework. The DID program, sponsored by Street Law, Inc., and the Constitutional Rights Foundations for both Chicago and Los Angeles, is one such program.

During the fall of the second year, candidates participate in the DID program. The program uses a structured academic controversy format to examine controversial issues from a global perspective. The university students are trained in the process and then deliberate a topic from those being addressed by high school teachers and students involved in the program around the world. The transferable skills addressed in the process include active listening, the clear articulation of positions, restatement of the perspectives of others, and a discussion of issues that involves consideration of the views held by others. Where possible, areas of agreement or consensus are identified.

The program students bring this training into the professional development high school with which the university is a partner. In one visit they meet the students and teachers involved in the DID program at the school. They return to observe several deliberations and then debrief on site to discuss the outcomes and compare the results with their own deliberation experience. The teacher education students then return for a third visit, during which time they facilitate a deliberation, again followed by an on-site focus group debriefing. The program students overwhelmingly cite the process as effective and report that it does permit a reflective consideration of diverse views and experiences. They find the engagement of the high school students to be positive and indicate that they find the procedures involved to be an effective way to address controversy in secondary classrooms. The website for the DID program (www.deliberating.org) offers assessment data that demonstrate the effectiveness of the program in meeting a wide range of objectives, all of which supports the contention that the program is beneficial to teacher education candidates.

During their third year, the candidates work with urban schools involved in another internationally recognized program, Project Citizen. Designed and administered by the Center for Civic Education, the program teaches students to recognize problems, identify solutions and agree on one to pursue, and then develop (and implement if time permits) an action plan. Teacher candidates learn the Project Citizen process, and then a number of things happen. The nature of many of the urban schools in the area means that the program involvement may vary from year to year. Unexpected challenges, administrative changes, and frequent teacher reassignments have required flexibility. The program's preferred approach over several years has been to bring students to the school site, where they go into classes and work with a group of middle-school students to pursue the project. Each group of university students is assigned to work with the middle students on one of four panels. The university students provide help with research, advise on the clarity of written and visual products, and discuss the practicality of the plans and work. The university students have reported that the experience has positively changed their perception of the urban school experience (Daly, Devlin-Scherer, Burroughs, & McCartan, 2010). They cite high-quality teaching and learning as evidenced throughout their work with the middle-school students.

For a variety of reasons, the teachers and schools with whom the program works and the arrangements for involving the university students may need to be modified. This past year the project had the university students working as virtual mentors. Each week they electronically monitored the work of urban high school students using a combination of interactive multimedia documents hosted on Google and Ning social technology. Unable to arrange a visit, the students at both schools exchanged introductory videos and video comments as well as advice about the project.

Both the on-site and the virtual work arrangement allow teacher education candidates to actively work with diverse students in a range of different settings. Debriefings occur immediately after each physical and virtual visit to maximize the potential learning for program students at an urban school (Proctor, Rentz, & Jackson, 2001). This type of structured field experience enables them to develop awareness and sensitivities too often overlooked

(Thompson & Smith, 2004). Follow-up discussions are essential for addressing and potentially eliminating misinterpretations of what is experienced. In these sessions, university students have identified unfamiliar and personally uncomfortable conditions and behaviors that—left unexamined—could easily reinforce stereotypes of urban schools. It is from these shared experiences that candidates enter the social studies methods class.

The Methods Course

The social studies methods course is offered in the first semester of the candidates' last year, immediately before student teaching. The class builds on the prior experiences students have had, and all have worked with the instructor in previous courses and experiences as well as through advisement. Thus, references are routinely made to programs, projects, and activities in which the students have already been involved.

Diverse views, experiences, and worldviews can all be a cause of conflict. Exploring alternative perspectives and examining materials beyond the safety of the textbook are perceived as controversial. Thus, the methods class seeks to address the teaching of controversial topics in a variety of ways. Hess (2009) offered compelling evidence that teachers of social studies do not address controversial topics often or well. Nelson (2003) warned that, in times of threat and great stress, teachers are unwilling to deal with controversy. These are surely such times, and in the larger society controversies are so many and so complex that it is impossible to avoid them. However, in social studies classrooms, the one place where controversial issues could be carefully considered and examined, they appear to be largely unaddressed. Censorship and self-censorship surely help to account for this. In addition, Cuban (2001) suggested that corporate, academic, and governmental elites have refocused the role of schooling from one primarily addressing civic and moral imperatives to an economic justification. Thus, the teacher candidates may be entering classrooms with a focus more on preparing workers to compete in a contentious global economy than preparing citizens dedicated to maintaining a republic. This change within a high-stakes testing environment makes the challenges for the teacher candidates significant.

Awareness of and support for academic freedom have the potential to protect preservice teacher education candidates as they enter classrooms, providing them with needed support for dealing with controversy. The methods class focuses on this concept. Teacher candidates need a range of skills that can assist them in teaching their classes how to actively listen and examine competing perspectives on issues of importance. Program students need to see secondary students actively engage in exploring diverse views on a wide range of topics. The methods course builds on prior work and seamlessly infuses active work in a range of programs and projects.

Students in the methods class participate for a second time in the DID program. Over the years, students have typically reported that they believed in the importance of teaching controversial topics, but felt that schools did not value or promote this. This seems to be consistent with what much research has suggested is true of social studies practitioners. Beale (1936), Barr, Barth, and Shermis (1977), Giroux and Penna (1979), Shermis and Barth (1979), and Engle (1985) are among the chorus of voices that have lamented the dearth of classroom teachers of social studies dealing with controversial topics. Of particular interest, Miscoe and Patterson (2007) reported on a range of limitations that teacher education candidates cited as restricting what could be taught. Given such a long and consistent history, the need to provide specific classroom-ready opportunities to engage teacher education candidates and secondary students in thoughtful consideration of controversial issues is important.

The deliberation process is again presented as a way in which to engage students in a reflective consideration of views and perspectives that may not be shared or even welcomed by many audiences. Its nature, focused on active listening and clear communication, leading to discussion and potentially to compromise, avoids many of the problems encountered in large-group discussions and debates. A review of the deliberation process precedes another class deliberation; this is done in the context of dealing with controversial issues and academic freedom.

The students share their views and experiences with teacher education university students from a pedagogical university in Eastern Europe trained in the same DID process. Using video and a section of the DID discussion board devoted to this university partnership, students discuss differences and similarities in perspectives on controversial topics. Double debriefing permits the university students to explore the dimensions of the issues, the content behind various perspectives, as well as the deliberation process with its technological component as a pedagogical strategy. The students at both universities have access to view the postings of thousands of high school students from the United States and Eastern Europe who deliberate on a range to topics. A wealth of information about the process as a teaching method as well as of a process to help young people learn about and appreciate differences is available. During the 2010–2011 academic year, a second European university joined in this work.

Examining diversity in teaching and learning from different geographic regions within the United States is also addressed through video exchanges with a large western public university. Students in the methods course at both schools are assigned a common reading on diversity. The video conferences provide an opportunity to share reactions and focus on specific issues. At the first video conference in the fall 2009 semester, a group of students from an urban history-themed magnet school near the studied campus joined their principal and a teacher in discussing school experiences as African-American and Latino students. The students at the western university found the activity valuable because their educational and personal experiences included few with students of color. The students from the program university enjoyed the chance to interact with the other university students and the high school students, teachers, and administrators both during the conference and at a lunch following the event. The high school students shared their sense of what they expected and needed from teachers, and the principal addressed the issues from a broader context. The second video conference between the two university classes focused on differences between rural and urban teaching. When one student from the other site described his hometown, one of the students in the examined program's class exclaimed that there were more people on his block than in the other's entire town. The students freely discussed their preparedness to design lessons for audiences different from themselves and their concerns about doing so. A discussion board was created to permit follow-up conversations. A common reading on the impact of poverty on teaching and learning served as the foundation for the first video conference of 2010–2011. Both classes worked on the newly opened discussion board, with additional video conferences scheduled.

Another requirement for the methods class is participation in the state-wide We the People—The Citizen and the Constitution competition. In the class, students explore the materials and resources developed by the Center for Civic Education. They then report to the State House in the capitol, where they are assigned as facilitators, timekeepers, or observers. They spend the day watching hundreds of high school students demonstrate an interest in—often a passion for—the Constitution. They get to see students from urban and suburban schools as well as from private and public schools. In the panels they see the diversity of the state. They see the students answer follow-up questions with a solid grasp of current issues and controversies. The university students see hundreds of parents and families proud of their children and happy to see them knowledgeable and skillful in civic educa-tion. Our students have served on panels and had conversations with former State Supreme Court Justices, members of the State Board of Education, political leaders, attorneys, corporate officials, and members of various organizations. Throughout the day, the class gets a chance to speak with students and their teachers. Over the years, the focus group debriefing has typically resulted in the reporting of a new awareness and appreciation for what high school students can do and a recommitment to bringing civic education to life in their own future teaching. A number of students volunteer to return in following years.

The university students in the methods class also examine the concept of academic freedom. Throughout their years in the program, the need for them to address controversy and explore diverse perspectives and worldviews has been an ongoing expectation. Having already examined approaches and considered programs that can assist them to do so, in this class, the students read from one of two views on the topic—namely, one for and one opposed to precollegiate academic freedom. The students create expert groups and prepare to teach their view to others. Debriefing corrects misunderstandings and clarifies remaining questions. The class is then given a case study based on Janet Cooper's experience with the Kingsville Board of Education (Daly, Schall, & Skeele, 2001). A moot court process provides the framework for examining the issues. The class is divided into three groups. Attorneys for Janet Cooper are directed to build compelling arguments for her appeal based on the readings supporting teacher academic freedom. Attorneys for the School Board are to do the same with readings in opposition. The third group serves as judges; they are directed to create questions to ask of attorneys from both sides using all of the readings. All three groups are then given short summaries of major court decisions that have had an impact on the concept of teacher academic freedom. Triads of one judge and one attorney for the board and one for the teacher then convene throughout the class. In a moot judicial conference, the judges from all of the triads share their reactions to the case made by both sides and their immediate response to the appeal. The decision of the actual 5th Circuit Court of Appeals is then reviewed, and a review of the mix of court cases is considered. The class is directed to either an electronic learning station or a reading addressing recommendations from national organizations (including NCSS) on ways in which schools should prepare for challenges and deal with them when they occur. With this information, students are directed to examine the school sites in which they are working to determine whether the recommendations have been followed in those schools (Daly, Roach, Evans, & Mitchell, 1995).

The work on academic freedom builds on the concept of responsibility. The class examines the responsibilities that teachers of social studies have to prepare their students to be citizens in a republic. The demands of knowledge require that the young know multiple perspectives and competing views of topics of concern and importance. Dealing with conflict is thus essential as disagreement on important ideas creates controversy. It is imperative to prepare teacher candidates to develop pedagogical skills to bring controversy into their classrooms in ways that promote listening and consideration.

Conclusion

Diversity represents a body of knowledge too broad to be effectively addressed in one class. It presents challenges too significant to be considered in a traditional university classroom. The range of skills needed to plan, teach, and assess in diverse settings is broad, and providing experience and practice in developing and improving them is time consuming. One class in one program cannot do justice to the students being trained. One approach is what has been described here. The attempt has been to build a coherent and integrated experience that builds on program faculty and education courses, fieldwork, and required university courses and opportunities. From the first semester to the last, students in the program discussed herein are confronted with the concept of diversity. They examine it in the context of history, religion, philosophy, and education. They study it in film and music as well as both ancient and current literature. Program faculty work in the required university core courses to become familiar with and lead the students through these experiences. Students' fieldwork provides opportunities for them to work in diverse schools with a range of learners. The program coursework is infused throughout the students' experience projects and opportunities to work with learners different from themselves. Electronically and in a variety of classrooms, students in the program participate in and learn how to implement national and international programs that develop skills and dispositions essential to successfully address diverse learners.

References

Barr, R. D., Barth, J. L., & Shermis, S. S. (1977). *Defining the social studies.* Arlington, VA: National Council for the Social Studies.

Beale, H. K. (1936). *Are American teachers free: An analysis of restraints upon the freedom of teaching in American schools.* New York: C. Scribner's Sons.

Bishop, B., & Cushing, R. (2008). *The big sort: Why the clustering of like-minded Americans is tearing us apart.* New York: Houghton Mifflin.

Cuban, L. (2001). *Oversold and underused. Computers in the classroom.* Cambridge, MA: Harvard University Press.

Daly, J. K., Devlin-Scherer, R., Burroughs, G., & McCartan, M. (2010, Spring). The status of civic education: A preservice program response. *The Educational Forum, 74*(2), 117–128.

Daly, J. K., Roach, P., Evans, S., & Mitchell, G. (1995). Building support for intellectual freedom. *Contemporary Education, LXVI*(2), 92–95.

Daly, J. K., Schall, P., & Skeele, R. (Eds.). (2001). *Protecting the right to teach and learn:*

Power, politics and public schools. New York: Teachers College Press.

Engle, S. H. (1985). Late night thoughts about the new social studies. *Social Education, 50,* 20–22.

Giroux, H. A., & Penna, A. N. (1979). Social education in the classroom: The dynamics of the hidden curriculum. *Theory and Research in Social Education, 7,* 21–39.

Hess, D. (2009). *Controversy in the classroom: The democratic power of discussion.* NewYork: Routledge.

Miscoe, T., & Patterson, N. C. (2007). A study of preservice teachers' conceptualizations of academic freedom and controversial issues. *Theory and Research in Social Education, 35*(4), 520–550.

Nelson, J. (2003). Academic freedom, institutional integrity, and teacher education. *Teacher Education Quarterly, 30*(1), 65–72.

Proctor, T. J., Rentz, N. L., & Jackson, M. W. (2001). Preparing teachers for urban schools: The role of field experiences. *Western Journal of Black Studies, 25*(4), 219–227.

Shermis, S. S., & Barth, J. L. (1979). Defining social problems. *Theory and Research in Social Education, 7*(1), 1–19.

Thompson, S., & Smith, D. L. (2004). Creating highly qualified teachers for urban schools. *The Professional Educator, 28,* 1–2.

CHAPTER TWELVE

E Unis Pluribum:
The Search for Diversity in Southeast Ohio

Frans H. Doppen

This chapter focuses on efforts in the Patton College of Education at Ohio University to raise its candidates' awareness of the influence of context and culture on behavior at the programmatic level as well as in social studies methods courses. Nearly two-thirds of the preservice teachers come from urban and suburban areas around the state and typically have a White, middle-class background. Unfortunately, there is not a great deal of racial diversity in the region. However, it is noticeable with respect to the region's culture, low levels of socioeconomic status, and large numbers of students with disabilities.

To broaden preservice teachers' experiences with diversity, the university also offers two significant programs, the Rural Urban Collaborative (RUC) and the Consortium of Overseas Teaching (COST), which give students a unique opportunity to gain experiences in culturally diverse settings outside of southeast Ohio. The purpose of the collaborative is to enhance preservice teachers' understanding of the similarities and differences between rural and urban education as well as offer an exchange of field experiences. Meanwhile, to promote global diversity experiences, the COST program has been sending candidates overseas to student teach in countries around the world. Preservice teachers who have participated in the COST program report significant increases in cross-cultural understanding and describe their future teacher roles as those of cultural mediators.

The social studies methods courses include an emphasis on making connections between local and global events, particularly by developing a unit plan that situates primary documents from a local archive within a global topic. In addition, each course includes a service learning component in which the preservice teachers learn and serve in a regional or global context. A series of field trips as part of the social studies methods courses helps the preservice teachers get out of "the Athens bubble" and have led to the creation of a course on the Appalachian experience in southeast Ohio that seeks to enhance the preservice teachers' understanding of how the microregion's history continues to impact its culture, environment, and educational institutions today. The course culminates in a service learning project that benefits the local community.

The Mwanje project is a global service learning project to benefit a primary school in Malawi that, through self-selected activities, seeks to raise funds to drill a bore hole for safe drinking water. The preservice teachers' reflections about the Mwanje project are generally positive.

Ohio University is located in southeast Ohio in Athens County, 1 of the 32 counties that together make up the Appalachian region in Ohio. All 32 counties are members of the Coalition of Rural and Appalachian Schools (CORAS) (see http://www.arc.gov/counties). The mission of CORAS is to advocate for and support the public schools of Appalachian Ohio in the continuous improvement of educational opportunities available to all the region's children. However, nearly two-thirds of the preservice teachers at Ohio University come from urban and suburban areas surrounding Cincinnati, Columbus, and Cleveland. Before coming to Athens, most have grown up in White middle-class neighborhoods and have had little experience with diversity. In 2007, 36% of all families in southeast Ohio lived below the poverty level, which more than twice exceeded the 16% state average. In 2008, the average daily median expenditure of $1,798 per student was 37% below the state median of $2,930. That same year, 5.02% of all students in families in the Appalachian school districts received support through the Ohio Works First (OWF) poverty program, which exceeded the state average of 3.17% by 58.36%, while the median income in the region was $27,161—$5,299 below the state median of $32,460 (Coalition of Rural Appalachian Schools, 2010). It is against this background that the Patton College of Education at Ohio University has developed a core mission to prepare future teachers who are committed to holistic learning; engage in collaborative and professional service to society; address changing human/social needs through inquiry, research, assessment, critical thinking, problem solving, and proactive use of technology; appreciate the variety of human cultural expression; employ multiple approaches to inquiry; use knowledge and practice for the benefit of a diverse society and promote social equity and justice for effective civic engagement; and engage in self-reflection and professional development for continuous personal growth and to inspire such practices in those they serve.

The college seeks to make its preservice teachers aware of the influence of context and culture on behavior; it does so at the programmatic level as well as through individual courses. There is not a great deal of racial diversity in the region. According to Local Report Cards published annually by the Ohio Department of Education (see http://ilrc.ode.state.oh.us/), White students typically make up close to 100% of the students in each of the 32

Appalachian school districts. However, diversity is noticeable with respect to differing levels of socioeconomic status and the number of students with disabilities. The Appalachian school districts, in which the university's preservice teachers participate in field experiences and clinical practice, typically have a population in which one third to two-thirds of all students are considered economically disadvantaged and about one-fifth to one-fourth have been identified with learning disabilities. The college seeks to address issues of diversity using multiple approaches; this chapter highlights three of these different approaches (i.e., through an institutional partnership, an overseas student teaching program, and service learning projects in social studies methods courses). Pseudonyms are used throughout the discussion.

Rural Urban Collaborative

The Rural Urban Collaborative is an institutional partnership among Ohio University, Ohio Dominican University, Columbus City Schools, Hocking School District, and Southern Local School District. Its purpose is to enhance preservice teachers' understanding of the similarities and differences between rural and urban education. The collaborative seeks to build multicultural competence in preservice teachers through diverse classroom and community experiences. In part, in response to National Council for the Accreditation of Teacher Education (NCATE) mandates, the collaborative's goal is to find avenues to better prepare preservice teachers for teaching in socially, eco- nomically, ethnically, racially, and culturally diverse environments by offering preservice teachers from Ohio University field experience opportuni- ties in inner-city school settings in Columbus and offering those same opportunities to candidates from Ohio Dominican University in the Appala- chian region. Building on similarities and differences between rural and urban educational settings, the collaborative seeks to determine how cultural diversity and geographic differences can be used to create constructive, enriching learning experiences for preservice teachers.

Preservice teachers in both rural and urban settings often enter the teach- ing profession with insufficient understanding of or experience with the diverse characteristics and needs of children in the geographic regions outside their university location. They typically complete field experiences in schools close to their universities or hometown. Their universities usually offer limited opportunities to learn about schoolchildren and communities with distinctly different backgrounds. However, multicultural competence is increasingly recognized as an essential qualification for instructional profi- ciency and effective teaching as well as for gaining employment and achiev- ing success in future teaching careers. The Patton College of Education at

Ohio University believes that its preservice teachers must take advantage of opportunities to gain multicultural competence.

The RUC seeks to promote multicultural competence, place-based education, educational partnerships, and learning organizations. Ladson-Billings (2001) recommended that "educators who are prepared to help students become culturally competent [must be] themselves culturally competent" (p. 97). They must come to understand the role of culture in education and learn about and use student culture as a basis for learning. Likewise, emphasizing the importance of multicultural education, Gollnick and Chinn (2009) and Manning and Baruth (2009) provided the RUC with both a conceptual structure and practical strategies for using diversity in the classroom. Furthermore, Theobald's (1997) notion of "place-based" education supports the RUC model's rural component by particularly recognizing the contribution of local communities to rural schools' curriculum and pedagogy.

In addition, organizational theory offers an institutional understanding of educational partnerships. Ravid and Handler (2001) identified the conceptual elements of partnerships and illustrated these with numerous cases of school–university collaboration. Senge's (1990) concept of a "learning organization" offers an additional framework for understanding the functioning of the RUC and its benefit to all partnering institutions. Building from his "systems thinking" concept, in which organizations gain skills and capacity through external relationships, Senge extended the original "learning organization" metaphor to education itself in *Schools That Learn* (Senge et al., 2000), offering models and case studies to advocate that schools engage with various stakeholders beyond their immediate walls to encourage organizational development.

Reflections from preservice teachers who have participated in the RUC suggest a deeper awareness of culturally relevant pedagogy as they reflect on their own preconceived notions and how the RUC experience has impacted their thinking. They report having had preconceived notions of urban schools as having loud, unruly students and exhausted teachers who lack classroom management skills, whereas rural schools were often thought of as being small and poverty-stricken. For example, one preservice teacher wrote, "A stereotype that I had before going to the rural school was that it would be small, and not be technologically advanced." Meanwhile, upon arriving at her urban placement school, Petra noted that she was "excited to see if there was any recognizable difference in this urban setting compared to the schools I have observed in within rural settings." Often their stereotypes were dispelled, as Chelsea suggested when she admitted that, "One stereotype that I have seen completely dispelled is that urban students care less about their academic careers."

More often than not, the RUC participants reported similarities rather than differences between urban and rural schools. "I was surprised that the rural school setting was similar to the urban schools that I have seen." The main similarity the participants repeatedly noted was that school children are the same regardless of where they go and that "children will be children." In a typical comment, Kayla wrote not to "judge a book by its cover. Students in inner city schools get a bad reputation. A ton of these kids are gifted and talented, and most of them are smart as a whip." Several participants also suggested that all students, despite cultural or geographical differences, encounter the same issues one may expect among adolescents, such as wanting to date and having more independence. They also repeatedly noted that students in both urban and rural settings often come from similar low socioeconomic backgrounds and frequently receive free or reduced lunches.

Another surprising similarity that stood out to many of the participants was the school facility. Many of the rural participants were surprised to find out that the middle school in which they were placed was located in a newer building. Likewise, the urban participants were surprised by the new buildings in which many rural schools in southeast Ohio are located. Thus, the RUC experience often dispelled stereotypes they held about outdated facilities and the lack of resources. Instead, they often ended up positively commenting on the quality of the school buildings.

Yet another similarity that the participants found and enjoyed was that teachers in both settings were interested in their students' lives outside of school, recognizing that there is more to academic success than classroom instruction. Kayla thought this was particularly important in any urban or rural setting because,

> the most important aspect in being a successful teacher and building a strong relationship with every student is to build strong connections, getting to know them inside and outside the classroom, and taking interest in the individual person they are. Mr. Smith could tell me about each student's family background, academic background and extracurricular background. It showed that he is involved with his students for more than just a 45-minute class period.

William echoed this same sentiment:

> I think the most important thing that I learned from my experience at the urban school is that it does not matter if a student attends a rural or an urban school, the teachers must follow the same standards of teaching.

Meanwhile, Eric wrote that, "The teacher professionals said they know their students as well as possible because they must know their students to teach their students the way each student learns best."

Finally, the RUC participants suggested that cultural competence is the most important skill to have in teaching because it enables students and teachers to relate and open a dialogue so the teacher can familiarize him- or herself with each student's interests, family life, and extracurricular activities. After participating in the RUC, Chelsea wrote, "As educators, we should instead celebrate cultural differences." Similarly, Kayla argued that "understanding cultural diversity in the classroom is a concept that cannot be ignored and is one of the most important aspects for future educators" whereas Sheryl wrote that, "My observations have definitely given me further insight into what cultural competency is and might mean." Overall, the RUC has been a positive experience for its participants. Many of the participants reported having grown professionally as well as personally, and they gained a deeper understanding of their own perspectives and beliefs. Most also suggested that they learned some important techniques for managing different classrooms and gained skills for working with multiple and diverse students. As Sheryl suggested in her final reflection, "I have grown a lot in my own cultural competency and sociopolitical consciousness. Being able to see that growth in myself is one of the most rewarding things that I have experienced."

Overseas Student Teaching

Since 1992, preservice teachers at Ohio University have also had the opportunity to complete their student teaching in an international setting. As a member of the COST program, the college has sent student teachers overseas to countries such as Mexico, Costa Rica, Ecuador, the Netherlands, Germany, England, Ireland, Greece, South Africa, Australia, and New Zealand. To be accepted into the COST program, the preservice teachers must complete a rigorous application process. In addition to submitting an extensive application, including two major essays on personal educational experiences and their reasons for wishing to student teach in an international setting, prior to departure all prospective COST students must complete a student teaching practicum. They must also complete a course on cross-cultural understanding. While student teaching abroad under the supervision of a cooperating teacher, they are evaluated at least twice by a local university supervisor and are required to submit regularly scheduled topical reflections on their teaching and cultural experiences to their COST coordinator at Ohio University. Finally, upon their return, they are required to submit a digital photo essay as well as complete a survey of their COST experience.

Cushner (2004) observed that increased globalization has led to a homogenization of the travel experience of many people as they venture only into rather similar and familiar environments. As such, many travelers never deeply engage in the culture of the country they visit, nor do they experience its—let alone their own—national identity. However, Cushner also reminded us that overseas student teaching mirrors the original concept of travel as a learning experience. Because overseas student teaching typically involves an extended period of time (three to four months), these "travelers" have the opportunity to immerse themselves in intercultural learning.

Bennett's (1993) Developmental Model of Intercultural Sensitivity provides a framework for understanding individual development and awareness along a continuum of six stages from ethnocentrism to ethnorelativism. The denial stage, which refers to the inability to see cultural differences, is followed by the defense stage, which is characterized by the ability to recognize differences but adhere to the superiority of one's own culture. Next is the minimization stage, in which people tend to minimize differences by believing that all humans are essentially the same. In the acceptance stage, individuals begin to analyze cultural differences that lead them into the adaptation stage, when they become competent in communicating across cultures. In the final integration stage, they have multiple frames of reference and are able to move relatively easily between different cultural groups.

To promote reflection during their overseas student teaching experience, COST students from Ohio University are required to submit reflective essays focused on their intercultural adjustment (see Wilson & Flournoy, 2007). Significant themes in these reflections include observations about lifestyles, economic inequalities, diversity, politics, and perspectives on American identity.

The perception of a different pace of life in the host country has stood out immediately and intensely to many student teachers as they describe a "laid back" lifestyle to characterize the slower pace of life in contrast to the fast pace of life in America. In a typical passage, Marissa wrote that,

> Americans…are always rushing. Even when we are in a hurry we need to go faster in order to feel that we have accomplished something. There are not enough hours in the day to complete everything that needs to be done to make a good impression that we tend to lose sight of what is really important in life.

Many student teachers have also reported observations about disparate economic conditions in their host country while some have related personal experiences as well. For example, after visiting a township school, Candace felt "sorry for the 'poor children' who had to attend school there every day." Contemplating whether such disparities exist in the United States as well, she realized that just as there are "haves and have-nots in Third World countries...there are people as bad off at home." Although Candace reflected on her COST experience as "an opportunity to reflect on [her] own privilege in a real way," Liz thought back to her field experience in a school at home [in the States], where "some students couldn't even pull together enough clean clothes for a week."

Several student teachers explicitly shared their thoughts about race and ethnicity. For example, Jesse observed that her host city was a residence for immigrants with "many cultures...from indigenous people to Europeans, to Asians, to South Africans, to North and South Americans, to Australians. Time to time we talk about the different countries we are from and what our daily norms are." Describing South Africa's culture as "extremely interesting," Candace noted that although White South Africans refer to "the black people as 'blacks' or 'Africans,' they don't refer to themselves as 'Africans' even though most of them have lived in Africa their entire lives with generations before them." Marla noted similar racial and ethnic distinctions in Ecuador between "*blancos*, or white people [of] mixed European/Latin American descent" and "the indigenous [who] have pure heritage from the native tribes."

The student teachers reported numerous experiences with stereotypes about Americans in their host country. They discovered that their students and the adults they encountered in their host country were extremely eager to talk about politics in America. However, these discussions were a mixture of pain and pleasure as these students and adults were often quick to criticize the United States. The student teachers also often encountered perspectives on America based on stereotypes acquired through media such as television, movies, and newspapers.

Interestingly, the student teachers almost exclusively reported negative stereotypes of Americans, who were characterized as being ignorant about the world, arrogant, superficial, loud, and materialistic. Many reported that Americans are thought of as being wealthy and intimately associated with celebrities, having large houses and many cars, and being obese, egocentric, overly involved in others' affairs, loud, and ignorant. For example, whereas Molly wrote that her Irish "students feel like America is this fabulous land where you can see plenty of celebrities just walking down the street," Bernice observed that "Americans in Greece are perceived as entitled, involved in the world, concerned with issues when Americans or America is involved, and wealthy.... Greeks feel Americans have an entitlement attitude where the world owes Americans everything." Although at times these stereotypes were "understandable," at other times they were "hurtful" and made them feel "sad." In several instances, the student teachers admitted they knew little about the world. For example, Kendall admitted that she was "guilty" of being an "example of the common stereotypical American." Consequently, some student teachers, like Jennifer, became determined to "prove those American stereotypes wrong."

The COST program broadens global awareness and cross-cultural understanding while helping student teachers move from ethnocentrism to ethnorelativism. Moving beyond minimization, they begin to analyze cultural differences and become competent in communicating across cultures. Realizing that cultural immersion was responsible for personal growth, Jocelyn wrote that, "being constantly surrounded by people of a different culture gives one certain insights into his/her own culture that might be otherwise unattainable." Similarly, Marcilla reported having gained a desire to help her future students become more culturally aware by suggesting that "[m]y experiences here have immensely broadened my global awareness." Finally, Jennifer echoed this same sentiment: "Going to other countries has broadened my global awareness by leaps and bounds because I now know that I have a tangible connection to the world."

Service Learning

Whereas cultural diversity is addressed throughout the curriculum offered by the teacher education program, the social studies methods courses for preservice middle and high school teachers include a special emphasis on making connections between local and global events. This is especially accomplished by developing a unit plan that situates primary documents from a local archive within a global topic. In addition, each methods course includes a service learning component, in which the preservice teachers learn and serve in a regional or global context.

Originally a series of field trips that were part of a social studies methods course sought to get the preservice teachers out of "the Athens bubble" to learn about the Little Cities of Black Diamonds, a microregion in southeast Ohio that experienced a coal mining boom around the turn of the 19th century and a subsequent economic decline. These field trip experiences subsequently led to the creation of an elective course designed to help preservice and inservice teachers develop a deeper understanding of the Appalachian region in southeast Ohio through classroom and field-based activities. In this course, they learn how the history of the Little Cities of Black Diamonds region continues to impact its culture and environment today. In addition, they gain an understanding of the role of education in not only preserving the region's culture, but also preparing its youth to be stewards of the land. By stressing the uniqueness of the Little Cities, the course seeks to counter stereotypes of Appalachia and help these preservice teachers become advocates of a promising future for this often poorly understood region. Finally, the course includes a service learning component in which each participant, after having learned about the microregion, develops a project that will benefit the Little Cities community.

Support in higher education for service learning has recently gained great momentum. However, service learning means a lot of different things to different people. According to Saltmarsh (2005), service learning is one of many avenues to promote civic engagement, as are democratic education, political engagement, citizenship education, and moral education. Arguing that historical knowledge contextualizes community-based problem solving, he emphasized the important role of community in shaping student learning.

Recently, McDavis (2008), president of Ohio University, suggested that what makes the "Bobcat" (i.e., university community) spirit unique is its emphasis on serving not only the nation and state, but also the region as well. This spirit is expressed by formally introducing all Freshmen to a core set of values: community, citizenship, civility, character, and commitment. According to McDavis, each of these qualities affirms "the value of citizenship as expressed through political engagement and public service" (p. 2).

In 2000, the National Council for the Social Studies (NCSS) issued a position statement that defined service-learning as "an essential component of citizenship education" (p. 240). According to NCSS, service learning differs from community service in that the service is integrated with academic skills and content as well as engages students in reflection activities. Effective service learning activities not only use the community as a learning laboratory, but also emphasize "solv[ing] community problems, meet[ing] human needs and environmental needs, and advocat[ing] for changes in laws to promote the common good" (p. 240). Effective service learning projects teach students that "they can make a difference" (p. 240).

In higher education, Batchelder and Root (1994) have found that college students who engage in service learning make greater gains in their thinking about social problems and prosocial decision making than students in traditional classes; Strage (2004) found more modest long-term academic benefits. According to Hammond (1994), faculty members in higher education who engage in service learning are predominantly driven by curricular concerns and derive satisfaction from service learning activities because they provide a sense of meaning and purpose and generate positive feedback from students and colleagues.

Service learning has also become part of teacher preparation programs at many universities. Preservice teachers often live in a bubble because they "just go to school [and] then plan to leave" (Boyle-Baise, 2005). As a result, they are often completely alienated from the local communities that surround their college town. As they first venture out into a local community, they often find themselves in unfamiliar culturally mixed or low-income settings in which they are forced to confront their own stereotypes (Baldwin, Buchanan, & Rudusill, 2007). However, as they become increasingly familiar with the surrounding communities, they learn to appreciate the importance of building reciprocal partnerships based on trust, mutual understanding, and shared values, thereby inspiring them to become potential advocates for social justice and agents of change (Boyle-Baise et al., 2007; Carrington & Saggers, 2007; Chen, 2004; Ethridge, 2006, McKay & Rozee, 2004; Perry & Katula, 2001; Swick, 2001; Wade & Yarbrough, 1997). As these partnerships help students and faculty break down the perception of the university as an ivory tower, they meet community needs while empowering communities as a resource for learning (Boyle et al., 2007; McKay & Rozee, 2004). An additional goal of teacher preparation is to prepare culturally responsive, asset-based (rather than deficiency-driven) community-centered teachers who understand that the community may not always welcome social justice-driven "do good" service learners and will see things differently (Boyle-Baise, 1998, 2005; Boyle-Baise & Langford, 2004). Finally, a special goal of teacher preparation programs is to help preservice teachers—especially those who hope to teach social studies—gain an appreciation of service learning as an enriching method of democratic education they will implement in their own future classrooms (Dinkelman, 2001; Swick, 2001).

Service learning provides a unique opportunity to engage students in place-based education. According to Smith (2002), place-based education reveals five thematic patterns as students study local culture and nature, identify and solve local problems, help the local community through internships and the creation of entrepreneurial opportunities, and become engaged in the community decision-making process. According to Blank, Johnson, and Shah (2003), place-based education uses a "community as text" model that includes service learning.

Little Cities of Black Diamonds. Social studies preservice teachers at Ohio University who have participated in Little Cities of Black Diamonds (LCBD) service learning projects report having learned more about the local environment and culture than they would have through a textbook. For example, Elsa reported, "I learned that the history of the LCBD has been much more diverse than previously believed. I really enjoyed learning about the cultural framework of the region and how it influenced cultural movements in metropolitan America." Students who came from the region also appreciated the project. Bryn stated, "Something so influential in American labor history began just down the road from my home." Overall, students who participated in this local service learning project reported positive experiences. Darby summed up the students' sentiments well when, after being asked what they had learned about the Little Cities, she wrote, "Lots of very interesting things. I enjoyed visiting the little towns and seeing and learning about the historic sites."

Students also reported learning about the microregion's environmental issues. According to Loraine, "The Earth isn't as large as many like to think and the lifecycle is easily polluted as evidenced by the mine runoff. If more responsible decisions had been made, there would be less hassle." Some students, such as Julian, focused more on the positive aspects of environmental learning: "I did learn...what steps were being taken to improve the environment such as the use of dosers and rerouting of the streams. I found both processes to be interesting." All students, whether they chose to focus more on the problems or solutions that characterize the Little Cities, became more environmentally aware. Rebekah's culminating remark with regard to the environment read, "Most of these things are in the process of being corrected, but it will be centuries to restore the environment to its initial state prior to all the damaging mining." Students in the elective course were required to complete a project of their choice that would be of service to the Little Cities. In choosing their projects, they had to identify problems that were in need of solutions and then decide how they could help solve the problems. For example, Tamara stated that she "chose to participate in a service project because I wanted my efforts to have a direct and immediate effect on the area." Kaye echoed similar sentiments:

> I can only hope that my project "made a difference" in the life of the Little Cities. I wanted to provide a tool for others learning about the Little Cities and the commitment of those who made the Little Cities revival possible. Hopefully, I filled this goal of mine.

Nearly all students reported positive feelings of accomplishment related to the service learning projects, saying, like Rhonda, that, "I felt really good about completing it. I only wish that I could do more."

Students felt positive not only about the projects, but also about the course and overall experience. Kellie stated, "I thought it was great to go around to all the Little Cities and see how they began and what their current economies are like." Some students even remarked that the course was similar to a local study-abroad program. Ginger took time to appreciate the hands-on aspect of the course, a sentiment shared by many of the partici-pants: "The hands-on application was terrific. If we had spent five days watching videos and reading, without actually seeing the area—that would've been a waste." Simply, yet elegantly put, Becky's final remark with regard to the course was that she "absolutely enjoyed the course!"

Mwanje school. Similar to the service learning project in the Little Cit-ies, the preservice teachers who participated in the Mwanje project reported having learned a great deal about Malawi, a country many were ignorant of prior to becoming engaged in the project. Mike stated, "It seems to be a very interesting country with a very distinct national pride and culture." Many students reported feeling more culturally competent because of the project. For example, Barbara wrote, "Not only did I gain knowledge about Malawi from this project, I also gained an understanding of how important it is to treat everyone with equal respect and to not be stereotypical." Coming in personal contact with those whom the project was to benefit was often credited as an eye-opener. Indeed, Susan remarked about the phone conver-sation between the class and the principal of the Mwanje school: "This was a very cool, very helpful way to get to know a little bit more about the school, and to take a more personal approach to the project."

Students also reported on what they learned about the local environment. For example, Jeanne admitted that, "the poverty in the country...does surprise me. I wasn't aware that a country with cities and an official infrastructure in Africa could be capable of so much poverty." Others remarked on the beauty of the land:

> One picture that struck me as beautiful was a picture of Lake Malawi. I had no idea how pretty the lake was. I pictured in my mind a muddy mess but in reality it was crystal clear waters. It made me want to go visit Malawi one day to see the lake, schools, and cities.

Many reported that the environment in which the project was set, combined with the personal contact and new cultural knowledge, was a motivating factor for them. Anja stated,

> The school has no running water, or water source near enough for them to all have water to use during the school day. The school is used by ten villages and is in one of the poorest communities in Malawi.... The school needs clean drinking water for its teachers and students.

Finally, students reported learning a great deal about service learning and its implementation as well as having a positive experience while completing the project. "I think it is good to do service learning projects because it helps students make connections with the people and places they are working with." Similarly, Mia stated, "Overall, I felt like this was a really cool idea to use for a class. It's a way for students to learn about a different culture and help out others in a way many have never done before." This theme was repeated again and again in students' statements about their participation in this service-learning project. "Overall, I thought this was a great project that allowed our class to become more global thinkers, which I hope everyone takes with them in their teaching careers."

Conclusion

Although being a teacher educator in an ethnically homogenous region and at a university with a nearly homogenous student population poses its unique challenges, helping preservice teachers appreciate the variety of human cultural expression is not an impossible task. Efforts to make preservice teachers aware of the influence of context and culture on behavior can occur at the programmatic level as well as through individual courses. This chapter has highlighted three different approaches used to help teacher candidates at Ohio University become culturally competent by creating an institutional partnership, offering an overseas student teaching program, and including service learning projects in social studies methods courses. Each of these approaches engages preservice teachers in cross-cultural learning experiences, heightens their self-awareness, and helps them develop a sense of accomplishment as well as a new and deeper appreciation of issues of diversity they will need to address in their future classrooms.

Although our history as a country of immigrants has been based on a coming together as one people, *e pluribus unum*, we must confront the reality of our changing demographic composition by acknowledging and respecting the diversity within, *e unis pluribum*. Only by committing ourselves to truly appreciating cultural differences between people—at the local, national, and global level—will we be able to make this world a better place.

References

Baldwin, S. C., Buchanan, A. M., & Rudusill, M. E. (2007). What teacher candidates learned about diversity, social justice, and themselves from service-learning experiences. *Journal of Teacher Education, 58*(4), 315–327.

Batchelder, T. H., & Root, S. (1994). Effects of an undergraduate program to integrate academic learning and service: Cognitive, prosocial cognitive, and identity outcomes. *Journal of Adolescence, 17*, 341–355.

Bennett, M. (1993). Towards ethnorelativism: A developmental model of intercultural sensitivity. In M. Paige (Ed.), *Cross-cultural orientation* (pp. 27–69). Lanham, MD: University Press of America.

Blank, M. J., Johnson, S. D., & Shah, B. P. (2003). Community as text: Using the community as a resource for learning in community schools. *New Directions for Youth Development, 97*, 107–120.

Boyle-Baise, M. (1998). Community service learning for multicultural education: An exploratory study with preservice teachers. *Equity & Excellence in Education, 31*(2), 52–60.

Boyle-Baise, M. (2005). Preparing community-oriented teachers: Reflections from a multicultural service-learning project. *Journal of Teacher Education, 56*(5), 446–458.

Boyle-Baise, M., Bridgwaters, B., Brinson, L., Hiestand, N., Johnson, B., & Wilson, P. (2007). Improving the human condition: Leadership for justice-oriented service-learning. *Equity & Excellence in Education, 40*, 113–122.

Boyle-Baise, M., & Langford, J. (2004). There are children here: Service learning for social justice. *Equity & Excellence in Education, 37*, 55–66.

Carrington, S., & Saggers, B. (2007). Service-learning informing the development of an inclusive ethical framework for beginning teachers. *Teaching and Teacher Education, 24*, 795–806.

Chen, D. W. (2004). The multiple benefits of service learning projects in preservice teacher education. *The Delta Gamma Bulletin, 70*(2), 31–36.

Coalition of Rural Appalachian Schools. (2010). *Vital statistics 2007–2008*. Retrieved from http://coras.org

Cushner, K. (2004). *Beyond tourism: A practical guide to meaningful educational travel*. Lanham, MD: Scarecrow Education.

Dinkelman, T. (2001). Service learning in student teaching: "What's social studies for?" *Theory and Research in Social Education, 29*(4), 617–639.

Ethridge, E. A. (2006). Teacher modeling of active citizenship via service-learning in teacher education. *Mentoring & Tutoring, 14*(1), 49–65.

Gollnick, D. M., & Chinn, P. C. (2009) *Multicultural education in a pluralistic society* (8th ed.). Columbus, OH: Pearson.

Hammond, C. (1994). Integrating service and academic study: Faculty motivation and satisfaction in Michigan higher education. *Michigan Journal of Community Service Learning, 1*(1), 21–28.

Ladson-Billings, G. J. (2001). *Crossing over to Canaan. The journey of new teachers in diverse classrooms*. San Francisco, CA: Jossey-Bass.

Manning, M. L., & Baruth, L. G. (2009). *Multicultural education of children and adolescents* (5th ed.). Columbus, OH: Pearson.

McDavis, R. J. (2008, Fall/Winter). Citizenship 101. *Ohio Today, 2*.

McKay, V. C., & Rozee, P. D. (2004). Characteristics of faculty who adopt community service learning pedagogy. *Michigan Journal of Community Service Learning, 10*(2), 21–33.

National Council for the Social Studies. (2000). Service-learning: An essential component of citizenship education. *Social Education, 65*(4), 240–241.

Perry, J. L., & Katula, M. C. (2001). Does service affect citizenship? *Administration & Society, 33*(3), 330–365.

Ravid, R., & Handler, M. G. (Eds.). (2001). *The many faces of school–university collaboration: Characteristics of successful partnerships*. Englewood, CO: Teachers' Ideas Press.

Saltmarsh, J. (2005). The civic promise of service learning. *Liberal Education, 9*(2), 50–55.

Senge, P. M. (1990). *The fifth discipline: The art and practice of the learning organization.* New York: Currency Doubleday.

Senge, P. M., Cambron-McCabe, N., Lucas, T., Smith, B., Dutton, J., & Kleiner, A. (2000). *Schools that learn: A fifth discipline fieldbook for educators, parents, and everyone who cares about education.* New York: Doubleday.

Smith, G. A. (2002). Place-based education: Learning to be where we are. *Phi Delta Kappan, 83*(8), 584–594.

Strage, A. (2004). Long-term academic benefits of service-learning: When and where do they manifest themselves? *College Student Journal, 32*(2), 257–261.

Swick, K. J. (2001). Service learning in teacher education: Building learning communities. *The Clearing House, 73*(5), 261–264.

Theobald, P. (1997). *Teaching the commons: Place, pride, and the renewal of community.* Boulder, CO: Westview Press.

Wade, R. W., & Yarbrough, D. B. (1997). Community service learning in student teaching: Toward the development of an active citizenry. *Michigan Journal of Community Service Learning, 4*(1), 42–55.

Wilson, A., & Flournoy, M. A. (2007). In K. Cushner & S. Brennan (Eds.), *Intercultural student teaching: A bridge to global competence* (pp. 34–56). Lanham, MD: Rowman & Littlefield.

CHAPTER THIRTEEN

Changing Perspective: Service Learning as Multicultural Pedagogy in a Graduate Teacher Education Program

M. Gail Hickey

This chapter focuses on the implementation of three required 10-hour service learning for diversity field experiences in a graduate teacher education program. Students' responses to program-driven diversity education are examined over time, and inservice teachers' diversity perspectives are analyzed. Three emergent patterns are identified in student narratives. The majority of students perceive the field experience in one of three ways: eye-opening experiences, seeing through a new lens, or a catalyst for change.

Prior to the implementation of new service learning for diversity field experience degree requirements, graduate students tended to associate diversity assignments with individual instructors and/or individual courses rather than with their work as inservice teachers. Consequently, these students were less likely than current students to perceive connections between the P-12 instructional environment and their training as multicultural educators. However, once university faculty worked together to create and implement a teacher education program that included mandated service learning experiences in diverse settings coupled with post-experience written reflections, graduate students' perspectives toward the need for multicultural education began to change.

The Indiana University–Purdue University Fort Wayne (IPFW) College of Education and Public Policy's Department of Educational Studies introduced a new graduate degree program model in January 2005. Responding to National Council for Accreditation of Teacher Education (2002) standards that both preservice and inservice teacher candidates "develop proficiencies for working with students from diverse backgrounds; dispositions that respect and value differences, and skills for working in diverse settings," the Educational Studies department faculty implemented a 30-hour service learning for diversity field experience degree requirement (10 hours in each of three required courses). This chapter explores students' responses to the 30-hour diversity field experience degree requirement and considers students' perspectives regarding diversity training needs. As an instructor for two courses requiring 10-hour field experiences (curriculum and educational research), the author is uniquely positioned to respond to the new program requirement.

The Setting

Professional teacher training programs have traditionally relied on a combination of field experiences and assignments in individual courses to facilitate teachers' cultural proficiencies. IPFW's geographic setting permits many opportunities for diverse field experience settings. Fort Wayne is the second largest city in Indiana (approximately 300,000 residents) and has an increasingly diverse population. Two local urban area school corporations, Fort Wayne Community Schools (FWCS) and East Allen County Schools (EACS), provide multiple opportunities for university students to engage in diverse field settings.

Current statistics show that FWCS is 53% White, 26% African American, 12% Hispanic, 3% Asian, 1% Native American, and 5% multiracial (FWCS, 2010). All FWCS schools include at least four racial/ethnic groups while most schools enroll students representing five or six different racial/ethnic groups. Of the 31,549 students in FWCS, 63% receive free or reduced-price lunch. State standardized test pass rates for all tested grades in FWCS were 64.2% (mathematics) and 61.1% (English/language Arts), compared with state averages of 75.1% and 72.4%, respectively. Eighty-five identified languages are spoken in the FWCS corporation.

At the individual FWCS building level, racial/ethnic, socioeconomic, and academic performance levels vary. For example, one Title I school's enrollment is 10% White, 34% African American, 48% Hispanic, and 8% multiracial. Ninety-seven percent of this school's students receive free or reduced lunch. The average state standardized test pass rate is 34.5% at this school, compared with 71.4% statewide. In contrast, at a largely suburban school located in a higher socioeconomic neighborhood, the school's enrollment is 74% White, 16% African American, 5% Hispanic, 1% Asian, 1% Native American, and 3% multiracial, and 26 percent of the suburban school's students receive free or reduced lunch. The average state standardized test pass rate at the suburban school is above 88%.

Meanwhile, as a whole, the EACS corporation is moderately urban with 70.0% White, 13% African American, 8% Asian, 4% Hispanic, and 5% multiracial (EACS, 2010). Forty-five percent of the student body receives free or reduced lunch. State standardized test pass rates for all tested grades in EACS were 65.6% (English/language arts) and 64.5% (mathematics). As with FWCS, individual building-level diversity varies widely in the EACS

corporation. For example, at a Title I school, the student population is 41%
White, 36% Asian (mostly Burmese), 13% African American, 6% multiracial, and 3% Hispanic. The state standardized test pass rate is 31%. In
contrast, at a suburban school located in a higher socioeconomic neighborhood, the student population is 82% White, 8% multiracial, 5% African
American, and 3% Asian. The state standardized test pass rate at the suburban school is 60.3% compared with state averages of above 70%.

The U.S. Department of State identified Fort Wayne, Indiana, as a
Burmese refugee resettlement site in the early 1990s. Secondary Burmese
migration related largely to family reunification has resulted in the rapid
influx of Burmese students in both FWCS and EACS corporations. Fort
Wayne's Burmese-speaking population, totaling approximately 7,000, is
the largest outside Myanmar. As a result, IPFW education students have
an even greater opportunity to experience diverse P-12 populations
through FWCS and EACS corporations. Yet many students continue to
exhibit resistance to such opportunities. Several possible reasons exist for
this resistance. The majority of students enrolled in the IPFW teacher
education programs, like the majority of teachers in U.S. K-12 schools, are
White and predominantly Protestant (Newman, 2005). Conversations with
IPFW teacher education students reveal that, as K-12 students, their
teachers were mostly White; as university students, their professors are—
for the most part—White. Furthermore, judging from students' self-
reported preferences, the majority hopes to teach at neighborhood schools
similar to those they attended. Research confirms that White teachers who
plan to teach in schools with predominately White populations do not
recognize a need to understand students from diverse groups, nor do they
comprehend the ramifications of the rapidly changing U.S. population
(Glazer, 1997; Ogbu, 2003).

The department's reliance on diverse field experiences alone had not
done enough to prepare students to teach in diverse educational settings.
Faculty realized that change was needed if students were to move toward
cultural proficiency. It became apparent that the necessary changes would
have to begin in the degree programs. The process of program redesign has
been addressed in a previous paper (Choi & Hickey, 2008).

Theoretical Frameworks

In "Diversity within Unity: Essential Principles for Teaching and Learning in
a Multicultural Society," James Banks (2001) noted that the findings of the
4-year Multicultural Education Consensus Panel included 12 essential
principles. Principle 1: Teacher Learning, states:

Professional development programs should help teachers understand the complex characteristics of ethnic groups within U.S. society and the ways in which race, ethnicity, language, and social class interact to influence student behavior. (p. 2)

The literature on service learning in teacher education offers a contextual rationale for the new graduate degree program requirements. Service learning in teacher education programs blends learning and service in such a way that "both occur and are enriched by the other" (Anderson, Swick, & Uff, 2001, p. xi). Unlike community service projects, which emphasize the needs of service recipients, service learning links community service activities with the curriculum. Students address community needs as they engage in community activities and reflect on their community experiences (Cairn & Kielsmeier, 1991). Seven essential principles serve to guide service learning programs: (a) high-quality service to prepare students to address an actual, recognized community or school need; (b) integrated learning to tie the service activities to classroom knowledge, skill, and value goals; (c) reflection to help integrate students' service experiences with the academic curriculum; (d) civic responsibility to promote in students a sense of caring for others and a commitment to contribute to the community; (e) student voice to ensure students take an active role in choosing, planning, implementing, and evaluating the service-learning activities; (f) collaboration so all partners (students, parents, school faculty and administrators, community-based organization staff, service recipients) benefit from the service project and contribute to its planning; and (g) evaluation to measure progress toward the learning and service goals (Anderson et al., 2001, pp. xi–xii).

Teacher education programs that effectively incorporate multicultural service learning opportunities may result in teachers becoming positively oriented toward their schools' diverse communities (Wade, Boyle-Baise, & O'Grady, 2001). Teachers involved in multicultural service learning opportunities expand their "emotional comfort zones" (Dahms, 1994, p. 92) while exploring issues related to cultural diversity. Such programs also facilitate teachers' appreciation for the funds of knowledge that exist between and among cultures, as well as their thinking about home–school connections (Moll, 1992). Miller-Lane, Howard, and Halagao's (2007) concept of multicultural education as civic multicultural competence is also relevant for the service learning for diversity field experience program requirement. This model demonstrates the intersections between civic responsibility and cultural understandings.

Program Requirements

Department of Educational Studies faculty members' concept of the graduate field experience requirement (IPFW, 2004) includes a description of the scholar-practitioner model, a vision statement, a definition of service learning, guidelines for completing a 10-hour diversity field experience for service learning, a form to document individual students' completion of a 10-hour field experience, a format for developing a written reflection about the 10-hour field experience, and a rubric by which faculty assess individual students' progress in two tenets drawn from the School of Education's conceptual framework (i.e., Democracy & Community: Foster a democratic, just, inclusive learning community with all stakeholders; and Experience: Integrate field and/or clinical experiences that reflect the diversity of educators, students, and schools and help educators assess those experiences).

The scholar-practitioner model emphasizes the preparation of educators who "address the challenges of population growth issues, cultural diversity, policy analysis and design, problem solving, and the change process" (IFPW, 2004). A scholar-practitioner, according to Bentz and Shapiro (1998), is a person who "mediates between professional practice and the universe of scholarly, scientific, and academic knowledge and discourse" (p. 66).

The Department of Educational Studies' vision statement informs students that the faculty seeks to build scholar-practitioner learning communities with "our students, our stakeholders, and ourselves" in an effort to engage teacher education candidates "in a democratic and diverse society." As part of the vision statement commitment, teacher education students should have opportunities "to observe, interact with, and learn about populations of diverse learners" in an effort to enrich educators' "understanding of and sensitivity to diversity issues" (*Program Guide & Unit Assessment System*, 2005). Drawing on Miller-Lane and colleagues' (2007) concept of multicultural education as civic multicultural competence, students should also be of service "to the educational or service agency where they are placed." Service learning for diversity field experience instructions inform students that the School of Education faculty believe service learning experiences benefit constituents at the service site as well as graduate students engaged in the degree program.

IPFW School of Education faculty adopted Bringle and Hatcher's (1995) definition of service learning for inclusion in the description of graduate degree program requirements. Bringle and Hatcher's definition states:

> Service learning is a credit-bearing, educational experience in which students participate in an organized activity that meets identified community needs and reflect on the service activity in such a way as to gain further understanding of course con-

tent, a broader appreciation of the discipline, and an enhanced sense of civic responsibility and personal values. (p. 112–122)

IFPW students are encouraged to engage in "authentic" service learning experiences. Eyler and Giles' (1999) common characteristics of authentic service learning experiences are elaborated upon for students' benefit and include:

- being positive, meaningful, and real to the participants;
- involving cooperative rather than competitive experiences, thereby promoting the development of skills associated with teamwork, community involvement, and citizenship;
- addressing complex problems in complex settings rather than simplified problems in isolation;
- offering opportunities to engage in problem solving by requiring participants to gain knowledge of the specific context of their service learning activity and community challenges, rather than only drawing on generalized or abstract knowledge such as that which might come from a textbook;
- offering powerful opportunities to acquire the habits of critical thinking (i.e., to identify important questions or issues within a real-world setting); and
- promoting deeper learning as results are immediate and uncontrived (no "right answers" found in the textbook).

As a result of this immediacy of experience, service learning is more likely than classroom-based learning to be personally meaningful to participants, generate emotional consequences, challenge values as well as ideas, and support social, emotion, and cognitive learning and development (Eyler & Giles, 1999).

Students are cautioned that authentic service learning experiences also share other common characteristics—namely, what authentic service learning is *not*. Service learning, according to Eyler and Giles (1999), is not:

- an episodic volunteer experience,
- an add-on to an existing school or college curriculum,
- simply accumulating a predetermined number of community service hours in order to complete degree requirements,
- required community service assigned by the courts or school administrations as a form of punishment,
- only intended for high school or college students, or
- beneficial only to the student or to the community.

The 30 hours of field experience for graduate students is divided into three separate 10-hour blocks, each of which is connected with one course required for degree completion. All students register for a noncredit EDUC M501 Service Learning for Diversity (satisfactory/unsatisfactory) while they register for one of the required courses featuring a 10-hour diversity field experience. Graduate students are expected to arrange their three 10-hour diversity field experiences for service learning themselves. Faculty members provide lists of recommended sites, such as English language learners (ELLs) language classes located outside their places of employment, organized tutoring experiences on campus and elsewhere, and other options. Students may choose one of the recommended options or, after reading the 10-hour diversity field experience for service learning requirements, may suggest an alternative site.

Following the completion of the 10-hour field experience, students are required to develop a formal written reflection based on two tenets of the academic unit's conceptual framework. Students attach their written reflection to the signed and dated form that documents their personal involvement in the 10-hour field experience. Faculty members assess students' written reflections using the rubric provided in the Unit Assessment System (UAS; IFPW, 2004). University instructors apply rubric standards for each graduate student who returns a completed written reflection. A copy of the blank rubric is attached to each written reflection, and university instructors assess students' narratives according to a 4-point Likert scale:

4   The reflection shows extensive learning and understanding in this category of the conceptual framework (CF) and identifies connections to practice.
3   The reflection shows meaningful learning and understanding in this category of the CF.
2   The reflection shows basic learning and understanding in this category of the CF.
1   The reflection shows little learning and understanding in this category of the CF.

Analysis and Discussion

Prior to 2004, master's degree students were not required to submit written reflections based on CF items. However, during one graduate social studies methods class prior to 2004, the author asked students to respond to an assignment intended to foster awareness of diversity within area schools and encourage teachers to use culturally responsive strategies (Hickey, 1999).

Student comments on a required diversity assignment prior to 2004, although sometimes supportive, nevertheless included such statements as:

- "We don't *have* any racial diversity in our school—even the *janitor* is White!"
- "As far as this being an educational issue around here, I don't know about that."
- "I am trying to find some way that this applies to myself in a rural school. I can't do it!"

Students entering the IPFW elementary or secondary education master's degree program since January 1, 2005, are required to complete three 10-hour service learning for diversity field experiences. The service learning model differentiates the field experience requirement from diversity assignments connected with individual courses (such as the one used in the author's social studies methods course) in several ways. First, the field experience setting must be outside students' normal workplace. Second, students follow the field experience with a debriefing, which is delivered in both written and verbal format. Teacher education students who participate in service learning activities should be involved in organized debriefing activities (Wade, 1997). Third, the 10-hour requirement is documented by a signed and dated form completed by a third party who verifies the student's involvement.

Two of the author's assigned courses, EDUC E535 (Elementary School Curriculum) and EDUC E590 (Research in Elementary Education), include 10-hour field experience requirements. Content analysis (Gall, Gall, & Borg, 2007) of students' written reflections from recent years shows several emergent patterns. For most graduate students, the service learning for diversity field experience was an eye-opening experience, helped them see through a new lens, or served as a catalyst for change. A general "other" pattern was also identified.

Eye-opening experience. Several researchers in multicultural education have noted that their students describe activities and assignments intended to increase exposure to diversity as "eye-opening" (Carpenter-LaGattuta, 2002; Fraser-Abder, 2001). A number of students enrolled in the author's courses followed this tradition when describing their 10-hour diversity field experience for service learning in the written reflection. For example:

> Hearing someone's story of their life in another country can be a real eye-opener to each of us.... I now have a better understanding and compassion for [the non-English-speaking mothers of several students in my classroom this year].

[Interviewing a foreign exchange student] was very eye-opening.... It is a refreshing reminder that [our annoying everyday] problems really are small in comparison to the issues [occurring] around the globe.

[Observing in an ELL classroom taught by an untrained volunteer to meet NCLB requirements] opened my eyes to a different kind of classroom and a different style of teaching. I was not aware that standards exist to help ELL students acclimate to the Indiana State Standards. These standards also help the teacher know where to begin to help these students meet adequate yearly progress (AYP) under No Child Left Behind (NCLB).

As a [secondary] language teacher, I teach students to communicate in another language [and] to respect other cultures. [Interviewing an immigrant] enabled me to see [my instruction] from a different perspective.... [I also confronted] some of my own feelings and perceptions about Hispanic immigration issues, and [now realize] I had let that color my relationships with [Hispanic] students. This opportunity has opened my eyes to some things, and I think it will help me be a better teacher.

My observation of an ELL classroom [helped me improve my own teaching]. I had never thought about using a child's first language as links to what I was trying to teach. I think I was too concerned about teaching my own agenda [to realize ELL students' unique needs].... This experience has opened my eyes to some of the challenges second language learners have in our schools.

[Interviewing an immigrant] is very enlightening. If you take getting to know the differences in cultures ...in an inquisitive light, you learn a lot and many [ethnic] idiosyncrasies will be explained.

This service learning experience has enlightened me as an educator—to the social and economic world [where] financially strapped members of my community and particularly their children exist. While I have always known of the differentiation between the [economic] classes, it is an entirely new experience [to me] to walk through it with another person who cannot just walk away from [poverty] at the end of the day.... This experience has taken me far from my comfortable, safe, and sterile world.

Seeing through a new lens. Other graduate students felt the 10-hour diversity field experience for service learning permitted them to view diversity "through a new lens" or, in some cases, forced them to perceive issues through a new lens. For example:

[Interviewing an immigrant] has provided me with a different lens in which I [now] see the world. It is one thing to read and be knowledgeable about other people's history, and [it is] a completely different experience to speak to and listen to a person who has lived it.... [T]his experience has helped me understand there are communities of learners that bring with them completely different experiences than my own. We cannot begin to understand and include them in a just, inclusive learning community until we listen to their story.... I [now] have a strong desire to integrate my students' own histories with a social studies/language arts [instructional unit]. It is important that students realize they are all different and have experiences which are uniquely their own and affect them in ways they do not even realize.

[Interviewing an immigrant] enabled me to develop a new perspective on how individuals live in other countries. It also gave me a non-American point of view on how our nation is different from [others].

[Time spent in an immigrant's home] provided a unique learning experience positioning me as the student.... More than the knowledge itself, it has brought a unique aspect of another's experiences that will broaden my mind and make me a more tolerant educator.

[Interviewing a foreign exchange student] gives me another perception.... I think we are taught to think we are better or at a higher level than others, but when it boils down to it, we are the same.... The more we are diversified as a country the more of a blending of students we are going to encounter.

[Interviewing an immigrant has] opened my life up to new experiences and [created] an appreciation for the struggles families experience when learning a new culture and language.

Watching [English Language Learners] strive to learn has enabled me to view them through a critical literacy lens.... Even though we had language barriers and it sometimes made it hard [for us to] communicate, this experience taught me that caring is a universal language and, regardless of the language spoken, students can sense when a teacher genuinely cares and wants to be of service to them.

Catalyst for change. Multicultural curriculum should serve as a catalyst for classroom change (Goldstein, 2001; New, 2000). When education for diversity includes appropriate curriculum for diverse learners, educators become change agents as the result of their own experiences with diversity. For example:

Not only did I get to observe [an adult ELL classroom], but I was [also] able to work individually with people who have moved to America and are motivated to learn the English language.... [This experience] has definitely motivated me to take the teaching skills [learned] and use them [in my own classroom with ELL learners].

By [observing in an ELL classroom], I now see the many challenges that face ELL teachers and their students.... I plan to incorporate more bilingual literature in my classroom and learn more about the challenges that face students coming from other countries.

[Observing in an ELL classroom] helped me grow in fostering an inclusive learning community in my classroom. Every year I have a very racially diverse [class]. I believed [inclusiveness] was my specific strength. [Then] I received a student who spoke no English [and I did not know how to teach her].... This field experience will help me reach ELL students I have in the future.

Time spent in an immigrant's home] provided a unique learning experience positioning me as the student.... More than the knowledge itself, it has brought a unique aspect of another's experiences that will broaden my mind and make me a more tolerant educator.

Experiences like [interviewing foreign exchange students] are important. Had I not had this assignment, I am fairly sure I would not have spoken with these exchange students as I did [or] asked these questions.

At [my school], we do not have the wide range of diverse learners as [at] other schools. [Observing at a different school] showed me the importance of treating students equitably regardless of their cultural background.

I have tried [since the service learning for diversity field experience], and will continue to try, to create the type of environment in my classes every day which will challenge the students and encourage them to keep trying, too.

[After interviewing an immigrant who was educated outside the U.S.], I have become more aware of the difficulties in communication and am more patient when encountering individuals who do not use English as their main language.

Other. The written reflection excerpts included here could not be easily formed into recognizable categories. However, these excerpts do illustrate graduate students' growth toward increased awareness of diversity issues. For example:

[Interviewing an immigrant] made me pause and think about the way American students are being educated.... [The interview] helped me grow and understand [a different] culture. It also caused me to reflect on my own teaching habits and believe I will be more open and sympathetic if I have a student in my class from an immigrant family.

[After observing in an ELL classroom, I realized] these are our students. We have to make them feel welcome in our classrooms, not feel like outcasts. Sometimes we simplify our [expectations] of ELL students because we think they cannot handle it. After this observation, I am not so sure that is true.

[After observing in an ELL classroom] I have a better understanding of the language barriers faced by these students, and the cultural adaptations they have to make in order to function [at school]. This experience also caused me to think about how ELL students have to take [state tests] in English. It makes me wonder if someday the [tests] will be offered in Spanish.

Not everybody. With the best of intentions and advance planning, new program model experiences may not positively affect all students' dispositions toward diversity. For example, one student wrote in her service learning for diversity field experience reflection paper:

[Interviewing an immigrant] has opened my eyes to what I already knew—we are very fortunate to live in a country where everyone receives a free and appropriate

education and everyone is valued. Although I do not believe the intent of this experience was for me to grow a deeper love for my family and country, it has. I am a
loved person and count my blessings daily.

Such comments seemed to point to the need for Educational Studies Department faculty to better understand students' perceptions about diversity
training in teacher education. A colleague and the author decided to develop
a survey to help learn more about students' perspectives. The survey was
administered to students in the author's graduate social studies methods class
and in the colleague's undergraduate educational foundations course.

Student Survey

The survey questionnaire was designed in an effort to better understand
students' perceived needs regarding diversity education (Choi & Hickey,
2007) and administered over a two-semester period. Questions included:

- How do you describe yourself (race/ethnicity, age, gender, religion,
  socioeconomic status)?
- Do you feel comfortable dealing with diversity in your classroom?
  How is your background helpful or a disadvantage in this?
- How well did your teacher education program prepare you to work
  in diverse settings?
- What kind of program modification could help you to better prepare
  yourself for working in diverse settings?

Students enrolled in both the graduate course and the undergraduate
course indicated that they feel positively about the issues addressed in the
brief questionnaire. However, subtle differences emerged among fast-track
graduate students' responses compared with those students enrolled in the
undergraduate course.[1] The majority of Transition to Teaching (T2T)
students expressed vague ideas concerning their abilities to work effectively
in diverse educational settings. Some believed they can work effectively in
diverse settings as a result of their teacher training, and some T2T students
think their life experiences and personal experiences in diverse social
settings will help them be effective teachers.

Responses to survey questions by the foundations course students
showed several differences from the T2T student response pattern. Undergraduate students felt many teachers in rural schools have not had experience
working in diverse educational settings. Those currently completing internships in urban settings who, as children, had attended parochial or rural K-12
schools (where the population tends to be more homogenous) felt unprepared

to work in the diverse educational setting where they now found themselves, and they expressed acute frustration at their lack of preparation.

The question "How well did your teacher education prepare you to work in diverse settings?" inspired some T2T students to reflect that, although there is not much in their training to help prepare them to work effectively in diverse classroom settings, they were skeptical about whether teacher education programs could prepare them for the task at all. Instead, these students tended to think that, as they gained experience in school settings, issues of diversity would resolve themselves. Foundations course students working in urban settings at the time tended to be critical about what they perceived to be an absence of diversity training in their teacher education program. Understandably, those who took multicultural classes during their undergraduate years appreciated the contribution that such classes made to their confidence in working effectively in multicultural settings.

In response to "What kind of program modification could help you to better prepare yourself for working in diverse settings?" a majority of T2T program students expressed that "practical classes" such as internships and student teaching were most helpful. While agreeing that such practical classes are essential, foundations course students stressed a need for more academic courses that would provide deeper understandings about issues related to social interaction.

T2T student responses may be skewed somewhat in favor of White males. Survey results indicated that a greater percentage of White males are represented in the T2T program than in graduate courses enrolling predominantly inservice teachers. Moreover, T2T student responses may not accurately reflect master's degree students' perspectives in general because T2T students (while technically considered graduate students) are not and have not been inservice teachers.

Students' perceptions revealed through the survey questionnaire analysis indicated that students feel comfortable dealing with issues of diversity in K-12 settings, believe their backgrounds sufficiently prepared them to deal with issues of diversity, and tend to value life experiences over formal instructional experiences for preparing educators to work effectively in diverse settings. Inservice teachers were more likely than T2T students to recommend that teacher education programs include more academic courses designed to promote a deeper understanding of the social issues connected with diversity.

Survey responses by teacher education students who did not participate in the required service learning for diversity field experiences indicate that these students feel unprepared to work effectively in diverse classrooms. Overall, survey results support the concept behind service learning-oriented teacher education programs. The survey results also illustrate teacher education students' perceived need for multicultural education training at both the undergraduate and graduate levels.

Conclusion

This study has examined graduate students' perspectives of required diversity field experiences over time and analyzed these students' perspectives through multicultural lenses. When graduate students connect diversity assignments with individual instructors and/or individual courses, they are less likely to perceive connections between their work as teachers and their training as multicultural educators. Once university faculty collaborated on a teacher education program that includes mandated diversity field experiences and mandated post-field experience written reflections, graduate students' perspectives toward the need for multicultural education began to change.

Banks (2001) insisted that teacher education programs must "help teachers understand the complex characteristics of ethnic groups" and how intersections of "race, ethnicity, language, and social class" (p. 2) affect K-12 students. As instructors in individual courses, the faculty at IFPW took Banks' (2001) recommendation seriously, yet they failed to see widespread change in students' cultural dispositions. Clearly, the program needed significant changes to be brought into line with current thinking regarding cultural competency.

By applying Miller-Lane et al.'s (2007) civic multicultural competence model of multicultural education to the graduate degree program through multiple mandated service learning experiences within the community, faculty members were able to make two important changes to the program that ultimately benefited students as well as members of the community. The first change was a program-wide commitment to reflect on experience, in which critical reflection for social action is an integral component (Leland & Harste, 2005). The second change was recommending service learning options to give students one-on-one time with individuals in their communities whose worldview and/or ethnicity are likely to differ from their own.

For the author's students, participating in a degree program with reflection-driven service learning for diversity field experience helps them begin to think critically about their preconceptions toward others. The service learning experience sometimes results in students working in settings and/or circumstances that take them outside their comfort zones. Meanwhile, entering uncomfortable settings as teachers with knowledge and skills to share—and under the protection of a degree program requiring their participation in service learning opportunities—permits these students a degree of latitude they might not otherwise enjoy. One African-American student, for example, had been teaching the children of Burmese refugee families for six years when she entered the new degree program. This teacher yearned to know more about her Burmese students' home lives, yet school administrators had never encouraged home visits. Recommended options for the 10-hour service learning for diversity field experience requirement for one of her graduate courses suggested that visiting the home of immigrant or refugee parents might benefit both the teacher and her immigrant or refugee students. As a result of participating in a degree program with a service learning requirement, this particular teacher felt empowered to ask her principal for the services of an interpreter while visiting a local Burmese family whose children attended the school. An interpreter was found, appointments for home visits were made, and—from the perspective of her newfound knowledge regarding Burmese families—the teacher wrote in her reflection:

> Many Burmese have differing levels of education [upon arrival in the U.S.]. Some graduated from secondary school, some attended only primary school; however, many of them have never been enrolled in school. [These Burmese parents] have few skills and limited knowledge. [...] As a teacher, these interviews brought to my attention a yearning to promote democracy in [my] classroom learning environment. Many [of my] students have comfortable lives [and parents who can] aid in their educational process. [Neither they nor I] have to worry about things like where to get the next meal or where to sleep at night. The concept of democracy has come into focus for me as I recognized the abuse of the rights of refugees [in Burma], in addition to [refugees' experiences with] poverty and insecurity.

Reflecting on their 10-hour service learning for diversity assignment was a life-changing experience for many students. Some believed that the service learning experience opened their eyes to the ethnic experiences and/or differing home lives of their own students. Others believed that the 10-hour experience caused them to view their community through a new lens. Still other graduate students began to think critically (perhaps for the first time) about the U.S. educational system within which they were educated and now work. Sadly, a few students felt the 10-hour service learning for diversity field experience for diversity only underscored their positions as privileged Americans. It is to be hoped that—in a program where students are required to participate in three such diversity experiences—these few students' perspectives about diversity will eventually be broadened.

Finally, the analysis of student questionnaires revealed multiple and varied in-school experiences that appeared to facilitate development of cultural competency in practicing teachers. Such experiences, in conjunction with reflection-driven service learning, may be essential to teachers' understandings about the complexity inherent in intersections between and among ethnicity, race, and class.

Note

All students enrolled in the social studies methods course were involved in a Transition to Teaching (T2T) program or fast-track licensing for students already holding a bachelor's degree. These graduate students are not required to complete three 10-hour service learning field experiences.

References

Anderson, J. B., Swick, K. J., & Uff, J. (Eds.). (2001). *Service-learning in teacher education: Enhancing the growth of new teachers.* Washington, DC: American Association of Colleges for Teacher Education.

Banks, J. A. (2001, April). Diversity within unity: Essential principles for teaching and learning in a multicultural society. *New Horizons for Learning.* Retrieved from http://www.newhorizons.org

Bentz, V. M., & Shapiro, J. J. (1998). *Mindful inquiry in social research.* Thousand Oaks, CA: Sage.

Bringle, R., & Hatcher, J. (1995, Fall). A service learning curriculum for faculty. *The Michigan Journal of Community Service-Learning*, 112–122.

Cairn, R. W., & Kielsmeier, J. (1991). *Growing hope: A sourcebook on integrating youth service into the school curriculum.* Roseville, MN: National Youth Leadership Council.

Carpenter-LaGattuta, A. (2002). Challenges in multicultural teacher education. *Multicultural Education, 9*(4), 27–29.

Choi, S., & Hickey, M. G. (2007, April). *Developing cultural competency in U.S. teacher education programs: A case study.* Chicago, IL: American Educational Research Association.

Choi, S., & Hickey, M. G. (2008, November). *Developing cultural competencies in U.S. teacher education programs: A case study.* Seoul, Korea: Center for Women's Studies, Sungshin Women's University.

Dahms, A. M. (1994). Multicultural service-learning and psychology. In R. J. Kraft & M. Swadener (Eds.), *Building community: Service learning in the academic disciplines* (pp. 91–103). Denver, CO: Colorado Campus Compact.

East Allen County Schools. (2010). *Indiana Education Statistics.* Retrieved December 10, 2010 from http://mustang.doe.state.in.us/TRENDS/corp.cfm?corp=0255&var=pctmin.

Eyler, J., & Giles, D. E. (1999). *Where's the learning in service-learning?* San Francisco, CA: Jossey-Bass.

Fort Wayne Community Schools. (2010). *Indiana Education Statistics.* Retrieved December 10, 2010 from http://www.eacs.k12.in.us.

Fraser-Abder, P. (2001). Preparing science teachers for culturally diverse classrooms. *Journal of Science Teacher Education, 12*(2), 123–131.

Gall, M., Gall, J. P., & Borg, W. R. (2007). *Educational research: An introduction* (8th ed.). Boston, MA: Pearson.

Glazer, N. (1997). *We are all multiculturalists now.* Cambridge, MA: Harvard University Press.

Goldstein, T. (2001). "I'm not white": Anti-racist teacher education for white early childhood educators. *Contemporary Issues in Early Childhood Education, 2*(1), 3–13.

Hickey, M. G. (1999, April). *Reflecting on diversity through the use of teaching cases.* Research in Social Studies Education SIG Sponsored Paper, American Educational Research Association, Montreal, Ontario.

IPFW. (2004). *Unit assessment system.* Retrieved April 1, 2007 from http://www.ipfw.edu/ educ/programs/ graduate/elementary.shtml.

Leland, C. H., & Harste, J. C. (2005). Doing what we want to become: Preparing new urban teachers. *Urban Education, 40*(1), 60–77.

Miller-Lane, J., Howard, T., & Halagao, P. E. (2007). Civic multicultural competence: Searching for common ground in democratic education. *Theory and Research in Social Education, 35*(4), 551–573.

Moll, L. (1992). Bilingual classroom studies and community analysis. *Educational Researcher, 21*(2), 20–24.

National Council for the Accreditation of Colleges of Teacher Education (2002). Standards for Professional Development, Standard IV Diversity. Retrieved May 10, 2004 from http://www.ncate.org/standard/m_stds.htm.

New, R. (2000). *Reggio Emilo: Catalyst for change and conversation.* Champaign, IL: Clearinghouse on Early Childhood Education. Retrieved from ERIC Digest (ED447971)

Newman, J. (2005). *American education* (12th ed.). Boston: McGraw-Hill.

Ogbu, J. U. (2003). *Black American students in an affluent suburb: A study of academic disengagement.* Hillsdale, NJ: Lawrence Erlbaum Associates.

Program Guide and Unit Assessment System (n.d.). Retrieved from http://new.ipfw.edu/dotAsset/150596.pdf on May 7, 2012.

Wade, R. C. (1997). Empowerment in student teaching through community service learning. *Theory Into Practice, 34*(3), 184–197.

Wade, R. C., Boyle-Baise, M., & O'Grady, C. (2001). Multicultural service-learning in teacher education. In J. B. Anderson, K. J. Swick, & J. Uff (Eds.), *Service-learning in teacher education: Enhancing the growth of new teachers* (pp. 248–259). Washington, DC: American Association of Colleges for Teacher Education.

Part IV
Conclusion

Educating for Cultural Diversity in Small Colleges and Universities

M. Gail Hickey and Brian Lanahan

That teachers working in American P-12 schools need focused training in cultural competencies is now universally understood among faculty in teacher education programs. However, precisely how university instructors should go about educating P-12 teachers for cultural competency continues to be a matter of debate. One area of the professional literature that has not yet been adequately explored is how teacher educators at small universities and colleges with somewhat limited access to diverse P-12 settings effectively train teachers in cultural competency. This volume provides a series of snapshots illustrating instructional methods and strategies used by 15 teacher educators representing 12 small American colleges or universities. These instructional snapshots significantly add to the professional literature on multicultural teacher education.

The layout of our volume seemed to fall naturally into two main sections. The chapters in Part II deal primarily with strategies and experiences to help teachers understand themselves while learning to better understand others. Chapters in Part III deal primarily with the pedagogical constructs and concepts surrounding educating for cultural competency. In the paragraphs that follow, the editors summarize the relevant corpus of research supporting this volume. We also describe connections between the relevant research and authors' snapshots of teaching for cultural competency in teacher education programs located in small colleges or universities.

The majority of teachers in American schools are White. The experiences and perspectives of a predominately White population continue to shape schools and schooling in the United States. Experts in multicultural education agree that, as a result of a predominately White racial perspective, the American schooling experience negatively impacts students of color. The research demonstrates that teacher education students from dominant groups (i.e., White Euro-American) resist instruction aimed at reducing prejudice and/or increasing awareness of diverse cultural/ethnic groups. Additional research from the field of teacher education suggests that preservice and inservice teachers must recognize their own worldviews and biases before they can begin to understand and positively affect the worldviews of their own students.

Several authors in this volume describe instructional strategies and purposeful curriculum intended to facilitate teachers' recognition of their own worldviews and biases. For example, Melissa Marks (Chapter 1) described how first-year teacher education students at the University of Pittsburgh at Greenburg analyzed their own beliefs about diversity and the ways perspectives expressed in required coursework differed from beliefs and perspectives verbally espoused by individual students. Kristi Stricker (Chapter 2) explored how preservice teachers at Concordia University Chicago use their own written autobiographies to begin to understand the power of social location and develop an awareness of why their future students' social locations are important in the P-12 instructional setting. A second perspective on the use of written autobiographies is presented by Michele Phillips (Chapter 3) about preservice teachers' work at the College of Charleston. Brian Lanahan (Chapter 6) at the College of Charleston engaged White preservice teachers in an examination of their White cultural identity through the development and discussion of individual critical autobiographies and the use of a racial identity model.

Researchers also have found that, even when teachers do exhibit an ability to situate future students' lives in a broad social context, they continue to be unable to recognize institutionalized racism in school settings. Studies also support the finding that, at the end of their teacher education program, most White teachers are able to demonstrate little knowledge about diverse cultural or ethnic groups. Several chapter authors in this volume provide illustrative examples of teacher educators' attempts to gauge preservice and inservice teachers' ideas about diversity. Indeed, Catherine Gatewood and Kenneth Hall at Lock Haven University (Chapter 5) examined preservice teachers' understandings about diversity at both the entry level and exit level of Lock Haven's degree program, demonstrating that as preservice teachers progressed through the program they exhibited a greater degree of comfort when discussing issues of diversity than their classmates just entering the program. Janie Hubbard's (Chapter 10) undergraduate students interviewed foreign-born individuals whose cultural and/or ethnic backgrounds differed from their own and then developed digital stories based on their interviews and further research.

The literature on multicultural teacher education also documents that P-12 teachers in American schools need to learn about their students' cultures and learn to see the world through the diverse cultural lenses available within their own communities. Chapter authors in this volume whose research supports this finding include Laura Marasco (Chapter 8), whose graduate students at Salisbury University developed critical case studies about P-12 students from cultural or ethnic backgrounds different from their own after visiting the P-12 students' homes and interviewing their parents. Moreover, Bethany Hill-Anderson and Darryn Diuguid (Chapter 9) described their survey of cooperating teachers working with McKendree University undergraduate students, in which the cooperating teachers were asked to respond to questions about the multicultural literature resources available in their own classrooms. Frans Doppen (Chapter 12) elaborated upon two programs at Ohio University, both created in an effort to raise teacher education candidates' conceptual awareness of diversity issues.

A critical examination of White racism and privilege inherent in the American White middle-class experience is essential to changing P-12 teachers' perspectives about their own students' diverse home lives. Several chapter authors deal with this topic. Edric Johnson's (Chapter 4) preservice teachers at the University of Wisconsin–Whitewater developed a "cultural memoir" with P-12 students whose cultural backgrounds differed from their own in an effort to help the preservice teachers examine their own cultural backgrounds and belief systems while also learning to teach for social justice. Russell Binkley's (Chapter 7) undergraduate students at Western Carolina University engaged in service learning opportunities intended to facilitate understandings about social justice; Binkley recommended that teacher education programs offer "a deliberate, explicit curriculum" centered in authentic diversity experiences. James Daly (Chapter 11) described an undergraduate teacher education program at Seton Hall University in which students engaged in civic education experiences in an attempt to increase their exposure to diverse populations. M. Gail Hickey (Chapter 13) described her work at Indiana University–Purdue University Fort Wayne, where graduate students enrolled in a teacher education program requiring 30 hours of service learning experiences within diverse settings wrote critical reflections illustrating their growth toward a deeper understanding of democracy and instructional experience.

Authors contributing to this volume agree that instructors in teacher education programs located at small American colleges and universities experience unique pedagogical challenges while also enjoying unique opportunities for continued growth. Not all instructional interventions described here were effectively implemented during the initial attempt. However, each chapter snapshot offers our professional colleagues at other small colleges and universities firsthand accounts of potentially effective strategies for facilitating P-12 teachers' cultural competencies.

Russell Binkley is an associate professor of social studies education at Western Carolina University. He pursues research in race, class, gender, and sexuality in education and tries to influence preservice teachers to become social justice advocates. Russ may be contacted at rbinkley@wcu.edu.

James K. Daly is a professor of education at Seton Hall University in South Orange, NJ. He is interested in examining issues related to academic freedom, the impact of diversity (with a focus on international perspectives), and increased collaborative efforts within and between institutions to promote social education. Jim may be reached at james.daly@shu.edu.

Darryn Diuguid is an assistant professor in the School of Education at McKendree University. His teaching, service, and research interests include diverse children's literature, differentiated instruction, and students in high-poverty situations. Darryn may be contacted at drdiuguid@mckendree.edu.

Frans H. Doppen is an associate professor at Ohio University in Athens, Ohio. He teaches courses in curriculum and instruction, middle childhood education, and social studies education. His major research interests include civic, global, and multicultural education. He is an active member of the College and University Faculty Assembly and International Assembly of the National Council for the Social Studies as well as the Ohio Council for the Social Studies. Frans may be contacted at doppen@ohio.edu.

Catherine Gatewood is the interim associate dean for the College of Arts & Sciences and the College of Education and Human Services at Lock Haven University of Pennsylvania. Her research interests include diversity in higher education and assessment/accreditation. Catherine may be contacted at cgatewoo@lhup.edu.

Kenneth Hall teaches at Lock Haven University. Kenneth may be contacted at khall@lhup.edu

M. Gail Hickey is a professor in the College of Education & Public Policy at Indiana University-Purdue University Fort Wayne in Indiana. Gail has more than 25 years of experience as a teacher educator, gifted resource teacher/coordinator, and elementary classroom teacher. She is an active member of the National Council for the Social Studies. Her research interests include contemporary migration, gender and ethnicity, and multicultural education. Gail may be contacted at hickey@ipfw.edu.

Bethany Hill-Anderson is an assistant professor of education at McKendree University. Her research interests include cultural diversity in the classroom, educating and parenting gifted learners, and engaging assessment methods. Bethany may be reached at bghill-anderson@mckendree.edu.

Janie Hubbard is an assistant professor in the College of Education at the University of Alabama. She is a former K-6 educator, both in the United States and abroad, and is an active member of the National Council for the Social Studies. Janie's research interests include professional learning communities, social studies teaching and learning, and cultural diversity issues. Janie may be contacted at hubba018@bamaed.ua.edu.

Edric C. Johnson is an associate professor at the University of Wisconsin-Whitewater. His research interests include drama in education, critical pedagogy, and social studies teacher education. Edric may be contacted at johnsoec@uww.edu.

Hyun Young Kang earned her Ph.D. from The Ohio State University. She is currently a full-time instructor at Kyung Sung University in Pusan, South Korea. Her research interests include early childhood education, curriculum, and teacher education. Hyun Young may be contacted at kang.123@osu.edu.

Laurie Katz is an associate professor in early childhood education in the School of Teaching & Learning at The Ohio State University. Her research, teaching, and service have focused on teacher preparation of early childhood educators and inclusion issues. Laurie may be contacted at katz.124@osu.edu.

Brian K. Lanahan is an assistant professor of social studies education at the College of Charleston in South Carolina. During the 2008–2009 academic year, he was a Fulbright Scholar in Sarajevo. He currently teaches graduate and undergraduate social studies methods and history of education courses. His research interests include social studies methods, comparative democracy education, and education in post-conflict countries. He is a member of the National Council for the Social Studies. Brian may be contacted at lanahanb@cofc.edu.

Laura L. Marasco is an associate professor in the Seidel School of Education and Professional Studies at Salisbury University in Maryland. Her research interests include linguistic and cultural diversity in a democracy, critical pedagogy, geoliteracy, and social studies education. Laura may be contacted at llmarasco@salisbury.edu.

Melissa J. Marks is an associate professor of education and chair of secondary education at the University of Pittsburgh at Greensburg. Her research interests include multicultural education, diversity, special education, and teacher socialization. Melissa may be contacted at mjm37@pitt.edu.

Michele Phillips is an assistant professor at the College of Charleston in South Carolina. Her research interests include teacher beliefs and practices, multicultural pedagogy, and democratic classroom practices. Michele may be contacted at phillipsml@cofc.edu.

Kristi Stricker is an associate professor at Concordia University Chicago. Her research interests include multicultural pedagogy, social class in higher education, and social studies education. Kristi may be contacted at kristi.stricker@cuchicago.edu.

Z

Zeichner, K., 50, 60, 78, 92, 111, 112
Zimpher, N. L., 4, 11
Zittleman, K., 132, 141

Parent Stories Questionnaire, 121
parents, role of, in cultural diversity, 137
parent-school connection, 119
Patton College of Education (Ohio
  University), 169, 170, 171–172
peace education, 93
PeaceJam, 94–96, 103–107, 110–111
people of color, subordinate status of, 3
personal narratives, 147
Phi Kappa Phi, 134
Photo Story 3 (Microsoft), 147, 149
place-based education, 172, 179
post-assignment reflections, 82
poverty
  sensitive handling of topic of, 109
  statistics in southeast Ohio, 170
power structures, questioning of, 57
power struggles, examination of, 147
power systems, maintenance of, 54
practical inquiry, 78
Practitioner Research, 78–79
pragmatic open-mindedness, example of, in
  White racial identity exploration, 83–85,
  89–90
prejudices
  analyzing nature of, 159
  decrease in, 20
  increase in, 20
  increasing awareness of, 155
  learning of, 53
  perpetuation of, 3
  uncovering of, 25
preservice teachers
  examination of own cultural heritage, 37
  lack of recognition of institutionalized
    racism in school settings, 6
  lack of understanding and confidence in
    working with linguistically and
    culturally diverse students, 144–145
  need for diversity among, 111
  negative attitude of, 6
  potential ignorance of, 23
  potential lack of self-awareness of, 23
  potential naïveté of, 23
  preconceived notions held by, 145
  reflection on racial identities, 77
  using autobiographies, 34. See also
    autobiographies

privilege, identification of, 110
professional development, 8, 111, 136, 148,
  170, 188
*Program Guide and Unit Assessment
  System*, 189, 201
program-driven diversity education, 185
progressive educators, specifications of, 110
Project Citizen (Center for Civic Education),
  155, 161
projecting feelings or expectations, of an
  entire group onto one student, 72
prospective teachers, as struggling with own
  identities while working with diverse
  students, 50
pseudo-independence, as stage of White
  racial identity, 80
Pura Belpre award, 139
Putumayo, 137

R

race
  as area of diversity in research, 17, 20,
    38
  as cultural characteristic, 40
  as cultural identifier, 42–43, 45
  and interplay with racism and classroom,
    42
  and multicultural education, 5
  relevance and meaning of, 63
  as shaper of human experience, 4
  understanding construct of, 29
racial awareness, lack of, 29
racial diversity, lack of, as issue for College
  of Charleston, 39–40
racial identity
  assessment of, by White preservice
    teachers, 77
  Atkinson, Morten, & Sue model, 77
  deconstruction of, 29
  examination of White racial identity, 79
  Helms model. *See* Helms model of White
    racial identity
  students' experience of affirmation of, 72
  use of model of, 206
racism
  impact of, on persons of color, 4
  and interplay with race and classroom,
    42

US European Judeo-Christian sociocultural context, 3
US government, mandatory schooling laws, 3
US immigration, as of beginning of 21st century, 37
US population
changes in, 3
implications of rapid change in, 187
US school population
19th and early 20th century, 3
changes in, since 1965, 3
US schools/schooling
apartheid nature of, 110
demographics of, 143
mandatory schooling laws, 3
as shaped by predominantly White society, 4, 205

V

values, as acquired from family, 53
videoconferencing, 148, 163–164
Vilnius Pedagogical University, 155
virtual field experiences, 148
virtual work arrangement, 161

W

We the People–The Citizen and the Constitution (competition), 164
Western Carolina University, 207
White identity analysis, 79
White privilege
acknowledgment of, 79
consideration of, 30
discussion of, 8
examination of, 147
reaction to McIntosh article on, 65
teacher's worldviews regarding, 3
Whites' refusal to acknowledge, 89
White racial identity
examination and exploration of, 79–90
Helms model of. *See* Helms model of White racial identity
White racism, 207
Whiteness, 79
whole, as greater than sum of parts, 67
world music, 137
worldviews

diverse, as potential cause of conflict, 162
exploration of, 165, 198
impact of lack of experience with others', 16
influence of age and life experiences on, 86
influence of class membership on, 33
recognition of, 205–206
of students, as differing from that of teachers, 145, 206
unchallenged and challenged, 3–4

Barry Kanpol
General Editor

The Critical Education and Ethics series intends to systematically analyze the pitfalls of social structures such as race, class, and gender as they relate to educational issues. Books in the series contain theoretical work grounded in pragmatic, society-changing practices. The series places value on ethical responses, as prophetic commitments to change the conditions under which education takes place.

The series aims to (1) Further the ethical understanding linking broader social issues to education by exploring the environmental, health-related, and faith/spiritual responses to our educational times and policy, and (2) Ground these works in the everyday world of the classroom, viewing how schools are impacted by what critical researchers do. Both theoretically and practically, the series aims to identify itself as an agent for community change.

The Critical Education and Ethics series welcomes work from emerging scholars as well as those already established in the field.

For additional information about this series or for the submission of manuscripts, please contact Dr. Kanpol (Indiana University—Purdue University Fort Wayne) at kanpolb@ipfw.edu.

To order other books in this series, please contact our Customer Service Department:

> (800) 770-LANG (within the U.S.)
> (212) 647-7706 (outside the U.S.)
> (212) 647-7707 FAX

Or browse online by series at www.peterlang.com.